Global Project Management

This book is dedicated to my parents, who taught me the pleasure of reading, and to Joyce, who showed me the pleasure of living.

Global Project Management

Communication, Collaboration and
Management Across Borders

JEAN BINDER

Routledge
Taylor & Francis Group

LONDON AND NEW YORK

First published in paperback 2024

First published 2007 by Gower Publishing

Published 2016 by Routledge
4 Park Square, Milton Park, Abingdon, Oxon OX14 4RN

and by Routledge
605 Third Avenue, New York, NY 10158

Routledge is an imprint of the Taylor & Francis Group, an informa business

British Library Cataloguing in Publication Data
Binder, Jean Carlo
   Global project management : communication, collaboration
   and management across borders
   1. Project management 2. International business enterprises
   – Management
   I. Title
   658.4'04
   ISBN-13: 9780566087066

Library of Congress Control Number: 2007927132

ISBN 13: 978-0-566-08706-6 (hbk)
ISBN 13: 978-1-03-283780-2 (pbk)
ISBN 13: 978-1-315-58499-7 (ebk)

DOI: 10.4324/9781315584997

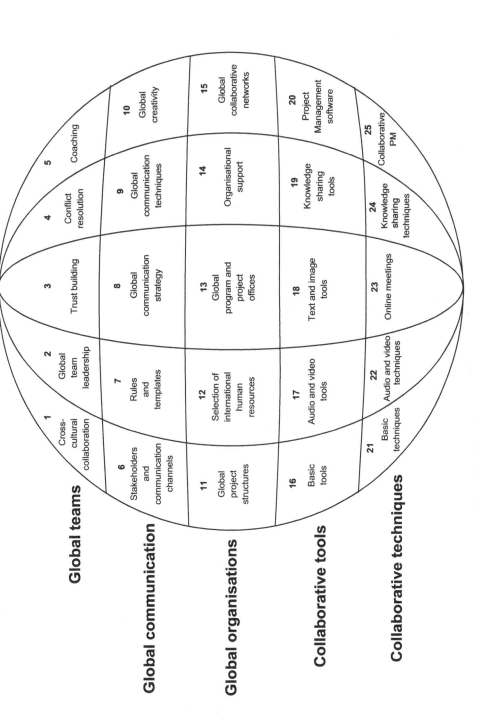

Global teams

1 — Cross-cultural collaboration
2 — Global team leadership
3 — Trust building
4 — Conflict resolution
5 — Coaching

Global communication

6 — Stakeholders and communication channels
7 — Rules and templates
8 — Global communication strategy
9 — Global communication techniques
10 — Global creativity

Global organisations

11 — Global project structures
12 — Selection of international human resources
13 — Global program and project offices
14 — Organisational support
15 — Global collaborative networks

Collaborative tools

16 — Basic tools
17 — Audio and video tools
18 — Text and image tools
19 — Knowledge sharing tools
20 — Project Management software

Collaborative techniques

21 — Basic techniques
22 — Audio and video techniques
23 — Online meetings
24 — Knowledge sharing techniques
25 — Collaborative PM

The Global Project Management Framework ©

Contents

List of Figures

List of Tables

Acknowledgements

I would like to thank the following people: Yannick Jolliet, who reviewed many parts of the book and gave me precious recommendations and testimonials; Marie-Paule Sottiaux, for the support, testimonials, review and lunch discussions; David Page, Carolyn McKellar, Marion Sachs, Belinda Freaney-Sadouk, Sophie Domine, Jean-Marc Genier, Jose Gonzalez, Jennifer Hyams, Mark Russell, Reddy Mandala, Viktor Puetzer, Annie Jordan, Patrick Vitzthum, Frank Bondoux, Thierry Sales and Paolo Lenti for the feedback during the interviews and initial brainstorming sessions; John Pelham for the insights on stakeholder management, communication strategies and cross-cultural experiences; Karel de Bakker for the nice suggestions on global risks; Paul Gardiner and Jim Ritchie for the support during my academic research.

Grateful acknowledgement is made to Geert Hofstede, Fons Trompenaars, Charles Hampden-Turner and Peter Wooliams who granted permission to reprint the definitions and classification tables of their cultural dimensions.

Sincere thanks to Jonathan Norman, Fiona Martin and Mike Brooks at Gower for all their trust and support.

Earnest thanks to my cat for the company, my daughters for the inspiration and my wife for the help and endless patience.

Preface

The need for this book

With the increasing trend for outsourcing, off-shoring and globalisation, many organisations are taking advantage of geographically distributed skills, round-the-clock operations and virtual teams. Small and medium sized businesses are linking up with major companies, forming supplier networks to deliver products and services, and customer networks of distributors, resellers and end-users. Global projects are now the operating units that establish an initial link among these cross-border networks and rely on information flows across the different partners and stakeholders.

Most projects in these global environments involve people from different companies, located in various countries. Currently, many companies struggle to obtain acceptable levels of efficiency and quality from global projects since the organisation structures and project management methodologies are not adapted to a multicultural environment, and because many project managers and team members still feel uncomfortable when they communicate over a distance. Many project managers still rely exclusively on the so-called 'hard' skills, such as planning, scheduling and controlling, to coordinate the projects. The 'soft' skills (for example, communication, understanding of cultural differences and team building) and the 'informal' project management techniques (such as networking, influencing and improvising) are essential for the success of global projects, and require special attention from organisations.

The framework described by this book is all about soft skills and informal project management, suggesting areas of knowledge that require special attention for effective global program and project management. Rather than providing 'one-size-fits-all' recommendations, the chapters of this book guide you in a quest to harvest your company's good practices, using them to develop and implement a Global Project Management Framework© in your company or project.

Intended audience

This book provides a comprehensive framework of good practices on global project management, and is primarily directed at project managers, program managers and project office members involved in the preparation and application of project management methodologies, and working on programs and projects involving different companies and locations around the globe. They can start by improving the project management and communication practices in their current portfolio of programs and projects, and later include these good practices in the company methodologies. They can also identify what types of tools can improve understanding over a distance, deploying them in their current work environment.

Senior executives can use the information in this book to understand the main challenges faced by global project managers and team members, and to identify how the deployment of tools and practices can improve the productivity of global project teams and the quality of the deliverables, while reducing travel and relocation costs. The senior board have a role model during the implementation of the framework, selecting the human resources to work on global projects, creating a project management office and providing organisational support. This book also provides various types of project structure – adapted to different needs – and some suggestions to improve the motivation of a project team that spans different locations, cultures and languages.

Finally, anyone participating in a global project as a team member or stakeholder can also find useful recommendations for smooth communication with people located in diverse countries, coming from other cultures, speaking different native languages or working in various time zones.

Academic researchers can make use of the framework presented in this book, performing new studies to investigate the impact of each chapter on the efficiency and productivity of global project teams, and to complete the Global Project Management Framework© with new developments, technologies, practices and theories.

The structure of this book

The introductory chapter presents the characteristics of global projects and programs, discusses how these peculiarities affect the work and efficiency of global project and program managers and summarises the main advantages and challenges of deploying a global team for a project or program. It presents a framework that helps global program and project managers to focus on the advantages and address the challenges of having project team members dispersed across the globe: the Global Project Management Framework©.

The chapters in Parts I to V explore in detail the five main categories of knowledge in the Global Project Management Framework©:

- Chapters 1–5 (Part I) present the core principles that allow the management of *people* across country and cultural boundaries.
- Chapters 6–10 (Part II) complement the learning on people management by presenting the *communication* strategies that facilitate the management of project team members in different countries, and make them collaborate more effectively.
- Chapters 11–15 (Part III) suggest *organisational* structures and practices that create all fundamental conditions for a good collaborative environment on global projects, and expedite the implementation of the people and communication strategies.
- Chapters 16–25 guide the development of good practices for the implementation (Part IV) and use (Part V) of the communication media and collaborative tools mentioned in the previous chapters: the *technology* that allows the management of people and the communication between stakeholders across country and cultural boundaries.

Part VI concludes the book, by presenting different strategies to adapt the recommendations according to the organisational cultures, standards, methodologies and requirements, obtaining buy-in from senior managers, project managers and project team members.

How to read the book

The book structure allows companies to understand the main domains that have an impact on the performance of global project teams, and then adapt their project management methodologies to a global environment. The sequence of the chapters aims to provide a progressive understanding of the needs and good practices. As an alternative route, project managers and team members may read each chapter independently and address specific issues to improve their efficiency on global projects. Many cross-references are provided to allow the chapters to be read in any order.

The main sources of information

There are different layers of information to consider when looking for good practices on global project management. The first and most important layer is the *experience* of other global project managers, team members and senior managers from different countries. One way to learn about this experience is to participate in networking events organised by associations such as the Project Management Institute and the British Computer Society.

The second layer is the foundation of knowledge on *project management* methods, tools, techniques and processes. This book does not redefine this set of principles, preferring to build on the information already established by existing bodies of knowledge. The main references for this book were the PMBOK® guide from the Project Management Institute, PRINCE2® from the Office of Government Commerce, the IPMA Competence Baseline (ICB) and the Gower Handbook of Project Management. However, a certain level of abstraction was adopted to allow companies using other methods and methodologies to consult this book without difficulty.

The third layer is the literature on *virtual teams and distributed project management*, which establishes the requirements and recommendations for projects involving people in different locations. The third layer is the literature on virtual teams and distributed project management, which establishes the requirements and recommendations for projects involving people in different locations. The main sources are described at the end of each part of the book.

The fourth layer is the knowledge gathered by the *intercultural studies* from Hofstede and Trompenaars, present in most chapters of this book.

Web companion

The website www.GlobalProjectManagement.org provides tools, templates and an open forum for the exchange of information related to the practices described in this book, also linking to different hardware, software and services solutions.

Introduction

This chapter defines the main characteristics of global projects and programs and presents a framework that will lead international companies to achieve maturity in global project management by helping global program and project managers to focus on the advantages of international teams, addressing the challenges of cross-cultural and virtual communication and presenting innovative solutions for collaboration over a distance.

By the end of this chapter, you will have learned the main dimensions of a global project and understand what challenges are faced by global program and project teams. You will also discover the Global Project Management Framework©, which will guide you throughout the book parts and chapters.

Traditional, distributed, international and virtual projects

In the project management literature we can find different types of projects, when comparing the number of organisations and locations involved in their implementation. In *traditional projects*, a large majority of the team members are working for the same organisation and in a single location. *Distributed projects* involve team members working in many locations, and can also be called *international projects* when they include people located across country borders. *Virtual projects* are composed of team members dispersed geographically and working in different organisations. Project managers may face specific challenges on virtual projects as they need to balance different interests, company cultures and working practices, and most communications occur over a distance. International projects require the collaboration of people from different country cultures and languages, sometimes with the added complexity of the locations over various time zones.

Global projects

This book addresses the combined challenges of international, distributed and virtual projects, being mainly dedicated to *global projects*. This novel category can be defined as a combination of virtual and international projects, which includes people from different organisations working in various countries across the globe. You can use the following dimensions to evaluate the level of complexity of your projects, and identify if you are experiencing the same challenges as other global project managers:

- **Number of distant locations** – The project team can be in a single room (project war room), in different rooms and in multiple locations. When all stakeholders are in geographical locations near at hand, face-to-face meetings can be easily organised and the positive influence of body language and social interaction on the efficiency is clear. In global projects, the team members are located at least in two different countries. When the distance among the team members is such that travel is required for physical contact, the use of phone and video conferencing becomes essential, requiring the application of communication strategies to ensure a high level of effectiveness.

- **Number of different organisations** – project team members can work for a single department in one company, for multiple departments or even for multiple companies. Project managers must adapt their people and leadership skills to the multiple policies, procedures and organisational cultures. The complexity of commercial and contractual processes is also increased, although outside the scope of discussions in this book.

- **Country cultures** – beyond organisational culture, the customs and traditions of different nations and regions can bring more diversity to the work environment, reducing the group thinking and improving the collective creativity. Motivation is often increased as many people prefer to work in cross-cultural environments because of the rich information exchange. Nevertheless, this diversity can sometimes be the source of conflicts and misunderstandings, and project managers must apply some basic rules and practices to take advantage of the cross-cultural communication, and to avoid its pitfalls.

- **Different languages** – international companies usually establish a common language for the exchange of information, although the way people communicate is highly dependent on their own native language. For example, if the common language is English, the effectiveness of communication by most non-English speakers will be limited by their knowledge of English expressions, vocabulary and often by their ability to make analogies and tell stories or understand jokes. On the other hand, native English speakers would need to limit their vocabulary to clear sentences and essential words, and carefully confirm the understanding of their ideas by foreign colleagues. The use of online meetings and visual communication are examples of practices discussed in this book that can be adopted by project managers to avoid misunderstandings and obtain a high commitment level from all stakeholders, independently of their native language.

- **Time zones** – the whole project team can be based in the same location or in different locations in the same time zone. On the other extreme, there are project teams with members in completely different time zones, ,making it difficult (or impossible) to organise meetings in common office hours. The effect is twofold. Program and project managers can use the different working times to their advantage, by creating a 'follow-the-sun' implementation, reducing the duration of sequential tasks by a half or a third of the time. The procedures and communication rules must be precisely defined among people in 'complementary' time zones (when there is low overlapping of working hours). On the other hand, important delays can happen, when the exchange of simple information takes a week to be completed, instead of a single day. Global organisations can implement standard communication rules and templates across locations to reduce the possibility of these problems occuring.

The above dimensions can be represented by a radial chart where the centre represents the lower complexity levels: single department, location/time zone, language and cultures (Figure I.1.). The combination of medium and high marks shows the higher complexity of projects across borders, with team members from different cultures, languages, and organisations working in different nations around the globe: the global projects.

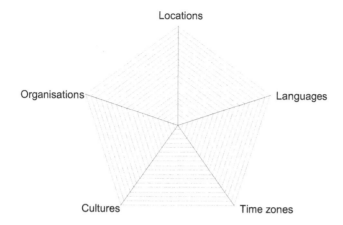

Figure I.1   Dimensions of global projects

© *Jean Binder 2007*

Organisations can use the scale above to establish comparisons among different projects, to decide when to apply the good practices and for risk management. More information on this is given throughout the book.

An alternative approach is to complete the scale with one colour to determine the level of complexity of the communication between the project manager and the project team members (where most or all recommendations in this book apply), and use a different colour to categorise the communication with other stakeholders (which requires trust building, conflict resolution and global communication). This can help the project managers to identify which sets of good practices are more important in each project. Some real-life examples can illustrate the usage of this approach.

Examples of global projects

- A software development project (Figure I.2) – the project team members are working in four companies in different locations (the software company in London, England; one development team in Curitiba, Brazil; two development teams in Bangalore and Mumbai, India) with team members speaking four different native languages (English, Brazilian Portuguese, Kannada and Tamil), all with different levels of fluency in English. There are three different country cultures, and the total difference in time zones is 8h30 in summer (GMT-3 for Brazil and GMT+5:30 for India). In addition to the team members, there are stakeholders from another three locations (three pilot customers in the USA, South Africa and Australia), elevating the number of country differences to six, and the time zone difference to 17 hours (GMT-8 for San Francisco, USA to GMT+10 for Sydney, Australia).

- A pharmaceutical project (Figure I.3) – the project team members come from a partnership of eight organisations, and are working in six locations (two quality assurance teams in England, the headquarters in France, two laboratories in Germany and one development team in South Africa) composed of people speaking three different native languages (English, French and German). There are four different country cultures, and the total difference in time zones is 1 hour in summer (GMT+1 for England and GMT+2 for the

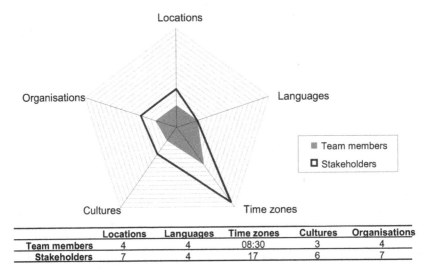

	Locations	Languages	Time zones	Cultures	Organisations
Team members	4	4	08:30	3	4
Stakeholders	7	4	17	6	7

Figure I.2   A software development global project

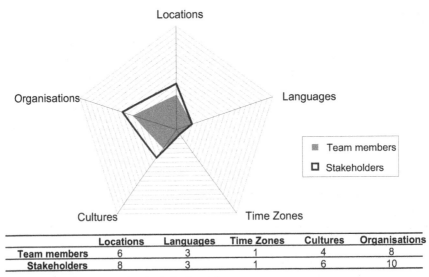

	Locations	Languages	Time Zones	Cultures	Organisations
Team members	6	3	1	4	8
Stakeholders	8	3	1	6	10

Figure I.3   A pharmaceutical global project

other countries). In addition to the team members, there are stakeholders from another two organisations in different locations (The European Commission in Belgium and one environmental agency in Switzerland), elevating the number of country differences to six, without changes in the number of time zones or languages.

- An organisational change project (Figure I.4) – the project team members from two organisations (the main corporation and one consulting company) work in 14 company offices in ten countries, speaking eight different native languages. The total difference in time zones is 14 hours in summer (from New York ,USA, to Melbourne, Australia). In this case, all the stakeholders are in the same locations as the project team members.

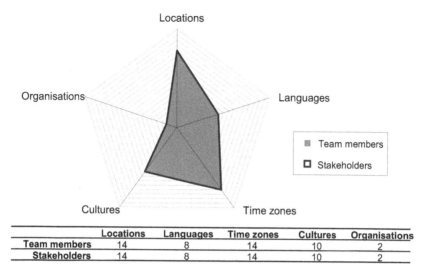

	Locations	Languages	Time zones	Cultures	Organisations
Team members	14	8	14	10	2
Stakeholders	14	8	14	10	2

Figure I.4   An organisational change global project

Global programs

PMI (2006a) defines a program as 'a group of related projects managed in a coordinated way to obtain benefits and control not available from managing them individually'. The program manager works closely with the program board, which is composed of senior stakeholders who provide guidance and make decisions affecting the program outcomes, and with other parties that have an interest in or are affected by the program. The program manager must also communicate with the Program Management Office (PMO), which oversees the management of programs. The program manager is responsible for providing direction and guidance to the project managers, and may receive assistance from a Program Support Office. Figure I.5 provides an overview of the relationship between the program manager and the program stakeholders.

The four main categories of programs take into consideration two dimensions: the location of the program stakeholders and the location of the different project teams (summarised by Figure I.6). One of these categories (traditional programs) includes programs where all stakeholders and project teams are located in the same country, which is not the focus of this book. The other three categories (global programs) will now be evaluated in detail.

The first category (local program of global projects) is a group of related *global* projects managed in a coordinated way to obtain benefits and control not available from managing them individually, where the program manager is located in the same country as all the project managers and members of the program board. While all the practices in this book are relevant to the project managers, the program manager may only require them to communicate with key stakeholders located around the globe. One example is a program to develop and implement a new software tool in five countries (Figure I.7), with a program manager located in the UK (represented by the 'PgM' circle), in the same location as all the project managers (represented by the 'PM' circles). The program is composed of a global project for the software development (project manager in the UK and the project team in the UK, Singapore and Mexico), the pilot implementation project in the UK (the whole project team located together with the project

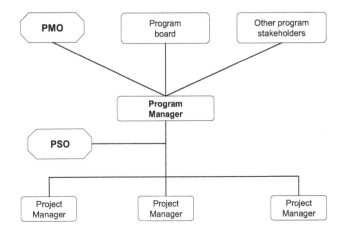

Figure I.5   Global program stakeholders

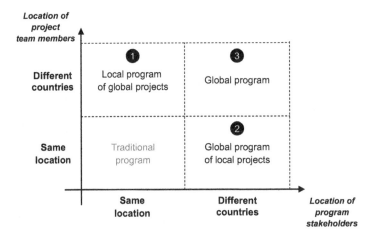

Figure I.6   Categories of global programs

manager) and the local implementation projects in the United Arab Emirates, Singapore, Mexico and Canada (all coordinated by project managers primarily based in the UK).

The second category (global program of local projects) is a group of traditional projects *deployed in various countries* and managed in a coordinated way, to obtain benefits and control not available from managing them individually *and in the same country*. This is the opposite of the first category, as the program managers will make use of most practices in this book when managing the project managers and communicating with the program board and other key stakeholders. Figure I.8 illustrates one global program that will implement standardised desktop computers in four countries, with the program manager in Brazil and project managers coordinating 'traditional' teams (all team members in the same location) in Australia, India, South Africa and Australia.

The third category (global program of global projects) is a group of global projects, with project managers located in different countries to the program manager and the program board. This category represents the true challenge of global programs, requiring excellent

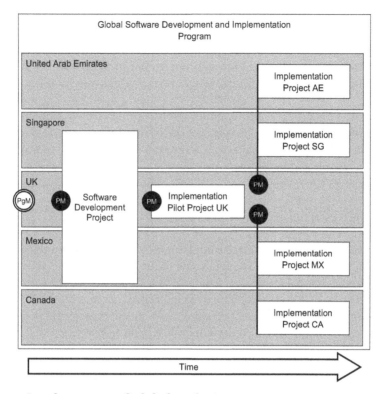

Figure I.7   Local program of global projects

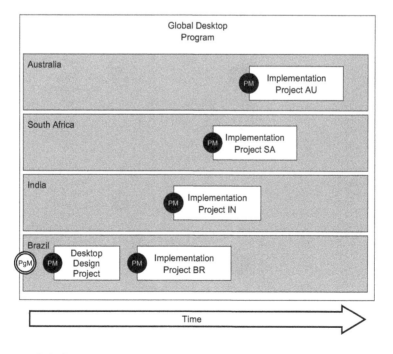

Figure I.8   Global program of local projects

interpersonal skills and open-minded behaviour from all stakeholders. The global program manager and all global project managers can apply the recommendations in this book to improve understanding and reduce conflicts. This is also true when a mix of the three categories appears (for example, traditional and global projects will be part of the same program, or only some of the project managers are in the same location as the program manager).

International companies often conduct global programs to implement Enterprise Management suites, with global projects for the different solutions. In the example illustrated in Figure I.9, the global program manager is located in France and the project managers and project teams are distributed in different countries.

Global projects and programs requirements

As discussed before, the processes, tools and methods assembled in the existing project management bodies of knowledge are applicable to most types of projects, whether they are traditional, virtual or global. However, what are the specific needs of global program and project managers that lead to the need for specific techniques and methods? A study on the available literature, complemented by interviews with global project and program managers, identified their main requirements, represented in Figures I.10–I.13.

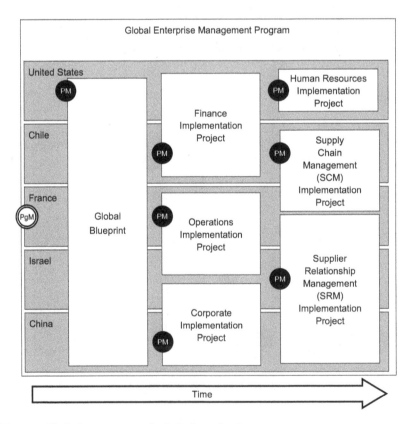

Figure I.9   Global program of global projects

Global Team Management

- How can I manage conflicts among team members working in different locations (to me)?
- How can I establish trust among virtual team members, particularly when they work for different organisations?
- How can I develop leadership skills that can be effective for team members in other locations?
- How can I learn to deal with different cultures, allowing other team members to thrive in a multicultural team?
- How can I perform team-building activities when the budget does not authorise all team members to be in the same location during the project initiation phase?
- How can I provide coaching to project managers and coordinators located away from me?

Figure I.10   Requirements of global project managers – global team management

Communication Across Borders

- How can I have more efficient and shorter meetings over distance?
- How can I adapt my company templates for meetings over distance?
- How can I track the project tasks and deliverables assigned to people located in other countries, and avoid misunderstandings created by the different languages?
- How can I conduct special meetings, like brainstorming, coaching and knowledge transfers over distance?

Figure I.11   Requirements of global project managers – communication across borders

Global Organisations

- How can my organisation adapt its structure and culture to thrive as a global company?
- What is the best way to structure the project team?
- What types of professionals work well over a distance, and how to select them?

Figure I.12   Requirements of global project managers – organisational culture

---

Collaborative Tools

- Which tools can my company deploy to enhance communication in global environments?

- Which tools can I employ to control and coordinate virtual teams working on my projects and programs?

- Which tools can I use to improve the quality of communication between program and project managers, enabling me to monitor the milestones without creating administrative overheads?

- How can my company deploy these tools at all organisational levels?

- How to foster the adoption of the tools?

Figure I.13   Requirements of global project managers – collaborative tools

If you are currently managing or are involved in a global project or program, it is likely that you have some of these questions in mind. The framework explained in this book aims to address all the above requirements, complementing the existing project management bodies of knowledge.

The answers to these questions are not universal as they depend on factors like the country and organisational cultures involved in the project, the number of locations, the different languages, the team size and the project duration, size and complexity. Therefore, the approach of the framework presented in this book is not to provide a 'one-size-fits-all' strategy, 'the right answers' or the 'best practices' in global project management. The framework contains guidelines and models that will help you to understand the cultural differences and sources of misunderstanding. You should determine the best alternatives for your own situation, based on the real-life examples and practices taken from other international companies. You will then be able to define an implementation model that suits the requirements of your global projects, adapted to the specific needs of your organisation.

To be or not to be … global?

In some situations, the location of the project team members from the main customers, suppliers and partners will define that a project must be global. One example is the development of a new product by a partnership of three companies, each with a specialised laboratory in a different country. In other cases, the location of the main project deliverables may determine the need for a global project team. This can be illustrated by the deployment of a new warehouse management system that requires the transformation of buildings located around the globe. Global projects can also allow companies to unite highly specialised team members in the same project without relocating them to other countries, or to delocalise certain project work packages or tasks in order to reduce the project costs. However, there is also a cost for companies to overcome the 'large distances between team members, lengthy travel times to meetings and the inconvenience of working across time zones' (Wild et al, 2000).

Before deciding to conduct global projects, each organisation must weigh up the higher level of innovation and the cost savings offered by having human resources distributed around the globe against the challenges created by the communication across borders, and the cost of implementing processes to ensure the deliverables will be produced as expected. Every situation will bring different results to the above equation and companies can define some principles of operation to guide project managers when developing human resource planning and assembling the project team. One example is the creation of centres of excellence, with a catalogue of the main standard services provided by them, and service level agreements specifying lead times to start activities, expected duration for common activities and the expected levels of quality. The organisation can then declare as mandatory the use of the services from these competency centres instead of developing local skills, recruiting local people or hiring third parties for specific project tasks.

When deciding to deploy a global team for important projects, organisations can evaluate the value of the main positive and negative aspects of having a global project, and then perform a cost-benefits analysis. Another alternative is to perform an evaluation of the strengths, weaknesses, opportunities and threats (SWOT analysis). A brainstorming session can identify the main factors applicable to each project, and the lists shown in Figures I.14 and I.15 can serve as a checklist to validate and complement the findings.

Organisational change and organisational theory

When organisations decide to start implementing global projects, or when they decide to increase the success rate of global projects, they must adapt their structures and their project management methodology. In order to succeed, this change process must focus on the whole organisation, from different perspectives. Harold Leavitt (1964) suggested that organisations

---

Advantages

- Access to technical experts
- Attracting the best workers independent of location
- Environmental benefits
- Global workdays (24 hours vs. 8 hours)
- Improved disaster recovery capabilities
- Increased flexibility
- Increased innovation (by reducing group thinking)
- Increased productivity
- Larger pool of potential job candidates
- More accurate picture of international customers' needs
- No need to relocate existing workers
- Proximity to customers
- Reduced labour costs
- Reduced office space requirements
- Reduction in travel time and expense

Figure I.14   Possible advantages of global projects

Challenges

- Adapt the organisational culture to home working
- Adapt the organisational structure to virtual teams
- Adapt the working hours to different time zones
- Build trust
- Cope with language differences
- Deploy collaborative software and licence costs
- Establish a team identity
- Handle divergent cultural values
- Manage conflicts over distance
- Provide communication and cultural training
- Provide communication technology

Figure I.15   Possible challenges of global projects

consist of four elements – task, structure, technology (tools) and people (actors), which are interdependent and interact with the external environment. A change in one of these variables will almost certainly have an impact on the others. Based on the model from Leavitt, Peter Clark (1972) suggested that, 'approaches to organisational change should take account of the possibilities presented by the four interacting variables to create multiple points of intervention'.

Laurie Mullins built on the organisational model from Leavitt to suggest five interrelated sub-systems to be used when analysing work organisations: task, technology (including physical aspects and methods, systems and procedures), structure, people and management. This organisational theory highlights the interrelationships between these variables, noting that, 'there is no one best, universal structure. There are a large number of variables, or situational factors, which influence organisational design and performance.' (Mullins, 1996).

A framework for global programs and projects

frame·work

4. A set of assumptions, concepts, values, and practices that constitutes a way of viewing reality.

The American Heritage® Dictionary of the English Language, Fourth Edition[1]

frame·work

2. A frame or structure composed of parts fitted and joined together.

Random House Unabridged Dictionary[2]

---

1   © 2000 Houghton Mifflin Company
2   © 2006 Random House, Inc.

The framework suggested in this book is based on the models from organisation theory, providing a flexible set of recommendations that can have a positive influence on the performance of global projects. Companies can select which areas of improvement are required, depending on their specific needs. They can also determine the order and priorities to implement the groups of recommendations, depending on their corporate cultures and the technologies available. Finally, they have the flexibility to select which particular recommendations are applicable to their global projects, considering their main characteristics (different languages, countries, cultures and time zones).

The organisational change foundation of the framework allows a holistic approach during the definition of new processes and practices, and the implementation of the recommendations. Global teams require a new set of people skills, interpersonal relationships and leadership styles. Novel communication techniques must allow the management of team members and other stakeholders over distance. Different forms of project structures and organisational standards must be in place to cope with project team members distributed around the globe. The organisational culture will serve as a basis for the selection and implementation of the collaborative tools – hardware, software and communications. New techniques, systems and procedures need to be available to all stakeholders involved in global projects to increase adoption of the new set of tools. Figure I.16 illustrates the resulting framework for global project management, and the five categories of information: global teams, global communication, global organisations, collaborative tools and collaborative techniques.

The practices, processes, measures, theories and case studies in the framework are grouped into different knowledge areas that allow a modular implementation. Five chapters exist for each category from the framework (Figure I.17), as follows:

- **Global team management** – the chapters in this category represent the main recommendations found in the literature for effective management of global project teams: cross-cultural collaboration, global team leadership, trust building, conflict resolution and coaching over distance.
- **Global communication** – the chapters in this category complement the communication processes as explained in the PMBOK® guide: global stakeholders analysis and

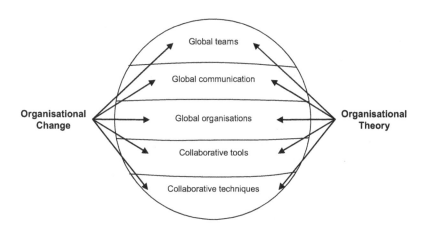

Figure I.16   The Global Project Management Framework©: five categories

© *Jean Binder 2007*

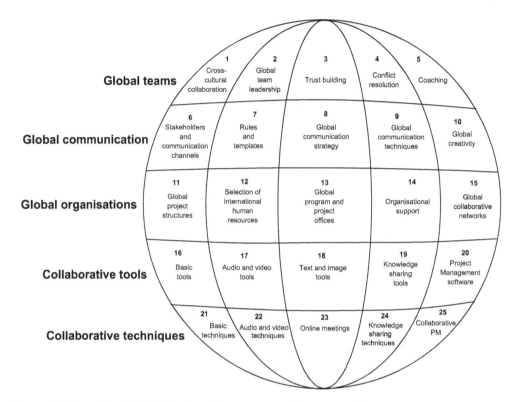

Figure I.17   The Global Project Management Framework©

© Jean Binder 2007

communication channels (main activities of the communications requirements analysis), communication rules and templates (input to the communications planning process), global communication strategy (part of the communications management plan), global communication techniques (knowledge gathering, distribution and exchange) and global creativity using online brainstorming techniques.

- **Global organisations** – this category contains the knowledge required by global organisations to improve the effectiveness of global projects: global project organisation structures, global human resources selection, global program and project offices, organisational support and global collaborative networks.

- **Collaborative tools** – this category provides generic strategies for the implementation of collaborative tools: basic technologies (e-mail and telephones), synchronous audio and video tools (audio and video conferencing), synchronous text and image tools (instant messaging and web conferencing), asynchronous knowledge sharing tools and asynchronous project management information systems. These knowledge areas represent the main solutions currently available to global projects, and can be expanded to include the new developments expected in the near future.

- **Collaborative techniques** – the chapters in this category provide techniques that allow the adoption of the collaborative tools by most project stakeholders: use of basic technologies (e-mail and telephones), effective audio and video conferencing, coordination of online meetings, knowledge sharing techniques and project management information systems.

The framework sources

Figure I.18 illustrates the main sources of information for the framework structure and contents. Academic papers provided the knowledge for the construction of the framework and for the structure of the 25 chapters. The main contents come from direct observations, round tables, interviews, surveys and personal experiences of successful projects. The observation and analysis of 'less successful' projects also provided an interesting comparison for the conclusions about the influence of the good practices on the project performance and on the quality of the deliverables. Other literary sources – usually based on different forms of theory, research, work experiences and case studies – provided additional information to validate and complement the academic findings and the real life experience. The main literary sources come from the following domains:

- Project management bodies of knowledge (for example, PMBOK® Guide, PRINCE2®, Gower Handbook of Project Management, International Journal of Project Management, Project Management Journal).
- Virtual teams (for example. Edwards and Wilson (2004), Haywood (1998), Fisher and Fisher (2001), Lipnack and Stamps (1997), Kostner (1996), and Hawaii International Conferences on System Sciences, see DeLone et al. (2005) and Katzv et al. (2000)).
- Virtual project management (for example, McMahon (2001), Mayer (1998), Rad and Levin (2003), Pauleen (2004), Goncalves (2005).
- Management and organisational behaviour (for example,. Buchanan and Huczynski (1997), Mullins (1996), Hannagan (1995)).
- Cross-cultural studies (for example, Hofstede (2001), Trompenaars (2003, 2005), Melkman and Trotman (2005), Magala (2005)).
- International business (for example, Wild et al (2000), Mead (2000, 2004)).
- Specialised magazines (for example, PM network, Project Manager Today).

The full references can be obtained from the bibliography section (see page 271).

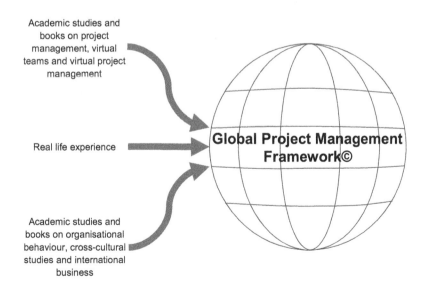

Figure I.18   The Global Project Management Framework©: sources of information

What the framework provides to global organisations

The framework implementation provides three main benefits to global organisations. Firstly, companies can deploy collaborative tools using the implementation templates supplied in this book. They may use the recommendations to increase the adoption rate of technology by the team members involved in global projects, by providing them with enough knowledge to master the essential functions of the hardware, software and communication tools. This will increase the efficiency of meetings, reduce the occurrence of misunderstandings and foster collaboration among team members in different locations.

The second benefit may be achieved when international companies implement a set of processes and good practices for global project management, based on the recommendations and templates provided in the different chapters. The project managers, program managers and PMO team members can form study groups, evaluating what recommendations are applicable to their specific situations, and develop new practices from their personal experience. The outcome will be a framework of good practices adapted to the organisational culture and to the cultures of the countries where the company operates. The framework can also be included in the project management methodologies. The organisations that opt for the Global Project Management Framework© as the structure for their good practices will simplify the exchange of information with other companies, the comparison of their practices and the creation of a set of practices specific to cross-company projects. These companies will benefit from an increased level of trust between team members, increased cooperation levels among people from different cultures, effective team leadership over distance and streamlined communication channels among all stakeholders.

Lastly, organisations can promote internal training on global project management, using the framework as a basis for the course structure and the contents, to increase awareness of and proficiency on the collaborative tools and global project management practices. The global project managers and team members attending the training can learn and discuss the main recommendations, practice coaching and brainstorming over distance, use the collaborative tools, rules and templates during the exercises and try the global communication techniques. Cross-cultural training can complement these sessions, with practical exercises on team leadership, conflict and negotiation skills, and cultural differences.

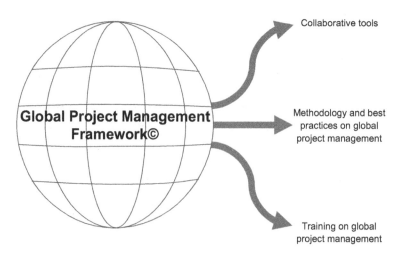

Figure I.19   The Global Project Management Framework©: the deliverables

The next steps

The framework explained in this book provides a comprehensive starting point for global organisations, project offices, global program managers and project managers to achieve higher levels of efficiency. After the implementation of the framework in their organisations, programs and projects, new practices and recommendations will start to appear, aiming for constant evolution and improvement.

The modular design allows a constant evolution of the framework through your feedback. At the end of each chapter, you will find questions about your opinions on the recommendations, practices, tools and techniques. You can also reflect on the applicability of each recommendation to your own environment, and voice your thoughts on the global project management forum (see www.GlobalProjectManagement.org):

- Are the recommendations applicable to most projects in your organisation, or only specific types (for example, large, critical)?
- Do you disagree with some recommendations, or have you tried different tools or practices with better results?
- Do you have any suggestions on how to improve the templates?
- Are you aware of different management theories that are more applicable to your country culture?

The goal of this knowledge exchange is to produce an improved framework of recommendations that can be exchanged among different companies and countries: an open framework for global project management. You can think about your own practices as a good way to improve the competitive advantage of your company, and therefore prefer to keep them confidential. However, the project management bodies of knowledge are there to prove the benefits of having a common set of good practices and terminology across organisations and knowledge areas. In this case, sharing is the best way to work together, in partnerships, in customer-supplier relations or when selling and providing services.

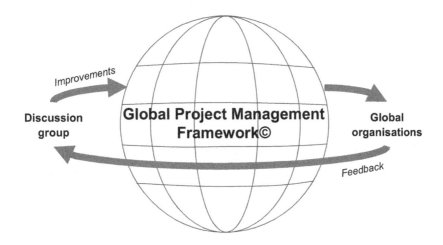

Figure I.20   The evolutionary Global Project Management Framework©

Key concepts

- Existing project management methodologies, bodies of knowledge and maturity models identify, but do not address, specific requirements from global project and program management. This book aims to build on their solid formalisation of processes and practices, adding a layer of knowledge on global projects and programs management.
    - Distributed Projects – projects with team members from the same company, based in different locations.
    - International Projects – projects with team members from the same company, working in different countries.
    - Virtual Projects – projects with team members from diverse companies, in different locations.
    - Global Projects – projects managed across borders, with team members from different cultures and languages, working in different nations around the globe.
    - Global programs – a group of related projects with aligned strategic benefits, normally associated with tactical organisation change, whose stakeholders are located in different countries.
    - Global project management requirements can be classified into tools, meeting management, people management and the organisational structure and culture.
- A cost-benefit analysis is required before deciding to deploy a global team to work on a project. The remaining chapters in this book will help in overcoming most of the challenges, but the residual cost and effort associated with training and organisational changes should not be underestimated.
- The Global Project Management Framework© was built on organisational change and organisational theories, allowing a consistent implementation of good practices and a good adoption rate by global project team members. The five categories of information in the framework are: global teams, global communications, global organisations, collaborative tools and collaborative techniques.
- The framework in Figure I.17 is a good reference tool for the preparation of a framework of good practices to be implemented in your company and projects.
- Global organisations following the recommendations in the framework will deploy collaborative tools with a good adoption rate, update their project management methodologies with good practices on global project management and have a comprehensive template for internal training.

Further reading

Desouza, K., Jayaraman, A. and Evaristo J. (2002) *Knowledge Management in Non-Collocated Environments: A Look at Centralized vs. Distributed Design Approaches*

This paper shows how projects changed from traditional (collocated) to virtual, suggests a typology of projects (from single collocated to multiple virtual) and provides some hints about centralised and decentralised approaches to development.

Van Fenema, P.C. (2002) *Coordination and Control of Globally Distributed Software Projects*

This thesis presents an academic definition of global projects and their main challenges.

Katzy, B., Evaristo, R., Zigurs, I. (2000) *Knowledge Management in Virtual Projects: A Research Agenda*

This study provides a research model and presents an interesting categorisation for projects, with the definition of traditional, distributed and virtual projects.

Zeitoun, A. (1998) *Managing Projects Across Multi-National Cultures: A Unique Experience*

This article presents the definition of Global Project Management and a checklist for working across cultures, discussing the main challenges in managing global projects and suggesting some strategies to tackle them.

Leavitt, H.J. (1964) *Applied Organization Change in Industry: Structural, Technical, and Human Approaches*;

Clark, P.A. (1972) *Action Research & Organizational Change*

These sources contain the early organisation change theory and the variables used as a reference for the framework of good practices.

Balogun, J. and Hailey, V.H. (2004) *Exploring Strategic Change*;

Thornhill, A. et al (2000) *Managing Change: A Human Resource Strategy Approach*

These books present more recent views on organisation change processes, from strategic change perspective (the former) and human resource strategy (the latter).

Mullins (1996) *Management and Organisational Behaviour*

This book provides a solid basis for the analysis of an organisation, for the preparation to an organisational change project, for the implementation of a new methodology on global project management and for an evolution of the organisational culture.

Turner, J.R. and Simister, S.J. (2000) *The Gower Handbook of Project Management*;

PMI – Project Management Institute (2004) *A Guide to the Project Management Body of Knowledge: PMBOK® Guide*;

IPMA – International Project Management Association (2006) *IPMA Competence Baseline*;

OGC – Office of Government Commerce (2002) *PRINCE2*

These sources provide a solid understanding of the main processes, techniques and skills applicable to project management. This book relied heavily on these sources to build the additional knowledge required by global project management.

Interactive section

- Participate in the online survey (www.GlobalProjectManagement.org) and let us know which types of projects and programs you are working on, visualising in the end how your projects fit within the global dimensions.
- Access the survey results on the same website to understand how the global projects from different companies are positioned in the dimension matrix, and how your project compares with them.

Using the discussion groups on the website, let us know your opinion on the framework:

- Do you see additional benefits to global projects in your environment, other than those represented in Figure I.14?
- Do you face different challenges in your global projects and programs, other than those represented in Figure I.15?
- Are you aware of organisational change theories that are more applicable to your geographical location and country culture?
- Can you identify any category of information missing from the framework?
- Do you have in mind a different use of the framework, other than those suggested in Figure I.19?

Global Teams

This part presents strategies to manage global project stakeholders, by understanding the differences in culture, language and time zones, and identifying how to transform these differences from challenges into opportunities.

One of the main challenges of team management across the globe is that most concepts and practices are dependent on the different personalities and cultures involved. You could ask a few people around you to define the terms that compose the titles of the chapters in this part: culture, leadership, trust, conflict and coaching. You would probably find as many definitions as the number of people you interviewed. When it comes to suggestions on how to be an effective leader, build trust and manage conflicts, you will also hear different – sometimes conflicting – recommendations. You must read the chapters in this section, as well as other books in these knowledge areas, with an open mind. The recommendations, methods and practices are not the absolute truth but 'hints' and guidelines that will help you to develop your own way of managing people, taking into consideration what works for you, and what fits the cultures you are dealing with.

1 *Cross-Cultural Collaboration*

'We need a certain amount of humility and a sense of humour to discover cultures other than our own; a readiness to enter a room in the dark and stumble over unfamiliar furniture until the pain in our shins reminds us where things are.'

(Trompenaars)

There are many studies analysing and defining the challenges of cross-cultural management, most of them based on Geert Hofstede's and Fons Trompenaars' cultural dimensions. These two theories were built around extensive surveys of managers in different countries, working for the same multinational company (IBM, in Hofstede's research) or in different companies (for Trompenaars').

This chapter starts with a review of the cultural dimensions and their implications on global projects, presenting a team building exercise that will help your team members and global project managers to recognise the differences among the country cultures in a participative way. It proceeds by reviewing some general recommendations for people working on global projects, and concludes with a real-life experience, to illustrate how you can adapt your management and communication style to working across cultures.

Defining culture

This chapter focuses on country cultures, not corporate cultures. Consider these three definitions:

- 'Culture (…) is the collective programming of the mind which distinguishes the members of one group or category of people from another. (…) The "mind" stands for the head, heart and hands – that is, for thinking, feeling, and acting, with consequences for beliefs, attitudes and skills. (…) Culture in this sense includes values: systems of values are a core element of culture.' (Hofstede, 2001)
- 'Our own culture is like water to a fish. It sustains us. We live and breathe through it.' (Trompenaars, 2005)

YOUR INTERCULTURAL EXPERIENCE

Before reading this chapter, think about a few people that work (or have worked) with you and are located in different countries. What memorable events have you experienced with these colleagues that would rarely happen with people from the same country as you?

Write on a list or mindmap the amusing and positive situations. Write on a separate list the negative conflicts you experienced, and how you would avoid these negative situations in the future.

- 'Culture is a fuzzy set of attitudes, beliefs, behavioural norms, and basic assumptions and values that are shared by a group of people, and that influence each member's behaviour and his/her interpretations of the 'meaning' of other people's behaviour.' (Spencer-Oatey, 2000, cited in Dahl, 2004)

Project managers must understand human nature and personalities in order to select team members, assign correct roles and responsibilities and perform stakeholder analysis. In addition to this, *global* project managers need to recognise how the different attitudes, beliefs, behavioural norms and basic assumptions and values can influence the collaboration among team members coming from multiple countries, and learn how to adapt their leadership style to the different cultures involved in the project.

Culture and project management

Culture is often represented as icebergs or onions, representing its visible and invisible aspects. According to Hofstede (2001), the visible components – also called practices – are manifested by *symbols* (words, gestures, pictures and objects), *heroes* (real or imaginary persons serving as good models of behaviour) and *rituals* (collective activities without a practical purpose but essential to keep the individual bound within the norms of the collectivity). You can observe all these manifestations when you visit other countries and when you receive foreign visitors. However, only insiders to those cultures can easily capture their real meaning. When managing projects abroad you must make an effort to:

- Discover the meanings of different *symbols* used by local people, in order to respect and follow their basic instructions. In project management, the symbols can translate into the specialised terms, techniques and diagrams;
- Know their local *heroes*, to understand the role models of behaviour. The organisational heroes can be the people who advance quickly in their career, employees receiving management awards or popular team members;
- Understand and respect the *rituals*, which in business are often present in the way people organise or attend meetings, in local practices for celebrating success, negotiation processes and by the demonstration of power when attending or rejecting meeting invitations.

Hofstede (2001) suggested that the 'invisible' core of culture is formed by the *values*, which broadly represent tendencies and preferences over different aspects of social or professional life. These are some examples of values that may affect global projects, as they differ depending on the geographical location of team members:

- Is it polite to decline meetings because they occur during your lunch hour? Conversely, is it acceptable to book regular meetings during the lunch hour? Is it acceptable to organise a meeting starting at 6pm on a summer Friday afternoon?
- Is it acceptable to request your project team to cancel their summer holidays to finish a late deliverable?
- Are project managers more effective when they use their formal power (their hierarchical position) or their expert power (based on their competences)?
- What is the preferred leadership style for project managers, in each part of the project life cycle?

- How important is the performance of the team members, when compared to the way they respect and relate to their colleagues?

The cultural dimensions defined by Hofstede

It is very important to understand what types of differences you can come across when working on global projects. The existing cultural studies identify and measure the relation of cultural aspects among various cultures, classifying them under distinct dimensions. The following classification summarises the dimensions defined by Hofstede (2001)[1]:

POWER DISTANCE

This dimension reflects how individuals from different cultures handle the fact that people are unequal, and how the project stakeholders are likely to be involved in the decision-making process. As an example, some team members coming from countries with *larger power distance* rates may find it more difficult to disagree with their project managers in front of other people than individuals from countries with *smaller power distance* rates. In order to understand if this general rule is applicable to your project team members, you can organise some one-to-one sessions with different individuals to validate their thoughts and compare them with the opinions they give (or not) during team meetings. You can then reduce this power barrier by organising 'round-table' discussions, asking all team members to give their opinions on key project decisions. When some of them give short affirmative or neutral answers, you can stimulate their thinking by raising questions that allow them to voice their opinions without a feeling of agreement or disagreement. One example, 'Have you seen a similar event in a previous project? How was it handled? Do you think we could have the same approach in this project?'.

Table 1.1 shows that power-distances are greatest in Malaysia, and smallest in Austria. All countries in between are ranked on a continuum for comparison purposes.

Table 1.1   Countries (regions) and their power distance relative ranks

Source: adapted from Hofstede (2001)

SMALLEST	Germany (F.R.)	Pakistan	East Africa	India
Austria	Costa Rica	Spain	Belgium	Indonesia
Israel	Australia	Taiwan	Turkey	Ecuador
Denmark	Netherlands	Iran	Salvador	Arab countries
New Zealand	Canada	South Korea	Colombia	Venezuela
Ireland	United States	Greece	Hong Kong	Mexico
Sweden	Jamaica	Uruguay	France	Philippines
Norway	South Africa	Portugal	Brazil	Panama
Finland	Argentina	Chile	Singapore	Guatemala
Switzerland	Italy	Thailand	Yugoslavia	Malaysia
Great Britain	Japan	Peru	West Africa	**GREATEST**

---

1   The analysis and tables provide a sample of the extensive work from Hofstede. For a complete analysis and the detailed results of the studies, please refer to the sources in the bibliography section.

INDIVIDUALISM AND COLLECTIVISM

This dimension classifies countries according to the relationship between individuals and societies, the extent of group cohesiveness, the importance of participating in a social group and the values attached to the working conditions and ambitions. Generally, team members with *individualist* mindset praise self-determination, are fond of having sufficient time for their personal lives, enjoy freedom on selecting the way they will execute the tasks assigned to them and thrive on challenging activities and competitive environments. Work tends to be performed better when the project objectives coincide with the team member's personal interests. The business aspect of the relationship between the workers and the project organisation is often prominent.

By contrast, the collective will of a group or organisation can determine the behaviour of team members from *collectivist* cultures, who are likely to give more importance to improving their skills, using their abilities and having good physical working conditions. A higher degree of achievement occurs when the project objective and strategies coincide with the interests of the groups represented by these stakeholders, who will probably see their relationship with the project manager on moral terms.

Table 1.2 shows the increasing ranks, from the United States (highly individualist) to Guatemala (highly collectivist).

Table 1.2   Countries (regions) and their individualism relative ranks

Source: adapted from Hofstede (2001)

HIGHLY INDIVIDUALIST	France	Argentina	East Africa	Pakistan
United States	Ireland	Iran	Malaysia	Indonesia
Australia	Norway	Jamaica	Hong Kong	Colombia
Great Britain	Switzerland	Brazil	Chile	Venezuela
Canada	Germany (F.R.)	Arab countries	Singapore	Panama
Netherlands	South Africa	Turkey	Thailand	Ecuador
New Zealand	Finland	Uruguay	West Africa	Guatemala
Italy	Austria	Greece	Salvador	**HIGHLY COLLECTIVIST**
Belgium	Israel	Philippines	South Korea	
Denmark	Spain	Mexico	Taiwan	
Sweden	India	Yugoslavia	Peru	
	Japan	Portugal	Costa Rica	

MASCULINITY AND FEMININITY

Using Hofstede's terminology, in the more *masculine* countries the degree of gender differentiation is high. Individuals tend to associate men with control, power and material ambition, and women with modesty, tenderness and focus on quality of life. The ideals are economic growth, progress, material success and performance. In the more *feminine* societies, the level of discrimination and the differentiation between genders tends to be low. Individuals are likely to treat men and women equally, and value the quality of life, human contact and caring for others.

Female project managers from feminine countries may need to be patient and assertive to overcome perceptions of the stakeholders from masculine countries. Male project managers from masculine countries must show modesty, humility and competency to win the confidence of team members located in feminine countries. Global project managers may need to encourage and support female team members from masculine countries to contribute and actively express their viewpoint.

Table 1.3 provides the decreasing rank of masculinity, from Japan (most masculine) to Sweden (most feminine).

Table 1.3   Countries (regions) and their masculinity relative ranks

Source: adapted from Hofstede (2001)

MASCULINE	Ecuador	Singapore	Uruguay
Japan	United States	Israel	Guatemala
Austria	Australia	Indonesia	Thailand
Venezuela	New Zealand	West Africa	Portugal
Italy	Greece	Turkey	Chile
Switzerland	Hong Kong	Taiwan	Finland
Mexico	Argentina	Panama	Yugoslavia
Ireland	India	Iran	Costa Rica
Jamaica	Belgium	France	Denmark
Great Britain	Arab countries	Spain	Netherlands
Germany	Canada	Peru	Norway
Philippines	Malaysia	East Africa	Sweden
Colombia	Pakistan	Salvador	**FEMININE**
South Africa	Brazil	South Korea	

UNCERTAINTY AVOIDANCE

This dimension reflects the resistance to change and the attitude to taking risks of individuals from different countries. As most projects are elements of change and involve risks, the stakeholder analysis and management activities can certainly be more complete and effective when the national differences are taken into account (see Chapter 6).

Individuals from countries with *stronger uncertainty avoidance* indexes are more inclined to avoid risks, enjoy working with tight rules and control systems and resist innovation. Team members are likely to enjoy tasks requiring precision, punctuality and hard work and feel more comfortable with detailed planning and more short-term feedback. Stakeholders from *weaker uncertainty avoidance* indexes enjoy innovation, accept higher risk levels and are comfortable with open-ended learning situations. The team members tend to resist stress better and accept work packages with lower levels of definition.

Having a good mix of people from different countries in the project team allows the organisation of a brainstorming exercise to identify how to win over the resistance and obtain buy-in from different types of stakeholders. The understanding that team members may have different tolerance levels for ambiguity or uncertainty will help you to determine the level of details required for the rules, conventions and standards in your project (see Chapter 7), as well as the level of definition of the work packages that will be assigned to team members from different cultures.

Table 1.4 lists the countries according to their uncertainty-avoidance rates, from the weakest (Singapore) to the strongest (Greece).

LONG-TERM ORIENTATION

The fifth dimension from Hofstede opposes long-term to short-term aspects of Confucian thinking. People from *long-term* oriented cultures tend to give high importance to values such as

Table 1.4   Countries (regions) and their uncertainty-avoidance relative ranks

Source: adapted from Hofstede (2001)

WEAKEST	New Zealand	Taiwan	Panama
Singapore	South Africa	Austria	Argentina
Jamaica	Norway	Pakistan	Spain
Denmark	Australia	Italy	Peru
Sweden	East Africa	Brazil	Yugoslavia
Hong Kong	Netherlands	Venezuela	Japan
Ireland	West Africa	Colombia	Salvador
Great Britain	Switzerland	Israel	Belgium
Malaysia	Finland	Mexico	Uruguay
India	Iran	South Korea	Guatemala
Philippines	Thailand	Turkey	Portugal
United States	Germany (F.R.)	Costa Rica	Greece
Canada	Ecuador	Chile	**STRONGEST**
Indonesia	Arab countries	France	

persistence when results are slow, thrift, savings and having a sense of shame. Stakeholders from these countries are more likely to support entrepreneurial activity and stimulate investments.

Individuals from *short-term* oriented cultures may aim to achieve quick results and give more attention to personal stability, protecting their reputation and respect for tradition. These stakeholders would like to see more frequent progress reports that clearly show the benefits already achieved and the short-term targets to be accomplished before the next reporting cycle.

Table 1.5 shows different countries and their orientation, from short-term (Pakistan being the highest) to long-term (China being the extreme).

Table 1.5   Countries (regions) and their long-term orientation relative ranks

Source: adapted from Hofstede (2001)

SHORT-TERM	Great Britain	Bangladesh	Japan
ORIENTATION	United States	Netherlands	Taiwan
Pakistan	New Zealand	Singapore	Hong Kong
Nigeria	Australia	Thailand	China
Philippines	Germany (F.R.)	India	**LONG-TERM**
Canada	Poland	Brazil	**ORIENTATION**
Zimbabwe	Sweden	South Korea	

The cultural dimensions from Trompenaars

Trompenaars defined a different set of dimensions during his cross-cultural studies, which can be an alternative (or a complement) to Hofstede's dimensions. The following classification shows the main dimensions defined by Trompenaars and Hampden-Turner (2005) and summarised by Trompenaars and Woolliams (2003). The comparisons with Hofstede's dimensions will help you to understand to what extent the two models can be used to complement each other[2].

---

2   The analysis and tables provide a sample of the extensive work from Trompenaars, with one example of the results for each dimension. For a complete analysis of the dimensions, other classifications and the detailed results of the studies, please refer to the sources in the bibliography section.

UNIVERSALISM VERSUS PARTICULARISM

The first dimension defines how people judge the behaviours of their colleagues. People from *universalistic* cultures focus more on rules, are more precise when defining contracts and tend to define global standards for company policies and human resources practices. Within more *particularistic* national cultures, the focus is more on the relationships; contracts can be adapted to satisfy new requirements in specific situations and local variations of company and human resources policies are created to adapt to different requirements.

Project and program managers from universalistic countries will prefer to define a clear set of standards for practices, processes and templates across different countries and companies, before starting to work together. By opposition, the more particularistics will favour the establishment of generic rules and concentrate on the deliverables, caring less if each project manager uses a different set of practices.

Table 1.6 shows a sample list of countries classified according to their universalism ranking – based on the answers to the 'car and the pedestrian' dilemma.

Table 1.6   Countries and their relative universalism ranking (according to the car and the pedestrian' dilemma)

Source: adapted from Trompenaars and Hampden-Turner (2005)

UNIVERSALISTS	Romania	Argentina	China
Switzerland	Germany	Singapore	Russia
USA	Hungary	Japan	South Korea
Canada	Czech Republic	Cuba	Nepal
Ireland	Brazil	Mexico	Venezuela
Sweden	Spain	Greece	**PARTICULARISTS**
Australia	Poland	Indonesia	
UK	France	Bulgaria	
Netherlands	Nigeria	India	

INDIVIDUALISM AND COMMUNITARIANISM

This dimension is similar to the 'Individualism and Collectivism' presented by Hofstede. It classifies countries according to the balance between the individual and group interests. Generally, team members with *individualist* mindsets see the improvements to their groups as the means to achieve their own objectives. By contrast, the team members from *communitarian* cultures see the improvements to individual capacities as a step towards the group prosperity.

The stakeholders from individualistic countries are inclined to accept that one representative makes a choice on behalf of a team or group. They will also be keen to use voting to take important team decisions without *losing* time. The drawback is that the stakeholders who do not understand the rationale – or simply don't agree with it – may ignore the group decision, or start lobbying to change it. This can increase the total time to implement the actions decided, affecting the project schedule.

Decision-making processes take much longer in more communitarian cultures. The stakeholders from these countries will prefer to have a group of representatives for each party, who deliberate until a consensus is reached. The decision is likely to be followed by all participants, as they all know the reasons for it. As a consequence, the time to correct problems created by dissidents will be reduced.

Table 1.7 shows the decreasing individualist ranks, from Israel (highly individualist) to Egypt (mostly communitarian).

Table 1.7   Countries and their relative individualism ranking (according to results of the quality of life' question)

Source: adapted from Trompenaars and Hampden-Turner (2005)

INDIVIDUALISTS	Spain	Germany	China
Israel	Australia	Pakistan	Brazil
Romania	UK	Italy	Philippines
Nigeria	Sweden	Ireland	Japan
Canada	Russia	Greece	India
USA	Bulgaria	Malaysia	Mexico
Czech Republic	Poland	Portugal	Nepal
Denmark	Belgium	Indonesia	Egypt
Switzerland	Hungary	Bahrain	**COMMUNITARIANS**
Netherlands	Norway	Singapore	
Finland	Venezuela	France	

ACHIEVEMENT VERSUS ASCRIPTION

This dimension, presented in Trompenaars studies, is very similar to Hofstede's *power distance* concept. People from *achievement-oriented* countries respect their colleagues based on previous achievements and the demonstration of knowledge, and show their job titles only when relevant. On the other hand, people from *ascription-oriented* cultures use their titles extensively and usually respect their superiors in hierarchy.

If you and most of your project team members are from achievement-oriented countries, and a group of people is located in one or more ascription-oriented countries, the role of the local managers will have a special importance. You may need to involve the functional managers in project review meetings and keep them copied in most e-mail communication. The team members are not likely to take important decisions before consulting their managers. In opposite situations, project managers from ascription-oriented countries need to understand that their team members from achievement-oriented countries will like to be consulted instead of given instructions; they can also have a high degree of independence from their managers to take decisions in their areas of specialisation. Table 1.8 illustrates Trompenaar's scale, starting from achievement-oriented countries (mostly Nordic and English speaking) into ascription-oriented (Nepal and Egypt).

Table 1.8   Countries and their relative achievement-orientation (according to results of the 'acting as suits you even if nothing is achieved' question)

Source: adapted from Trompenaars and Hampden-Turner (2005)

ACHIEVEMENT-ORIENTED	Germany	Mexico	Romania
Norway	Portugal	Russia	Hungary
USA	Kenya	Netherlands	Bulgaria
Australia	Singapore	Venezuela	Cuba
Canada	India	Oman	Spain
Ireland	Thailand	China	Czech Republic
New Zealand	Switzerland	Greece	Argentina
UK	France	Japan	Uruguay
Sweden	Italy	Austria	Nepal
Nigeria	Israel	Ethiopia	Egypt
Denmark	Philippines	Indonesia	**ASCRIPTION-ORIENTED**
Finland	Brazil	Poland	
	Hong Kong	South Korea	

NEUTRAL VERSUS AFFECTIVE

According to Trompenaars, people from *neutral* cultures admire cool and self-possessed conducts and control their feelings, which can suddenly explode during stressful periods. When working with stakeholders from more neutral countries you may consider avoiding warm, expressive or enthusiastic behaviours, prepare beforehand, concentrate on the topics being discussed and look carefully for small cues showing that the person is angry or pleased.

People from cultures high on *affectivity* use all forms of gesturing, smiling and body language to openly voice their feelings, and admire heated, vital and animated expressions. To improve the collaboration of stakeholders from more affective countries you may need to avoid detached, ambiguous and cool behaviour, appreciate their good work in previous projects and tolerate their excess of emotionality, evaluating the real contents of the messages beyond the adjectives and superlatives.

Table 1.9 shows this scale from Trompenaars, starting with more neutral countries (Ethiopia and Japan) and moving to more affective countries (Egypt and Kuwait).

Table 1.9   Relative positions of countries on the extent to which exhibiting emotion is acceptable

Source: adapted from Trompenaars and Hampden-Turner (2005)

NEUTRAL	Singapore	Belgium	Argentina
Ethiopia	Australia	Brazil	Russia
Japan	United Arab Emirates	Norway	Bahrain
Poland	Nigeria	Thailand	Philippines
New Zealand	Portugal	Greece	Venezuela
Hong Kong	Sweden	Israel	Saudi Arabia
Austria	Netherlands	Germany	Cuba
China	Hungary	Denmark	Spain
Indonesia	UK	Italy	Oman
India	Czech Republic	Switzerland	Egypt
Bulgaria	USA	Malaysia	Kuwait
Canada	Mexico	France	**AFFECTIVE**
Burkina Faso	Finland	Ireland	

SPECIFIC VERSUS DIFFUSE

Trompenaars researched differences in how people engage colleagues in specific or multiple areas of their lives, classifying the results into two groups: people from more *specific-oriented* cultures tend to keep private and business agendas separate, having a completely different relation of authority in each social group. The team members may have more authority – depending on their experience and knowledge level – when meeting their functional managers at non-professional events. They are usually precise, transparent and direct, preferring meetings with precise agendas and detailed plans.

In *diffuse-oriented* countries, the authority level at work can reflect into social areas, and employees can adopt a subordinated attitude when meeting their managers outside office hours. Stakeholders from these cultures will tend to be ambiguous, evasive and act indirectly, feeling more comfortable with free-form meetings and work packages defined in less details, allowing them to exercise personal judgement and creativity.

Table 1.10 shows a list of countries, from more specific-oriented (Sweden) into more diffuse-oriented (Nepal and China).

Table 1.10   Relative positions of countries on cultural-diffuseness, according to the 'paint the house' situation

Source: adapted from Trompenaars and Hampden-Turner (2005)

SPECIFIC	Ireland	Hong Kong	Egypt
Sweden	Germany	Malaysia	Bahrain
Netherlands	Belgium	Spain	Indonesia
Switzerland	USA	Japan	Singapore
Bulgaria	Norway	Mexico	Kenya
Czech Republic	Philippines	New Zealand	Venezuela
Finland	Australia	Thailand	Kuwait
Hungary	Oman	Greece	Nigeria
Denmark	Brazil	Cuba	Burkina Faso
UK	United Arab Emirates	Saudi Arabia	Nepal
France	Poland	India	China
Canada	Israel	Ethiopia	**DIFFUSE**
Russia	Pakistan	Austria	
Uruguay	Portugal	South Korea	

HUMAN-NATURE RELATIONSHIP (INTERNAL VS EXTERNAL CONTROL)

Trompenaars shows how people from different countries relate to their natural environment and changes. Global project stakeholders from *internal-oriented* cultures may show a more dominant attitude, focus on their own functions and groups and be uncomfortable in change situations. Stakeholders from *external-oriented* cultures are generally more flexible and willing to compromise, valuing harmony and focusing on their colleagues, being more comfortable with change. Table 1.11 shows a classification of country cultures according to another aspect of this dimension: the belief of internal control. Nationals from external-control countries (for example, Venezuela and China) are less likely to believe they are in control of their own fate than people from internal-control countries (like Norway, Israel and Uruguay).

Table 1.11   Classification of country cultures according to their relationship with fate

Source: adapted from Trompenaars and Hampden-Turner (2005)

EXTERNAL-CONTROL	Japan	Sweden	Ireland
Venezuela	India	Cuba	Switzerland
China	United Arab Emirates	Belgium	UK
Nepal	Ethiopia	Italy	Canada
Russia	Hong Kong	South Korea	New Zealand
Egypt	Poland	Thailand	Australia
Saudi Arabia	Kenya	Denmark	USA
Oman	Germany	Netherlands	Norway
Kuwait	Greece	Austria	Israel
Bulgaria	Finland	Argentina	Uruguay
Singapore	Nigeria	Brazil	**INTERNAL-CONTROL**
Czech Republic	Romania	Spain	
Portugal	Indonesia	France	

HUMAN-TIME RELATIONSHIP

Similarly to Hofstede's long-term orientation, Trompenaars identified that different cultures assign diverse meanings to the past, present and future. People in *past-oriented* cultures tend to show respect for ancestors and older people and frequently put things in a traditional or historic context. They can usually be motivated by reviewing previous success stories as a preparation for the project planning sessions. People in *present-oriented* cultures enjoy the activities of the moment and present relationships, tend to be less motivated for planning sessions and may show resistance to follow detailed plans. People from *future-oriented* cultures enjoy discussing prospects, potentials and future achievement, and tend to participate actively in the planning sessions.

A second division of country cultures is based on the time orientation, in which *sequential* cultures drive people to do one activity at a time and to follow plans and schedules strictly. People from *synchronic* cultures can do work in parallel, and follow schedules and agendas loosely, taking the priorities of the individual tasks being performed as a major rule.

The representation of the human-time relationship is too complex to be summarised on a table. Please refer to the books at the end of this part, or to Trompenaars' website (www.thtconsulting.com) for more details.

The impact of the dimensions on global project management

Before using these dimensions and the classification tables, make sure you understand the following considerations:

- The dimensions assess the structure of national culture's business communities. They are not intended to be guidelines for tourists and are not concerned with personality.
- They only give an illustration of the kind of issues you may face when working with people from various national value systems, and cannot be used to predict a person's effectiveness in another culture.
- These dimensions reflect general standpoints from national cultures, not taking into account other distinctions like gender, generation, social class, education or organisation. Trompenaars' longitudinal research also now reveals shifts and convergences in many cultures over the last 20 years and thus changes in the dimension scores.
- The classifications allow a cultural comparison between different countries according to their positions in the tables.

Global project managers can consider these dimensions when assigning roles and responsibilities to team members from different country cultures, and when forming working groups. During the project execution activities, these differences are potential sources of conflict that can bring advantages to the project and reduce group thinking when correctly managed. You should read the recommendations in the other chapters of this book using the cross-cultural lenses provided by the above dimensions, and share this information with all project team members.

You may want to refer to the 'further reading' section at the end of this chapter to find more information on each of the above dimensions, the full list of countries evaluated and their classification rates, and various recommendations for international managers dealing with different cultures, which can be useful to global project managers. Intercultural awareness sessions and cross-cultural team building exercises are powerful tools during project initiation workshops and kick-off meetings, well worth the investment for global projects with a high level of cultural complexity. You can evaluate this complexity by considering the different project locations and their positions in the cultural dimension classifications. The dimensions model provides a valuable framework for beginning to comprehend the relevance of culture in business. But, ultimately, it is not about simply understanding differences, but how differences can be both connected and harnessed through reconciliation as described in Trompenaars' more recent publications.

A 360° analysis of the cultural dimensions on your project team

When forming a cross-cultural team, you can develop an early understanding of the different cultures involved, getting information from the different team members on how they position their country cultures on the dimensions and how they see other country cultures. One suggestion for this exercise is to organise a team-building activity as follows:

1. Decide if you will use Trompenaars' or Hofstede's dimensions. When you have more experience of this exercise, you can opt to combine both dimensions.
2. Form small groups of two to three individuals, each group ideally containing only nationals from the same country. The participants who are left alone can join other groups or form a separate group, deciding which country they will represent.
3. Distribute two sheets of paper to each group, with the grid shown on Table 1.12 or Table 1.13.
4. Ask each group to write their country of origin on the first line of one sheet. Groups with mixed nationalities should make a choice, giving preferences to countries well known by all members.
5. Ask the groups to 'trade' their countries, in order that each group can make an independent evaluation on another team's country. Ask each group to write the name of that country on the second sheet of paper. Alternatively, you may decide on a single country to be evaluated by all groups, based on the future contacts your project team will make. As one example, if your project requires frequent contacts with an off-shore company, you may want to develop you team's cultural awareness on the nationals of that country.
6. Describe and explain each dimension from Hofstede or Trompenaars, asking each group to write their impressions on the two countries, one on each sheet. Use the websites www.geert-hofstede.com and www.thtconsulting.com to get more information from Geert Hofstede and Fons Trompenaars on their cultural dimensions.
7. Ask each group to read aloud both views and to make a comment when opinions about the same country are different. Mark the results on the evaluation sheets (Tables 1.14 and 1.15). Promote a discussion on how different countries compare on that dimension and what this may represent to the project (by using the information presented earlier in this chapter).
8. For each dimension, compare the participants' views with the position of the countries in the classification tables from Hofstede and Trompenaars, and discuss the similarities and differences with them.
9. To close the exercise, ask each participant to tell the audience about the main surprises in how other people see their own cultures.

10. Collect the results of this exercise and repeat it on the project closing session to evaluate how the impressions of other cultures evolved during the project, and how the differences affected communication, collaboration and the project deliverables.

Table 1.12   Cultural dimensions exercise (Sheet 1)

COUNTRY:	

Please indicate, by circling the appropriate number, the extent to which the following statements characterise the cultural behaviour of nationals from the above country.

Power Distance – *How frequently, in your experience, are team members from this country comfortable to express disagreement with their functional managers?*

1	2	3	4	5	6	7	8	9	10
Very frequently.						Very seldom.			

Individualism and Collectivism – The team members from this country are more likely to enjoy ...

1	2	3	4	5	6	7	8	9	10
... self-determination, having sufficient time for their personal lives, freedom on selecting the way they will execute the tasks assigned to them, and thrive on challenging activities and competitive environments.						... improving their skills, using their abilities and having good physical working conditions.			

Masculinity and Femininity – *The team members from this country are more inclined to value ...*

1	2	3	4	5	6	7	8	9	10
... economic growth, progress, material success and performance.						... quality of life, human contact and caring for others.			

Uncertainty avoidance – *Most team members from this country are likely to ...*

1	2	3	4	5	6	7	8	9	10
... enjoy innovation, accept higher risk levels and are comfortable with open-ended learning situations.						... be more inclined to avoid risks and resist innovation, and enjoy working with tight rules..			

Long-term orientation – *Most team members from this country will prefer to ...*

1	2	3	4	5	6	7	8	9	10
... achieve quick results and give more attention to personal stability, protecting their reputation and respect for tradition.						... give more attention to savings and be persistent when results are slow.			

Table 1.13   Cultural dimensions exercise (Sheet 2)

COUNTRY:	

Please indicate, by circling the appropriate number, the extent to which the following statements characterise the cultural behaviour of nationals from the above country.

Universalism versus Particularism – *Most team members from this country are likely to ...*

1	2	3	4	5	6	7	8	9	10
... focus on detailed rules, be more precise when defining contracts, and define global standards for company policies and human resources practices.						... favour the establishment of generic rules and concentrate on the deliverables, caring less if each project manager uses a different set of practices.			

Individualism and Communitarianism – *Most team members from this country are likely to think that ...*

1	2	3	4	5	6	7	8	9	10
... more individual freedom and development opportunities can increase the quality of life.						... quality of life improves when individuals take care of their fellow human beings.			

Achievement versus Ascription – *Most team members from this country usually respect their superiors based on ...*

1	2	3	4	5	6	7	8	9	10
... their previous achievements and the demonstration of knowledge.						... the hierarchy.			

Neutral versus Affective – *Most team members from this country tend to ...*

1	2	3	4	5	6	7	8	9	10
... admire cool and self-possessed conducts and control their feelings.						... use all forms of gesturing, smiling and body language to openly voice their feelings, and admire heated, vital and animated expressions.			

Specific versus Diffuse – *When meeting their managers outside office hours, most team members from this country tend to ...*

1	2	3	4	5	6	7	8	9	10
... treat them as equal.						... adopt a subordinated attitude.			

Human-nature Relationship – *When working on teams, most people from this country ...*

1	2	3	4	5	6	7	8	9	10
... usually show a more dominant attitude, focus on their own functions and groups and are uncomfortable in change situations.						... are generally more flexible and willing to compromise, valuing harmony and focusing on their colleagues, being more comfortable with change.			

Table 1.14   Cultural dimensions exercise (Evaluation sheet 1)

Please write the country names below the ranks given by each group

Power Distance (Hofstede)

	1	2	3	4	5	6	7	8	9	10	
Lower						Higher					

Individualism and Collectivism (Hofstede)

	1	2	3	4	5	6	7	8	9	10	
More individualists						More collectivists					

Masculinity and Femininity (Hofstede)

	1	2	3	4	5	6	7	8	9	10	
More masculine						More feminine					

Uncertainty avoidance (Hofstede)

	1	2	3	4	5	6	7	8	9	10	
Weakest						Strongest					

Long-term orientation (Hofstede)

	1	2	3	4	5	6	7	8	9	10	
Short-term						Long-term					

Table 1.15   Cultural dimensions exercise (Evaluation sheet 2)

Please write the country names below the ranks given by each group

Universalism versus particularism (Trompenaars)

	1	2	3	4	5	6	7	8	9	10	
Universalists						Particularists					

Individualism and Communitarianism (Trompenaars)

	1	2	3	4	5	6	7	8	9	10	
Individualists						Communitarians					

Achievement versus ascription (Trompenaars)

	1	2	3	4	5	6	7	8	9	10	
Achievement oriented						Ascription oriented					

Neutral versus affective (Trompenaars)

	1	2	3	4	5	6	7	8	9	10	
Neutral						Affective					

Specific versus diffuse (Trompenaars)

	1	2	3	4	5	6	7	8	9	10	
Specific						Diffuse					

Human-nature relationship (Trompenaars)

	1	2	3	4	5	6	7	8	9	10	
Internal oriented						External oriented					

REAL-LIFE EXPERIENCE

The use of the above exercise can be advantageous to the cross-cultural awareness of the project team but also has limitations. Compare your own opinion with these two testimonials:

'I worked on outsourcing projects, with a large group of people from different countries, and I can see some truth on the cultural dimensions. They really link to the real-life situations. The advantage of the exercise is to show the real side of the cultural dimensions, from the very people sitting next to you. It gives a higher level of trust than when you read them from a textbook.' (Patrick)

'I've lived and worked in different countries, and with people from many cultural backgrounds. When I meet a new colleague from a certain country, I tend to compare his or her behaviour with someone I knew in the past, coming from the same place. I prefer to rely on my first impression than on survey results, as people from certain countries may try to give you the answer they think you are expecting from them rather than the answer they really meant. I believe the exercise can bring more value to individuals without a large intercultural experience in helping them to realise this.' (Frank)

Avoiding generalisations

Most of the studies available on cultural differences reflect general observations and research on the national cultural level. You can use them as a basis to understand the most likely behaviour of your colleagues and team members from a specific country. They can also help you to accept certain attitudes and discuss them with other team members to resolve conflicts. However, you need to make sure that the global team members will use this knowledge to understand and accept the cultural differences, while avoiding negative generalisations and stereotyping.

Stereotyping is an exaggerated and limited view of the average group behaviour under the cultural lenses of the observer, taking a few examples of cultural encounters – or the information from the cultural dimensions – as the only reference. You will also find different behaviours when working with a team of people from the same country, as the values and norms discussed in the cultural dimensions are not only dependent on the nationality of team members. In your life, you can be part of different cultural groups, cumulating experiences that help make you unique. Some examples of characteristics that define your cultural groups can be:

- the region (inside the country) where you live
- your ethnic origin
- your religion
- your language
- your gender
- your age or generation
- your education level
- the industry you work in
- your company
- your job function

Perhaps the most important lesson for global project managers is the openness they should have in relation to the cultural dimensions. Take this example: Hofstede (2001) evaluated the relationship between the power distance dimension (PDI) and planning and control systems, concluding that, 'Lower-PDI control systems place more trust in subordinates; in higher-PDI cultures such trust is lacking.' Table 1.1 shows that Malaysia is higher than Austria in power distance. The wrong usage of this information is to relax on project control when dealing with activities performed by Austrian members, and adopt a directive approach to the Malaysians. The preferred approach is:

- Start using the same processes and management style for all team members – you can control the activities of the Austrian and Malaysian team members with the same frequency and using the same processes.
- Observe the different reactions and behaviours under the lenses of the cultural dimensions – observe if the team members are performing their activities on time, verifying the work executed. Identify if the Austrian team members really have less need for control than the Malaysians. This will not show a weakness from either team, simply a different behaviour.
- Be ready for surprises – in many cases, the team members are well adapted to the company cultures, and will react in a different way than you expect. The Malaysian team members may in fact work independently, with a reduced need for control.
- Adapt your style to the differences – if you notice that the team members from Malaysia require a more directive approach for control, you can organise a weekly meeting to follow their activities in more detail, while reviewing the overall project status together with the Austrians in a separate fortnightly meeting.

Building on the richness of a multicultural team: crossvergence and hybridisation

Global project managers can use originality to deviate from general norms and obtain competitive advantage, improving the likelihood of project success. An interesting concept from recent research is *crossvergence*, which according to Jacob (2005) is, 'all about fusing together management practices of two or more cultures, so that a practice relevant to a heterogeneous culture can be assembled'. Global teams can provide all elements for an effective fusion of different project management practices: people from various country and company cultures, enriched by different experiences and management theories, implemented by a team in different countries, with a wealthy mix of skills and beliefs. *Hybridisation* is another concept on multicultural management, which can be defined as the use of a common body of knowledge, enhanced with selective parts of successful practices from the countries where the project is being implemented, or from the team members' original culture.

When starting a global project in a new country, or when new project team members have a cultural origin that you never experienced before, the cultural dimensions (presented earlier in this chapter) can be a first source of reference to understand their general mindset, and the cultural patterns likely to be found in their culture. A second step is to read different sources of information on the country, not only to show the team members that you care for their culture, but to really understand how they live, think, and what the main sources of cultural and economic richness are. The third step – and certainly the most important – is to pay attention to the behaviour of the team members, to understand their values during informal conversations and to show respect for these values, while letting them know your own opinion, the project communication standards and the important norms that must be followed for them to be accepted by the other team members (Connaughton and Daly, 2004).

The development of these skills is not a simple task, and can only be achieved after some years of experience in multicultural teams. To reduce the time to master these skills, and improve the likelihood of success in your first global project, you can attend 'soft-skills' training sessions and request coaching from more experienced global project managers. Fisher and Fisher (2001) suggest that a good training plan will also include language lessons (for people in frequent contact with a foreign language), technical training (when there are different levels of understanding on technical disciplines that can create conflicts or risks to the collaboration) and cross-cultural training (when team members and key stakeholders come from different cultural backgrounds and there are many differences in the cultural dimensions explained earlier in this chapter).

REAL-LIFE EXPERIENCE

The level of information exchange required on the project can vary depending on the cultural patterns of the stakeholders. In one real-life example, the project implementation would affect the availability of the computer systems in various factories across the globe, requiring an early approval from six country representatives. In the first project phase, an overall description of the activity was distributed by e-mail and the electronic approval was requested by using an automated change configuration tool.

One country representative called the project manager on the same day, took the opportunity of the telephone call to have a lengthy informal discussion, and then promised a quick approval (this happened 3 days later). The representative from a second country called the project manager, spent a short time in informal introductions, and then discussed the activity at a detailed level. After receiving all the explanations on the risk assessment and understanding the contingency measures in place, the activity was approved on the same day.

While the project manager was thinking the approval process would be smooth, the third country representative sent a lengthy e-mail, copying two senior managers and the project sponsor, and explained in an abrupt language that the details supplied were not enough. The project manager needed to:

- Organise an audio conference immediately, to review the detailed project plan, all the risk responses and to introduce the project team members coordinating and executing the critical activities;

- write precise meeting minutes capturing the points discussed;

- reply to the e-mail, with a copy to everyone that received the original message, and including a link to the meeting minutes, remaining available for more information if needed.

After 1 week, the electronic approval was provided, without any informal telephone call or e-mail.

One week after the request, the other three country representatives had not replied. The project manager called the fourth country representative, who informed that the approval would never be provided without a detailed level of information. Four days after receiving the detailed documentation, the representative provided the electronic approval and forwarded one e-mail message that revealed a long thread of internal reviewers, who participated in an internal meeting to discuss the activity and validate all the project details.

When called, the fifth country coordinator apologised politely for the lack of answer (using the excessive amount of e-mails as a justification), and gave the electronic approval in 5 minutes.

After 3 weeks of e-mails (never replied to) and voice mail messages (never returned), the sixth representative provided the approval without any question or request for details.

The project manager considered all these behaviours and reviewed the project communications plan for the second project phase (that would require the approval of the same representatives):

- The information e-mail contained a couple of paragraphs with a brief description of the planned activities, the risks involved and the response strategies;

- the e-mail also contained a link to the project plan, to the detailed risk analysis and to the roles and responsibilities matrix;
- the last paragraph invited all representatives to an information session (by audio and web conferencing) aiming to discuss the activities in more detail and suggesting that they invite all colleagues who would be involved in the approval process;
- the country managers (senior to the representatives) were included in the distribution list of the same message, and requested to take action in case their subordinates were unavailable at that time.

The first two representatives called in the same day, again for informal discussions, and provided a quick approval. They declined the invitation to the explanation meeting, as they were satisfied with the detail level in the brief description.

The third and fourth representatives participated in the meeting, with other colleagues, and provided their approval in less than a week. The fifth and sixth representatives answered the e-mail after 1 week, with their apologies for the delay and for not attending the meeting, but with positive feedback on the information and giving their approval.

The revised approach was part of the lessons-learned documentation and applied successfully in later projects, with participation from different representatives from the same countries. While some of the behaviours above were similar between different representatives from the same country, an important part was not repeated, revealing personal or intra-cultural differences. The main conclusion of this experience is that the adoption of a holistic approach for communication, providing different levels of information to various stakeholders from distinct culture backgrounds, can improve understanding and reduce conflicts.

4-step framework for effective cross-cultural project management

- Learn the definition and different types of culture – the cultural differences exist across countries, but are also influenced by a diversity of age, gender, regions, religions and many other types of social groups. Consider the dimensions presented in this chapter as a starting point to build your own cross-cultural knowledge.
- Understand the cultural differences – use the cultural dimensions to know what differences to expect between people from different cultures. Employ a team building exercise to identify how your team and colleagues view these differences.
- Respect the cultural differences – keep the differences in mind when confronted with opposite views of the world. You must accept them and show respect for the different standpoints.
- *Vive la différence* – enjoy the richness of a multi-cultural team. Remember that you can build on the differences to identify and mitigate risks, to find alternative approaches and achieve the project objectives in better ways, and to increase the level of innovation and quality of your project deliverables.

YOUR INTERCULTURAL LEARNING

Revisit the list or mindmap created at the beginning of this chapter. Would you handle the negative situations in a different way? What conflicts would be hard to avoid, despite the learning from the cultural dimensions and strategies? Do you think that societies have evolved in the last few years, making the cultural classifications out-of-date? Now share your thoughts with other people and read about their own intercultural experiences (www.GlobalProjectManagement.org).

2 *Global Project Leadership*

Project leadership can be defined as *the creation of a vision about the project objectives that directs all team members to work towards it.* Good project leaders are able to influence the task prioritisation and the availability of the project team members towards achieving the project goals and strategies.

Different authors have captured the essence of leadership from various perspectives and defined theories and frameworks to increase the effectiveness of team leaders. This chapter is not dependent on any particular theory and presents only the challenges and recommendations on leadership that are applicable to global projects. Project managers that already have a good notion of leadership skills in traditional projects can use these recommendations to evaluate their current practices, complete their preferred leadership models and theories and effectively lead a project team composed of people located in different countries.

This chapter explains the differences between leadership and management, discusses the main leadership challenges to global project managers and provides some suggestions to increase the commitment and motivation of team members located around the globe.

Project management and leadership

Project managers make use of proven practices to plan project activities and monitor important elements such as cost, scope, time, quality and risks. Examples of these *management* practices are presented by bodies of knowledge such as the PMBOK® Guide, ICB and PRINCE2®. Project *management* is the application of these practices by using 'hard skills' such as planning, estimating and controlling. Project *leadership*[1] adds to the management practices and involves

---

YOUR EXPERIENCE OF LEADERSHIP

Before reading this chapter, think about some situations that occurred in your previous or current global projects. Were the team members committed to work towards the project objectives? Was it more difficult to obtain support from team members located in other countries? Why?

Now think about some situations when you worked for other program or project managers. What characteristics make them good managers? What makes them good leaders? What are the different leadership styles of project managers from different countries?

Summarise these thoughts on a list or mindmap, underlining the main challenges you faced, and the key characteristics of managers and leaders. You can complete the list while you read this chapter, and keep it for future reference.

---

1   The term 'project leader' is often a misnomer, when it refers to project managers that have less experience or responsibility.

providing direction, motivating the project team to achieve the project's objectives and obtaining commitment from the key team members and stakeholders. Project *leadership* is the application of 'soft skills' to obtain commitment, foster innovation, negotiate conflicts and create a team spirit that increases the quality of the deliverables and customer satisfaction. Good leadership can reduce the intensity and frequency of control activities on medium-sized projects, and is usually mandatory on large projects and programs.

Project managers can develop strong leadership skills to compensate for the lack of expert power (when they manage projects outside their main knowledge domains) and formal authority (when the project team members are subordinated to a functional manager or are part of a different organisation). *Program* managers usually have a stronger need to develop and make use of good leadership skills to inspire, motivate and provide coaching to the project managers and coordinators.

Global leadership

Each dimension of global projects adds a series of leadership challenges. Some of these challenges are listed below, together with strategies that can help you to surmount the global barriers:

- Number of distant locations – the geographical distances can be barriers to relationship building, as there will be fewer opportunities for informal discussions and team events. Leaders will need to structure the project vision in creative ways to communicate it equally across all the locations.
- Number of different organisations – team members working for different organisations can have competing interests and hidden agendas. Good leaders keep their eyes and minds open for the different perspectives, aiming to identify and reconcile the various factors of motivation.
- Country cultures – people coming from different countries can have various sources of motivation, diverse priorities and dissimilar values and ethics. Good leaders must consider all these factors and the cultural dimensions (evaluated in Chapter 1) to align, motivate and inspire the global team members.
- Different languages – team members with different native languages may not understand or may have imprecise interpretations of sentences in foreign languages. Good global leaders may find local allies that translate the project vision and constantly communicate it and reinforce it to the local teams, using local languages and expressions.
- Time zones – the development of motivation and relationship building without a 'shared time' can be extremely difficult and frustrating for project managers. The team members may tend to ignore the asynchronous communication or keep it as low priority. Few people will feel motivated or inspired by someone they rarely meet. Global leaders must plan for shared time, organise co-located team events, travel to meet the team members during key activities and coach key team members to function as local leaders during all project phases.

The next sections review the leadership activities in more detail, providing recommendations to global project managers.

Commitment

How can you obtain commitment from global team members? How can you develop followers in the different locations that can disseminate the project vision and make sure that all team members across the globe are aligned on the project objectives and strategies?

The strategies and practices depend on the organisational and country cultures, the project type, size and duration, and even on the different personalities involved. However, there are some broad recommendations for leadership competencies and activities, to win these challenges and increase the commitment from the team members located in other countries. The suggestions below must be evaluated according to the situations and projects you are involved in, and can be a starting point when you acquire and develop your project team:

- Set clear goals and directions at the project outset, with participation from key team members in different locations. Online brainstorming techniques (discussed in Chapter 10) can be very effective to collect feedback and obtain buy-in from people across locations.
- Build a vision that serves the interests of the main stakeholders and that can be translated into the achievement of the project objectives. Consider the cultural dimensions of the stakeholders involved in the project, and adapt the description of the vision to their trends on long-term orientation and human-nature relationships.
- Together with the key team members, develop a strategy to achieve the project objectives, and make sure that all or most team members agree on its feasibility. This is a good opportunity to gather representatives from every country in the same location for a few days and develop a good team spirit.
- Communicate the vision, goals and directions equally to all local and distant project team members. Obtain buy-in by asking for their feedback and suggestions on how to improve the project strategy, and how to achieve the objectives. Organise online sessions using the synchronous tools (see Chapters 22 and 23), and take this opportunity to launch the project website, publishing the vision, goals and directions, and organising polls to gather opinions and ideas (see Chapters 19 and 24).
- Provide appropriate and timely feedback to all suggestions and remarks. This will show your team members that you are open to their ideas, and align them to the project objectives. To the same extent, answer all questions within an acceptable time, using an appropriate media (See Part V – Adoption of Collaborative Tools).
- Empower the team; by delegating the control of important work packages, by nominating coordinators for complex knowledge domains and by developing leaders at distant locations. Distribute work packages to these coordinators and suggest the organisation of meetings to build a detailed plan. Attend the first meetings and provide coaching on leadership to the local coordinators.
- Build an informal network among all project coordinators, and make sure their behaviour remains consistent to the project vision and strategies during the whole project. This will facilitate the negotiations and conflict management processes, and foster cooperation and innovation.
- Discuss with the project coordinators the applicability of different leadership theories to the various countries and cultures.
- Encourage self-leadership behaviours by team members who are geographically separated from the other project team members.

- Build trust from the beginning, and maintain a high level of trust until project closure (see Chapter 3).
- Create a team environment that allows the work experience to be rewarding and enjoyable, where team members learn to understand and respect different cultures and have positive attitudes toward conflict resolution.
- Foster social interactions outside the project tasks, creating a strong personal relationship by face-to-face contacts and understanding of cultural values, communication norms and business ethics.
- Organise face-to-face team building exercises to reduce the feeling of isolation of global project team members located in remote offices.
- Foster use of communications technologies for teamwork including people from various locations. The availability of task-related information will increase the job satisfaction and commitment level.
- Consider the 'power-distance' cultural dimension as a starting point to understand which leadership behaviour you will apply to new team members from different countries: directive, supportive, participative or achievement-oriented.
- Act with integrity and consistency to the project vision and strategy, during the whole project and on all occasions. The communication of the vision and strategy will only increase commitment when they are synchronised with actions of the project manager.
- Inspire the team, by being always available and providing guidance, locally or remotely.
- Praise members with positive attitudes, and motivate others to follow their examples.

Motivation

> 'The study of motivation concerns those processes that give behaviour its energy and direction. Energy implies that behaviour has strength – that it is relatively strong, intense and persistent. Direction implies that behaviour has purpose – that is aimed toward achieving a particular goal'
>
> (Johnmarshall Reeve)

Motivation can be defined as an individual process that provides energy and direction to adopt a specific behaviour or perform a determined task. In project management, the *energy* must ensure the team members will complete their tasks on time, and the *direction* needs to lead the tasks performed toward the project vision, mission and goals, following pre-determined strategies. Each individual can initiate a self-motivation process by understanding how the task can satisfy personal or professional needs, suit expectations and beliefs and invoke positive emotions. The task of motivating other project team members can be harder, as you need to understand what their needs, expectations and beliefs are, and what 'makes them tick'. You need to pay special attention to their behaviour and carefully evaluate their reactions and emotions through verbal and non-verbal cues.

When working with team members from other countries over a distance, the challenge is higher, as suggested by Staples, Wong and Cameron (2004), 'Tasks may appear unconnected, the big picture is not always easy to visualise, and it may be difficult for employees to remain committed to the project.' The cultural dimensions are a good starting point to pre-empt the possible values and beliefs of people you seldom meet face-to-face. One-to-one telephone discussions and local coordinators can help you to obtain individual feedback from each key

REAL-LIFE EXPERIENCE

This is a tale of using effective leadership to recover a troubled project. After a turbulent project start, and when the trust level across companies and locations was at its worst, two experienced project managers were brought on board to establish a quick recovery plan and avoid slippages in the tight schedule.

As their first action, they visited the main stakeholders and project managers in the different project locations, identifying the main risks, problems, challenges and recommendations. They quickly identified that there were too many issues to be addressed, and prioritised the list according to the urgency of the recovery actions. They established a short-term goal: to succeed on a critical milestone planned to happen in 2 weeks. The strategy:

- establish quick daily meetings, well coordinated, to track the progress of actions in the critical path;

- nominate project coordinators and empower them to manage and own the main work packages, coaching them when needed;

- increase trust from the main stakeholders, by organising weekly information sessions and distributing daily summaries with the status of critical activities.

Despite the high pressure, long working hours and an endless list of activities, they kept their focus on their strategy and adopted a professional demeanour. All e-mail messages and requests for information were answered on the same day. The requests that could not be fulfilled immediately were replied to with a target date. The stressful moments were dealt with by using humour and patience, stepping back to take emotions out and find the right answers to the problem. At that moment, the team members knew they were being led to the right direction: the successful completion of the project.

When the critical milestones started to be achieved, the tight control was somewhat relaxed, motivating people by showing confidence in their technical and coordination capacities. The daily status meeting continued until the end of the project, with reduced duration and stress levels.

team member and monitor their reactions and emotions. You can compare these feedback elements to the original assumptions and adapt your attitude and leadership style.

Hofstede (2001) identified that motivation theories based on Western thinking and individualist societies (for example, Maslow, McClelland and Herzberg, explained in Mullins (1996)) may not be equally applicable to different country cultures, and that motivation is highly dependent on the different degrees of uncertainty avoidance and masculinity in various countries. You can understand better the relationship between motivation factors and cultural dimensions with the help of Table 2.1.

You can also increase the level of motivation by making use of the roles and responsibilities. A classic tool for this is McClelland's *achievement motivation theory*, which groups individuals according to their need for achievement, affiliation and power (adapted from Rad and Levin, 2003):

- **Achievement-oriented** individuals seek attainable but challenging goals and feedback on their performance. They can participate in the project charter preparation and are well-suited for virtual environments. You can refer to Trompenaars' dimension 'Achievement versus ascription' (see page 30) when working with a group of team members from another country, to have an initial feeling about how they tend to value achievement

Table 2.1   Factors of motivation in different areas of the world (adapted from Hofstede, 2001)

Countries and regions	Motivators
USA, Great Britain and their former dominions and colonies	Individual success in form of wealth, recognition, and 'self-actualisation'
Japan, German-speaking countries, some Latin countries and Greece	Individual security and wealth obtained by hard work
France, Spain, Portugal, ex-Yugoslavia, Chile, and other Latin and Asian countries	Security, relationships and group solidarity
North European countries plus the Netherlands	Success, belonging, quality of human relationships and the living environment

in comparison to your local colleagues. Furthermore, countries rated low on uncertainty avoidance (see page 48) and high on masculinity (see page 26) tend to have a higher number of achievement-oriented individuals. Achievement-oriented people can be motivated by being placed in roles involving the completion of challenging tasks, can benefit from electronic forums and collaborative environments, and may enjoy the recognition of project achievements announced using these electronic media.

- **Affiliation-oriented** people desire to be part of a group and have human interaction roles. Affiliation-oriented individuals may have difficulties when working in virtual and global projects, but can be motivated by acting as relationship managers for the global team, functioning as a communications expeditor, serving as a meeting facilitator, promoting camaraderie and following-up on action items.

- **Power-oriented** team members aspire to make an impact and to be recognised as influential and effective. They may find it most difficult to be a member of a global project, as they may not have the same impression of recognition as in traditional projects. Power-oriented team members can be motivated by performing critical roles such as leading team meetings and problem-solving sessions, mentoring colleagues, performing risk assessment and conflict management.

Becoming a good global leader

The main characteristics of a good leader are valid for most countries and cultures. When adapting common recommendations from the literature on leadership and motivation to global project management, the following suggestions appear:

- foster a positive and flexible culture, respecting the country differences and making the team members see the benefit of this diversity to the project;
- use the synchronous and asynchronous communication tools to coach, lead and support the team members, independently of their location, origin, gender and hierarchical position;
- search for cohesive solutions, adapting your negotiation skills to the different cultures involved in the conflicts and discussions;

- behave as a partner, not a 'boss', mainly when working with people from smaller power-distance countries;
- nurture creativity and innovation in team members from different locations, by deploying online and asynchronous brainstorming tools (see Chapter 10).

Brainstorming on global leadership

As well as using the recommendations above and from other books, you can understand what the people in your company think about leadership and motivation, and evaluate what practices would work in your situation. You can organise a brainstorming session, with a mix of project managers and team members from different countries, to understand their opinions on leadership. Alternatively, organise the session during your project kick-off meeting with your global project team members. You can keep the results on a mindmap posted in the project website and in the project 'war room'. Below, you can find some examples of questions to be asked during the session:

- Question 1 – Think of one of the most satisfactory and successful <u>local</u> projects you worked on as a team member. What are the main characteristics that define the leadership style of the project manager?
- Question 2 – Think about one of the most satisfactory and successful <u>global</u> projects you worked on as a team member. What are the main characteristics that define the leadership style of the project manager?
- Question 3 – Based on all points captured by you and your colleagues on the first two questions, how would you define a good leader of global projects?
- Reflection – Is there any difference between a good leader for local and global projects? How does leadership translate across different cultures?

You can use the result of the brainstorming sessions to complete the suggestions in this book, and prepare a set of recommendations to be used by all global project managers at your company. Revisit these good practices during lessons-learned sessions of strategic or complex programs and projects, to validate their applicability across borders, and adapt them to the new acquirements.

YOUR LEARNING ON LEADERSHIP

Revisit the list or mindmap created at the beginning of this chapter. Would you lead your global project teams in a different way? How can you adapt your leadership styles to the team members from different countries? What did you learn from the brainstorming sessions that confirmed or contradicted your original thoughts?

Now share your findings with other people, and read about their own learning (www. GlobalProjectManagement.org).

3 *Trust Building*

Trust is at the heart of global team management. Most books and academic research conclude that trust is the key element that allows effective communication, management and leadership over a distance. As an example, Lipnack and Stamps (1997) define trust as, 'the belief or confidence in a person or organisation's integrity, fairness, and reliability (...) [coming] from past experience, however brief or extensive,' and conclude that trust is an essential quality in productive relationships across borders. Bower and Skountzos (2000) suggest that 'with understanding comes trust and with trust comes the possibility for a synergistic relationship,' when multiple companies form partnerships for the project execution. Hofstede (2001) noted that the the personal relationship prevails over the task (and over the company) in collectivist societies, where project managers need to form personal relationships with key stakeholders and establish a trusting relationship before starting to plan and work on the project.

There is a high level of dependency between trust and all other practices in the Global Project Management Framework©. Implementing the recommendations from the Global Project Management Framework© in all remote locations can help to increase trust, as all the program and project managers will share common processes, tools and communication techniques with the stakeholders in different countries. On the other hand, building trust from the beginning will simplify the implementation of common processes, tools and techniques into a new project team, increasing adoption.

You can follow the steps described in this chapter to evaluate your needs and increase trust among the project managers and coordinators, team members and other stakeholders:

- identify the level of trust required;
- determine the weak communication channels in your project team;
- establish trust in the initial phases of the project;
- maintain trust during the project implementation;
- build on this trust to create a healthy and collaborative environment for future projects.

YOUR OPINION ON TRUST

Before reading the recommendations to evaluate and improve the trust on your project, think about some current or recent global programs and projects in which you were involved. Do you trust all team members, or only a few of them? What are the reasons for you to trust them? Do they trust you? What makes you trustworthy? Think about other programs and project managers and enumerate some of their qualities that inspire your trust. Can you establish a relationship between successful programs and trustworthy program and project managers?

Write on a list or mindmap the main reasons for trust and qualities that inspire trust. Write on a separate list some actions you can take to develop trust in people that will work with you in the future.

Identifying the level of trust required

Not all global programs need the same level of trust, requiring a different set of practices to be deployed depending on each situation. The main variables that can impact the level of trust required by global projects are listed below. You can use them to evaluate how much effort you need to put in place to develop trust between the key project stakeholders:

- **Project complexity** – the project budget, scope and risk level can add to the complexity of programs and projects, and increasing the level of trust among the stakeholders can be a good contingency to reduce the likelihood of risks. You can classify the complexity of your programs and projects by using the typology proposed by Khazanchi and Zigurs (2006): *Lean* projects have, 'low complexity, narrow scope and relatively low risk'; *hybrid* projects have, 'varying levels of complexity, scope and risk'; *extreme* projects have, 'high complexity, broad scope and high risk'.
- **Project schedule** – projects that have many parallel activities, and more than one critical path, will require more trust among team members to attain the cooperation level needed to achieve the milestones. Global projects will have increased levels of risks when these parallel activities are performed by team members working across borders, and when the dependencies among activities require communication between people in different time zones.
- **Number of different locations** – the need for trust development is greater, the more geographical locations involved in a project. For team members in the same location, sharing working and leisure time, trust establishment can be a natural process. Remote team members have less probability of sharing activities out of the office and having informal conversations. These activities must be stimulated in team-building exercises in order to build trust.
- **Number of different cultures** – the number of different cultural values and norms is a natural barrier in people trusting each other. These hurdles can be reduced or eliminated through cultural awareness training, exercises and brainstorming involving teams from different cultures.
- **Number of different organisations** – differences in organisational cultures, priorities and interests may damage the trust between partners, suppliers and customers. In many cases, the rules must be clearly formalised at a very early stage and followed strictly during the execution of project activities. Companies working in partnerships need to agree at an early stage on their roles and responsibilities for control and information sharing, and make sure all stakeholders involved in the project understand and respect these agreements.
- **Number of new relations** – trust develops over time, based on successful shared experiences. When a group of people have never worked together in previous projects, the trust development must start from the beginning, taking more time to mature.

Trust and communication channels

A second step to identify how to develop trust in a project team is to draw the chart of communication channels, drawing one line for each of the situations described in the previous section. This can be illustrated by the exercise below, taken from a real-life example.

Consider a global project with four key members in two locations (A and B) and you, the project manager, on a third location (C). Your company director classified this project as 'business critical' and told you the project must be completed on time. When preparing the project schedule, you noticed three critical paths composed of activities under the responsibility of different team members. You identified this as a risk with high probability and high impact on the schedule. You believe you can lower its probability by developing trust early in the project, and you want to develop this strategy further and calculate the mitigation costs to obtain management approval.

You can start by depicting a chart of the project manager, the team members and the geographical locations, drawing one line for the communications between people in the same site (as in Figure 3.1):

Consider – in this example – that locations B and C are in the same country, and draw an extra line between team members having the same country culture (as illustrated in Figure 3.2).

Consider now the team members who have already worked together on previous projects (as illustrated in Figure 3.3). You need to pay some attention to these relationships during the project, in order to identify if the previous experience was positive – generating good quality teamwork – or negative, marked by conflicts and mistrust.

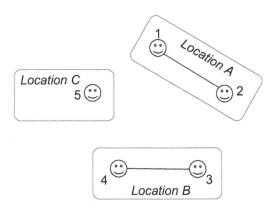

Figure 3.1   Communication channels in the same location

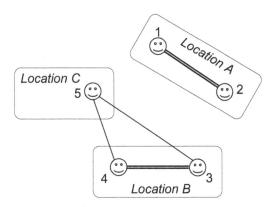

Figure 3.2   Communication channels not crossing country borders

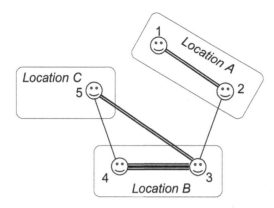

Figure 3.3   Communication channels built from previous experiences

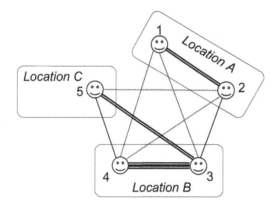

Figure 3.4   Weak communication channels that require trust building

As a final step, identify the missing links: the weak communication channels that you must build during project initiation for trust to be reinforced during project execution. Ignore for the moment the channels between people that have low probability of working together. Suppose that you will not manage team member 1 directly, as team member 2 will coordinate all activities for location A. This way the trust level between you and team member 1 will have a very low impact on the project outcomes and can be suppressed from the chart. Figure 3.4 shows the final stage of this exercise, serving as a reference for the next sections, which will illustrate different ways to develop and maintain trust. In this case, almost half of the communication channels are weak (represented in the figure by the dotted lines).

Establishing trust

A 'project planning workshop' is one of the most effective ways to involve the key team members from the beginning, to develop trust by team building activities and to produce a project management plan that will be accepted by the team. Here are some good practices for a planning workshop and for other meetings in the early stages of your project:

- Trust is extremely important between the project manager and the key team members and coordinators. These relationships must have the higher priority for trust establishment.
- Face-to-face meetings are a very good opportunity to build trust among your project team members. When you discover that most of the communication channels crossing country borders are weak (for example, Figure 3.4), identify this as a risk and suggest mitigating its probability by organising one face-to-face planning workshop. If the costs of such a workshop are unacceptable, organise a series of meetings using video conferencing and invest more time in team-building activities. Be aware that this second alternative can have reduced costs but will certainly increase the time and effort required to build trust, and is less likely to be effective.
- You can also identify the existing communication channels as opportunities to increase the likelihood of project success (for example, Figure 3.3), and enhance them by the same face-to-face or video conferencing workshops.
- Consider organising the planning workshop in a neutral location, where all team members can spend the same amount of time and cost on travel.
- When some key team members cannot travel, avoid isolating them from the rest of the team during a face-to-face meeting, preferring to use video conferencing to link all locations. As another alternative, you can travel to their locations after the planning workshop, taking your time to review the outcomes with the key team members, noting down their suggestions for a later discussion over video or audio conferencing with the rest of the team.
- Start your workshop by reviewing the project scope and building the Work Breakdown Structure (WBS) during a brainstorming session including all team members. Taking the team in Figure 3.4 as an example, involve all four team members in the WBS creation process. For large teams, consider organising groups to define the work packages for different project deliverables. Use the suggestions below to create groups that will help to develop trusting relationships.
- Build on relationships from previous projects. You can identify the informal discussions happening during the face-to-face contacts to know who worked together on previous projects. They can help you to expand the network of trusting relationships. Consider the communication channels when dividing the team members into groups to prepare the project plan or to execute some early activities, and include some individuals that know each other in the same group. Using the example in Figure 3.4, you can ask team members 1, 2 and 3 to develop the WBS for one deliverable. This would help to build the relationship between 1 and 3.
- Be careful with relationships from previous projects. Distrust can spread quickly when new team members did not share good experiences in the past. Be aware that more effort will be required to build trust with these people, helping you to set up priorities in the trust building process. As an example, observe the relationship and cooperation between team members 1 and 2 when they are working on the WBS preparation. When you notice a turbulent relationship, try to identify the sources of conflict and build on common ground to improve the level of trust.
- Build on your interpersonal skills to obtain trust from team members that have never worked on one of your projects. Using the previous example, use the conflict management skills (see Chapter 4) to transform the bad relationship between team members 1 and 2

into a source of creativity. As an example, you can use their different opinions to identify risks or to create different scenarios to be discussed with the rest of the team, building a trusting relationship between you and both team members.

- Build on shared personal interests. You can have informal discussions and identify common interests from different team members, as trust can develop naturally between people sharing the same passions or hobbies. As an example, you can ask people to mention their hobbies when introducing themselves at face-to-face workshops. If you notice a group of 'chess lovers', the project collaborative space can have some areas dedicated to announcing online chess tournaments after working hours, grouping people with the same interests. On some occasions, you may need to monitor the use of these spaces to make sure the number of informal contacts will not have more priority than the project execution tasks.
- Ask all team members to agree to the information that must be exchanged across different tasks, mainly when there is a dependency between activities performed in different locations. In the previous example, increase the trust level in the relationship between 1 and 4 by making them agree on the information they need to exchange in order to complete their activities, and make them define in advance the level of detail required by them to work on their own tasks. This will streamline the communication and reduce the probability of negative conflicts that can generate mistrust.
- Use all opportunities to demonstrate the integrity and competence of your team members to each other, by praising achievements and giving positive feedback during meetings or informal discussions. You might serve as a role model by showing your adherence to the project mission and objectives, being compliant to your company standards and ethics and demonstrating competence on the project management processes.
- The cross-cultural management practices are extremely important during trust establishment, as global team members must consider intercultural differences when evaluating other people. Review Chapter 1 with your project team and organise some brainstorming sessions on the topic.
- Use all the collaborative technologies (discussed in Chapters 16–25) to foster the exchange of information, as the team members will trust colleagues who are open to share their knowledge and exchange ideas through the accepted practices and communication tools.
- Project initiation tasks must establish the project mission and strategies in a clear and unambiguous manner. Review this and other suggestions in the leadership chapter (see page 43).

After a successful planning workshop and a series of well-organised meetings, our map of trusting relationships should be complete, as shown in Figure 3.5.

Maintaining trust

During project execution you should continue developing and managing your project team and the project stakeholders, to enhance project performance and keep the level of trust. This can be part of your monitoring and controlling activities. Some examples of good practices for maintaining the trusting relationships developed during project initiation and planning:

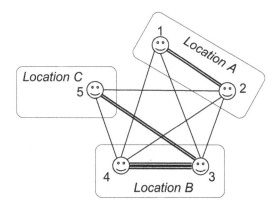

Figure 3.5   Trust in all communication channels

- Define ground rules and clear methods to monitor and control the project execution, informing all team members of the processes to be followed, and monitoring their correct deployment.
- Always follow the communications management plan, ensure all project team members are also following it and obtain suggestions to adapt the plan whenever applicable to improve understanding.
- Give a high priority to the interests of your stakeholders and evaluate their feelings to adapt your communication and leadership styles.
- Organise team-building activities during regular meetings. You can start your meetings with informal conversations around common personal interests identified during the planning workshop or organise 5-minute brainstorming sessions on soft-skills topics. You may also ask the team members to prepare short presentations on personal hobbies, or longer presentations on professional topics that can add value to the project.
- Take time to meet the key stakeholders face-to-face and have informal discussions whenever possible. Alternatively, use the telephone to make these informal contacts, without having a pretext of discussing the project work. You can increase the level of trust of your team members, and show openness for them to discuss their potential personal or professional issues that could affect their work on the project. You can then identify when trusting relationships are getting weak, and use problem-solving skills to address potential issues in advance.
- Reserve meeting rooms in advance. Team members working in the same location may prefer to sit together during meetings. This allows informal discussions to happen after the meetings are finished, building trust and simplifying the communication among these team members.
- When visiting a distant location, try to meet all team members working there, independently of their hierarchical position. This will reinforce the relationship between you and the project team, and show your openness to ideas and opinions coming from different sources.

REAL-LIFE EXPERIENCE

This is another tale of global project recovery. In some situations, projects start to deviate from the original targets and new project managers are brought on board to assess the problems and correct the situation. In one of these cases, the main problem was a general feeling of mistrust, diagnosed a couple of months before a critical milestone was due. The risk of missing the deadline was considered high and the potential impact to the company was very important.

The new project manager detected the problem during the first status meeting with participation from the three main teams involved, each in their own country attending by audio conference. Most of the meeting time was spent on complaints from the customer team about long-running open issues and actions not performed on time, angry reactions from the two suppliers challenging the need for the actions and the validity of the issues, and long discussions on technical topics that involved only a few participants.

After the meeting, the former project manager said that this meeting had been viewed as stressful since the beginning of the project and was considered impossible to change, as the personalities and organisational cultures were completely different. One hour was allocated to the meeting, but the effective duration was between 2 and 3 hours. The new project manager decided to travel to the different locations and listen to the opinions of the different participants.

Both supplier teams were extremely dissatisfied with the behaviour of the customer team members, who changed the scope and agreed dates too often and very close to the deadlines. This was creating a regular need for overtime at very short notice. Apparently, the suppliers only considered two members from the customer team as trustworthy, and they were not the ones leading the discussions.

A very similar opinion was given by the customer team: the supplier team members never understood the pace of change on the business, were always complaining about overtime and short reaction times and were not competent in their technical domains. The only exception was for one team member – who was appreciated for his technical expertise – and the team leader – who was trustworthy but, 'unlucky to manage such a poor team'.

The new project manager put the following strategy in place:

- Implement formal and simple change management procedures – this increased the trust of the project manager by both teams and improved the mutual understanding of the impact of changes on time and cost.

- Organise a risk identification session – the outcomes raised an awareness of potential changes on dates and requirements, allowing the suppliers to be prepared in advance.

- Appoint the 'trustworthy' team members as local coordinators – these coordinators needed to organise weekly meetings with their local colleagues 2 days before the status meetings. They were responsible for following up the open action points and providing reasonable explanations for deviations, with a brief impact and contingency analysis. The project manager participated in the initial meetings and provided coaching and support to the coordinators. This action reduced the number of open points and increased the mutual understanding of the deviations.

- Limit the participation in the meeting only to the coordinators and a few key players – this action eliminated the long technical discussions and increased the time available to the team members for the execution of the project activities. The general feeling of distrust disappeared gradually and the satisfaction level of both teams increased.

With these simple actions, the project was back on track and the project manager travelled to both locations every 2 weeks to identify other ideas for improvement, by analysis of the reactions, emotions and open suggestions from all team members.

Long-term trust

During project closure organise a face-to-face meeting in order to build on trusting relationships for future projects.

- Organise a brainstorming exercise during the final lessons-learned session, to identify positive aspects that contributed to increasing the level of trust during the project.
- Try to involve key stakeholders outside the project team in this brainstorming session, as they can give their impression of the project teamwork and trust levels.
- If you cannot involve suppliers, customers or other external stakeholders in this workshop, try to gather their opinions in advance, preferably by informal contacts.
- Identify during the same brainstorming session the reasons for reduced trust levels, gathering suggestions of how to avoid these in the future.
- Celebrate the project success, organising an informal event – sometimes a simple drink or a lunch with all stakeholders – and identify informal comments that can help you understand the reasons for trust – or its absence. Investigate beforehand local rules and customs for celebration.
- Make this information available to other project managers, who can work in the future with part of your project team members, or on similar projects involving teams in the same locations.

YOUR LEARNING ON TRUST

Revisit the list or mindmap created at the beginning of this chapter. Would you add any recommendations to your list? Have you identified any other qualities that inspire trust? Do you believe that any of the recommendations provided in this chapter are not applicable to your country or company culture?

How can you develop trust between the team members from different countries? What did you learn from the lessons-learned sessions that confirmed or contradicted your original thoughts?

Now share your findings with other people, and read about their own learning (www. GlobalProjectManagement.org).

4 *Conflict Resolution*

Conflict management can be seen as a process that begins when two or more parties have a different viewpoint on the same topic, hindering or improving the project performance. Many projects involve conflict, created by resource availability and by different priorities on costs, time, scope and quality. Global projects add the differences in country and organisational cultures to this list, which increases the probability of having stakeholders with diverse views on customer satisfaction, different reactions to change and various approaches to risk management. Furthermore, the reduced amount of face-to-face interactions increases the likelihood of negative conflict and aggravates the conflict resolution process. The deployment of solid communication techniques (described in Chapters 6–10) and collaborative tools (explained in Chapters 16–25) can reduce the occurrence of conflict due to misunderstandings and facilitate the resolution process.

On the other hand, conflicts are a 'necessary evil' that foster creativity, increase innovation and avoid a climate of apathy and stagnation. The optimal level of conflicts allows a positive movement towards the project goals, a good problem-solving environment and quicker adaptation to project changes. The main task for the program and project managers is to avoid conflict from degenerating into a breakdown in communication and collaboration, and to stimulate conflicts that can bring benefits to the project. The project team can handle conflicts as risks or opportunities, and prepare response strategies such as influencing the stakeholders to accept the project strategies, intercultural training and pro-active negotiation between conflicting parties.

This chapter discusses the types and sources of conflicts specific to global projects, providing some ideas on how to identify conflicts during risk analysis, how to foster *functional conflicts* (which support the project goals and improves its performance) and how to identify and resolve *dysfunctional conflicts* (which can hinder project performance).

YOUR OPINION ON CONFLICTS AND NEGOTIATION

Before reading the recommendations on conflict and negotiation, think about conflicts you have experienced in project situations. Have you seen the same types of conflicts in traditional and global projects? Did you employ the same resolution strategies for both situations? What are the added difficulties for conflict management on global projects? How do you cope with these challenges?

Write on a list or mindmap the types of conflict and resolution strategies for global projects. Write on a separate list the challenges you have faced on global projects and your suggestions to cope with them. When reading this chapter, add the key learning topics to the mindmap with a different colour pen.

Global sources of conflict

The characteristics of global projects (multiple locations, organisations, languages, time zones and cultures) can contribute to generate conflicts, some examples being:

- Cultural differences among stakeholders can increase the likelihood of diverse standpoints on risk acceptance and conflicting criteria for change approval and customer satisfaction.
- Different behaviours when coping with change can also create conflicts. As one example, stakeholders from countries with internal-oriented cultures (see the 'human-nature' dimension on page 32) tend to accept that people with strong convictions challenge change initiatives.
- Different native languages can generate misunderstandings, and the challenge of addressing personal concerns in another language is higher.
- Conflicts can be created by incompatible views from different locations and companies on the distribution of work, responsibilities and power. Some countries may fight to keep strategic job functions, while companies charging daily rates may struggle to own the tasks requiring more resources. Most organisational functions may wish to influence the strategies of projects involving organisational change.
- Stakeholders in different locations with asynchronous hours can have different understandings on acceptable times for meetings, and on the respect of work-life balance. In some countries, the employees prefer to have a sandwich in the office during lunchtime and go home earlier, while people from other countries opt for having a 2-hour lunch break and staying in the office later.
- Companies working as partners during the execution of highly specialised tasks can have different views on the strategies and techniques to be deployed, on the time required to accomplish them and the costs to be charged to the customer.
- Individuals working in foreign locations may suffer from ethnocentrism, which is the evaluation of their behaviours and working style according to local norms and standards, usually tending to be unfavourable. The local team can consider the visitor as being naïve or impolite, simply because their values are different. On the other hand, a large group of foreigners working in another country can have the same impression of the local workers, who will not act according to the same set of values and beliefs.

The project manager will need to be aware of the situations above and always foster discussions to identify potential reasons for conflicts, motivate constructive discussions and obtain a common understanding on the diverging topics. The above list can be completed with other situations specific to each company, improved during lessons-learned sessions, and used as a reference during risk identification exercises.

Conflict levels in global projects

Risk identification brainstorming exercises can consider two main categories of conflict: *intra-country* (when conflict appears among stakeholders sharing the same country culture) and *inter-country* (when the reasons for the conflict can perhaps be explained by different cultures, and these must be taken into consideration during the resolution). You can also start the brainstorming session by identifying the main *risk levels* with the team members, some examples being:

- Individual – conflicts can appear among the stakeholders, reflecting different opinions, beliefs and interests.

- Group – conflict can happen when groups of people that share the same location or job function agree on a certain aspect of the project, but have opposition from other groups of stakeholders.
- Company – many global projects are executed by stakeholders from different companies, which can have conflicting interests and clashing company cultures.
- Projects – global portfolio and program managers are likely to evaluate conflicting interests from the different projects under their responsibility that compete for priority and resources. Project managers can also identify potential conflicts with other projects and decide to escalate the risk to a program manager or the senior management, who can pro-actively define priorities in the allocation of resources.

Global perspectives on conflict

Many different perspectives exist on organisational conflict, depending on national and organisational cultures. The understanding of the basic differences among these perspectives is fundamental for global project managers to determine how the global stakeholders are expected to behave, to react according to these different behaviours and to choose the resolution method most adapted to each culture. According to Buchanan and Huczynski (1997), these perspectives are:

- Traditional or unitary – people with this perspective see consensus as the ideal state, and conflict as a malfunction with harmful effects on projects. The conflict reasons are often rooted in misunderstandings, poor organisational structure or in minority groups that mislead their colleagues into non-cooperative behaviours. The resolution method usually consists of identifying and eliminating the causes of conflict. Stakeholders from collectivist societies (see page 26) tend to have the traditional perspective on risk.
- Pluralist – people from individualist societies (see page 26) are usually educated under the pluralist perspective and see conflict as positive for the vitality, responsiveness and efficiency of organisations. As an example, the quality of risk management and the richness of the project planning can be improved by having stakeholders with different mindsets bringing innovative ideas, under the coordination of a global project manager, that drives the efforts into a consensus. Conflicts are seen as the inevitable consequence of having many separate but related interest groups pursuing their own objectives, and finding compromises that satisfy all parties to enhance the project performance. The preferred conflict resolution strategy under this perspective is to use the project plan, objectives and strategies to reconcile the interests of the different parties.
- Interactionist – this perspective sees group cohesion as bad for innovation and creativity, and encourages both conflict stimulation and management of conflict to move from 'groupthink' situations into self-critical and creative change processes that can improve the effectiveness of the project team.

Conflict management steps

When the project team has identified potential conflicting situations as threats to the project, the risk mitigation strategy can be to manage the conflicts and obtain an agreement among all parties. The steps below are general guidelines that can be used to adapt your current conflict management practices to global projects:

- **Act as a mediator** – show transparency, integrity and cultural understanding, making sure your main interest is to resolve the conflict in the best possible way for all parties involved. Cultural differences among stakeholders require more openness from all parties in order to understand the reasons for conflicts and to find a common ground. Foster this openness with team building activities, mainly when face-to-face contact is possible.

- **Appoint a third-party arbitrator** – when the program or project manager is part of the conflict, or needs to defend the interests of one organisation involved in the divergences. Usually the arbitrator will come from an independent body trusted by the project sponsor and the main stakeholders with interest in the results of the conflict negotiation.

- **Question the situation** – obtain information about the strengths, weaknesses, threats and opportunities of the different standpoints from all parties involved. You can organise online brainstorming sessions or send questionnaires to stakeholders distributed around the globe. Structure the information you have collected in a format that allows easy comparisons, and be ready to use online conferencing tools to share it with people in other locations.

- **Assess the situation** – evaluate the conflict under the lenses of the project objectives and the business strategies, with participation from 'neutral' stakeholders, as well as those involved in the source of conflict. This can depersonalise the situation, remove the negative emotion and focus on the desired outcome. Consider asking people from different countries and companies to participate in the process and suggest they voice their opinions and concerns privately on sensitive matters or to avoid emotional discussions.

- **Define the strategy** – using the information collected in the previous steps, and the suggestions on Table 4.1, define the best approach for the conflict situation. Prepare your arguments and anticipate the reactions from different participants.

- **Prepare the discussion** – define the communication media to be used during the discussions and negotiations. Avoid audio conferencing, as verbal agreements may generate misunderstandings after the meeting is finished. Prefer to have online meetings (see Chapter 23) or even face-to-face discussions when the decision is important to the project, and when it involves people with different personalities and cultures. Decide who needs to take part in the discussion, sending the meeting invitations and organising the logistics. Spend time building rapport with the key participants before the discussion.

- **Start the discussion** – introduce the participants, the reason for the conflict, the main differences on standpoints, the importance and impact of the decision for the project. Reinforce the project mission, goals and objectives that are relevant to the discussion. Share your opinions on the cultural dimensions (see Chapter 1) with the parties involved in the conflict situation, helping them to understand the reasons for the differences on their viewpoints.

- **Resolve the situation** – when there are many items to be resolved, start with the points on which you can reach an easy consensus, increasing the collaboration and trust level, and address the 'problem areas' afterwards.

- **Document and communicate the situation** – all parties must agree on a written statement of the decisions. Share a document that summarises the key decision areas by video or web conferencing, and request a verbal agreement from all parties. Distribute the outcome to the participants and key stakeholders, and ask for a written reply stating their agreement or comments.

- **Document the lessons learned** – summarise your learning during this conflict situation for future use: the reasons, the methods, the positive and negative strategies and consequences.

Table 4.1   Comparison of conflict resolution approaches

(The cultural perspectives were adapted from Hofstede, 2001, and the strategies adapted from Blake and Mouton, 1964)

Approach	Objective	Appropriate situations	Cultural perspectives (see Chapter 1)
Confronting (Problem solving)	Solve the problem, by evaluating objectively the different positions together with the conflicting parties (preferred approach)	- When the impact of the decision is important to satisfy the project customer's interests - To gain commitment from all parties - To avoid conflict reoccurrence	People from more individualistic cultures tend to feel more comfortable with confrontations and open discussions of conflicts; confrontations with people from more collectivist cultures should be carefully formulated to not hurt anyone
Compromising	Find quick and expedient solutions that bring some degree of satisfaction to all parties	- When time is important - When different parties have mutually exclusive goals	People from feminine cultures may have a penchant to compromise, by identifying the important points for the different parties, ideally under the lenses of their cultural differences. Individuals from high uncertainty-avoidance countries may consider dangerous to compromise with opponents
Avoiding (Withdrawal)	Retreat or postpone the problem	- When the people required for a decision are not available at the moment - When the issue is not relevant and cannot disrupt the project execution - When the stress level is too high and gets in the way of a healthy discussion	People from masculine cultures may try to "deny" the conflict until the use of a "forcing" approach is inevitable
Smoothing	Avoid distraction during critical periods	- When harmony and stability are more important in the short term, and the problem can be resolved at a later stage without impacting the project	People from more collectivist cultures may prefer to pretend an environment of harmony and consensus rather than facing and resolving the conflicts
Forcing	Avoid spending time in discussions	- To reinforce unpopular rules and discipline - When the reasons behind the solution are confidential - When quick actions are required and the moderator is able to make a quick judgement	People from masculine cultures can be more inclined to impose their views on their counterparts and fight until the 'best side' wins

REAL-LIFE EXPERIENCE

The last deliverable of a major offshoring project consisted of migrating one system from the old solution provider to a newly created support organisation. Two team members detected a security breach in one software component when performing the final tests. Migrating the system with this security flaw could potentially block the truck deliveries to 5 warehouses for more than a week, damaging the company business in that country.

The new support organisation considered the system not compliant with their security and service standards and rejected it. The old provider refused to extend the support contract beyond the agreed date, claiming that the probability of a problem occurring was very low, as the system had been working without issues for the past 3 years. The customer wanted to complete the project on time, and without risk of security failures.

The project manager decided to investigate the conflict situation directly with each party, and concluded the following:

- The security flaw was the consequence of a change to the system design as requested by the customer 2 years ago; no impact was identified until now.

- In the event of a security problem occurring, the impact to the customer was very high (the warehouses would not be operational for 3 weeks, and the company may face unacceptable financial losses).

- The probability of a problem occurring was the same for both situations: if the system remained in the current location, or if the migration was performed.

The project manager summarised the possible resolution scenarios, as a preparation for the negotiation:

- Migrate the system → security risk high; cost, scope and time not impacted (preferred solution).

- Do not migrate the system → security risk high; cost not impacted; scope and time impacted.

- Correct the security flaw before system migration → security risk lower; scope not impacted; time and cost highly impacted.

The project manager investigated the cultural patterns of the different parties using Hofstede's dimensions (see Chapter 1) and organised one-to-one discussions with the key stakeholders, to influence their position and stimulate a problem solving environment:

- Old provider = masculine country culture → the financial director from the old provider was forcing the project to complete on time, threatening to invoke contract penalties to cover the allocation of external contractors to support the system. The project manager presented the three scenarios, which convinced the director that the preferred solution (1) was the most likely to be accepted, and suggested a more constructive discussion to achieve this target.

- New support organisation = high uncertainty avoidance → the service director from the new support organisation preferred to avoid the conflicting situation, and invoked a clause of the contract specifying that, 'all systems being transferred must be working perfectly in the old environment'. The project manager explained the differences between the scenarios and the high impact to the customer and old provider of not migrating the system. The service director then agreed to negotiate, under the condition that the customer accepted liability for security risks during and after the migration.

- Customer = collectivist culture → the customer was quickly convinced that scenario 1 was the preferred option, and accepted liability for security risks if a task force was put in place immediately, to correct the security flaw as quickly as possible after the migration.

After the preparation, the negotiation process took place through audio and web conferencing, and achieved a consensus in less than 1 hour. The project manager moderated the discussion and captured the main decision points online, showing them to all parties:

1. The system migration is accepted by all parties, who understand the risk of the security breach, and the impact to the warehouses, should the risk occur.

    a) The customer accepts liability for the occurrence of the risk, under the reserve that all parties follow their commitments expressed below.

2. To mitigate the risk of a security breach, a task force will investigate and correct the problem.

    a) The task force will include two specialists, in security and programming, from the old provider. Their role will be to provide all background information on the problem and make suggestions for the resolution strategy.

    b) Three members from the new support organisation will lead the task force, with specialisations in security, programming and testing. Their role will be to decide on the resolution strategy, implement and coordinate the tests.

    c) Two members from the customer will be part of the task force, being responsible for the validation of the resolution strategy and obtaining the approval of the customer representatives in the warehouses. Their role will include the coordination of testing by the warehouse operators, and the negotiation of system downtime for the implementation of the security fix.

All parties agreed with the resolution strategy and confirmed their approval by e-mail 1 day after receiving the meeting minutes. The project manager tracked this decision using the formal change process, and requested the legal department make the amendment in the contract.

In the lessons-learned session, the project manager suggested that new projects must include this type of security problem in the risk management process, being ready with a similar mitigation strategy.

YOUR LEARNING ON CONFLICTS AND NEGOTIATION

Revisit the list or mindmap created at the beginning of this chapter. Did you discover new sources of conflict? Were you able to improve your conflict resolution strategy? What recommendations in this chapter are not applicable to your global projects? Will you include the evaluation of potential conflicts in your next risk identification session?

Now share your own experiences with other people, and read about their findings (www. GlobalProjectManagement.org).

CHAPTER

5 *Coaching Over Distance*

'*Coaching is fundamentally about helping people fulfil their potential by allowing them to recognise the things that hold them back and by helping them discover ways around them*'

(Somers, 2007).

Global project managers can improve the performance of distant team members by adopting a 'coaching' style and encouraging them to think for themselves. The increase in performance and self-confidence can reduce the need for monitoring and control, and the project manager can then monitor the work packages at a higher level. The coaching style is also beneficial when the project manager appoints local coordinators, who will be responsible for a group of work packages performed by a local team. Good program managers usually deploy an artful combination of coaching and leadership to empower and motivate the project managers.

The first main challenge faced by global program and project managers during coaching sessions is the distance, which inhibits the informal discussions and tends to reduce the frequency of meetings between coach and coachee (the person being coached). The second main challenge is the need for video and web conferencing facilities to allow the coach to use visual resources during the explanations. Finally, the cultural differences can also create barriers for the mutual understanding and trust required for an efficient coaching period.

The method suggested in this chapter gives you a powerful tool for coaching sessions across national boundaries: it formalises the exchange of knowledge and the evolution of learning, uses the collaborative tools to facilitate understanding and increases trust to the high level required for the learning process.

YOUR EXPERIENCE OF COACHING

Before reading this chapter, think about recent occasions when you provided coaching to other people. Were they located in different countries to you? If so, did you find any difficulty in overcoming the barriers of distance and culture? If they were in the same country as you, do you think your experience would be different if they were far away? If they were from the same country culture as you, do you think your experience would be different if they were from other cultures?

Write on a list or mindmap the positive experiences you would expect from cross-cultural coaching. Write on a separate list the challenges you experienced, and how you would deal with them in the future.

Coaching on global projects

Coaching can help global project managers during the whole life cycle. As an example, the social complexity of the project initiation and planning processes might justify coaching from more experienced program and project managers, during tasks such as (adapted from Gareis, 2000):

- organisational design;
- project plan development;
- moderating of the project kick-off meetings and workshops.

You will notice that many other examples of situations where global project managers can benefit from coaching are described in other chapters of this book. Think about conflict management, stakeholder management, use of the collaborative tools, definition of communication strategy and the preparation of the project documentation using the rules and templates. Therefore, a general recommendation is to have a program or project manager with previous experience on global projects coaching new project managers, using this book as reference during the four stages of the coaching process described below.

Global coaching principles

This chapter is based on a collaborative style of coaching, when the coach and coachees work together on generating thoughts, insights, ideas and changes (Starr, 2003). The principles of collaborative coaching for global program and project managers are:

- The coach usually masters the project management methodologies, tools, techniques or has expert knowledge. However, the coachees may know more about their local culture, language and working practices. The coaching process can then be a knowledge exchange, which will increase the confidence level of the coachee.
- The coach can use advanced skills of listening, questioning and reflection, in order to learn more about the local practices and the unique characteristics of the local project team, and to stimulate the coachee to think about the actions to be taken.
- The coach can motivate and guide the project managers and coordinators to use their local knowledge allied to project management skills, in order to complete the project deliverables.
- The coach can ask questions to learn the opinion of the coachees on the project management knowledge being transferred, and meditate if the general skills are applicable to that local team. Sometimes, local adaptations are required to allow the project management practices to fit into the cultural, social, technological or economic situations of individual countries and companies.
- The project managers must observe the coachees objectively and under their cultural perspectives, in order to identify specific behaviours and their consequences on the communication with the various stakeholders. Part of the coaching activities will consist of making clear links between these behaviours and their results, making people understand the consequences of their actions on people from other cultures.
- The coach must prefer to raise the awareness of the coachees of their feelings when performing the coordination of their activities, and of the reactions of other stakeholders.

- The coach must involve the coachees in deciding how the session should run, and what they must do to achieve their objectives. This will make them feel responsible for their learning and owners of their actions, increasing their self-confidence to progress after the coaching process is completed.
- The coach will need to trust the abilities of the coachees, encouraging them to believe in their own abilities and try the new methods and principles by themselves.
- The coach needs to build the trust of the coachees, by treating them with dignity and respect, keeping the exchange of personal information and feelings confidential, by referring back to examples of positive learning, and by accepting the failures and learning together from them.
- The coachee must trust the coaching process, and participate in the definition of the coaching context from the beginning, as discussed below.

Starr (2003) suggested four stages for effective coaching: the establishment of the context for coaching, the creation of understanding and direction, review of learning and completion. Global program and project managers can use a similar framework to provide coaching over distance to individuals from other cultures, with the five-step framework discussed below.

Establishing a global context for coaching

The first step in the framework is to build the supporting context for the coaching sessions, starting with the definition of the media and frequency of the meetings, setting up expectations and establishing objectives. In global projects, the main aspects are the following:

- At least the first session should happen face-to-face. This will help to build trust between the coach and coachee. When face-to-face contact is not possible, use some form of video conferencing to allow the use of body language and drawings.
- Agree in advance on the dates of the coaching sessions, at a time that is convenient for both parties. Be aware of the differences in energy, motivation and stress – when booking meetings in early mornings or late evenings – and the impact of these differences on the motivation of both parties.
- If you are fluent in the coachee's language, offer to use it during the sessions – even if this is not the official project language, or if you do not use it regularly when communicating. This can bring an extra level of confidence and make it easier for the coachee to express concerns and feelings. Depending on your level of fluency, you can suggest using your own language (if possible) when you have difficulty in explaining complex ideas or concepts. However, be aware that conversations in more than one language can bring more headaches than understanding.
- Start the first session by asking about other coaching experiences the coachee had in the past and their outcomes. Analyse this under the cultural perspective, by considering if these experiences would have been useful in your country, and evaluating if you can build from them and adapt your strategy.
- Review the coaching process with the coachee, ask for suggestions and make sure that you and the coachee agree on a process that will be effective in providing the desired change. The coachee must trust the coaching process.
- Understand the coachee's expectations, and build together a list of desired achievements and their expected timeframe.

Create a global understanding and direction

The coaching objectives must be clearly set at the beginning of the process and reviewed when starting each coaching session. Both coach and coachee need to set up these objectives together, making sure they are measurable and achievable. The coach can stimulate the coachee to include career-development objectives in order to increase the motivation level for the sessions. The understanding of project requirements and methods are objectives that allow the coachees to develop a better understanding of their new roles and responsibilities on the project, and to confirm if these are in line with their capacities and aspirations. As an example, the objectives for coaching sessions of local coordinators of global projects can be based on the different chapters in this book:

- The coachee must have an understanding of the collaborative tools employed by the project, and know how to set up and use all of them effectively.
- The coachee can suggest the use of other tools, evaluating what benefits they can bring to the effectiveness of the communication among the project team members.
- The coachee must know the different cultures of the project team members, and understand the main differences among them. As a proof of understanding, the coachee will identify the main risks of conflicts when the local team members communicate with these different cultures.
- The coachee will understand the different team leadership models, and identify which ones relate better to the local culture.
- The coachee will understand the strategies to develop trust and to manage conflict among local team members, and between these team members and stakeholders in other locations.
- The coachee will know the strategies to manage different types of meetings and communications over distance. The coachee will identify if these strategies are in line with the local culture, and add to them, based on previous experiences.
- The coachee will need to develop or improve some of the global skills (see Chapter 12).

When the coaching session is structured in this manner, the outcome can be a win-win situation: the coachee will understand the principles of global project management, under the perspective of the coach, and will contribute to improve the company good practices in this area.

The coach and coachee also need to know more about each other, to identify how the project and private objectives can coincide. As an example, a project coordinator who is soon to have a baby may need to develop the remote communication skills quickly, in order to be effective without constant travelling. Before requesting personal information, you must explain why these details are needed and understand if the coachee agrees and is comfortable with sharing certain details with you.

Review achievements and objectives

At the beginning of every coaching session, achievements made since the previous meeting must be reviewed and compared against the objectives previously agreed. The goal is to understand if the coaching sessions are useful and if the coaching style and process are working for both coach and coachee. The format used to get this understanding can vary. One possible method for coaching sessions over distance is to establish a document containing the objectives, updated during every session using web conferencing software, so that both coach and coachee can agree on the comments and changes. See Table 5.1 and Table 5.2 for examples of entries on a coaching log, adapted from real-life situations.

Anatomy of a coaching session

During the coaching sessions, the coach will make the coachees understand their capacities and feelings, and will stimulate them to devise a strategy and achieve their goals. The main activities and behaviour during every coaching session are as follows:

- ask questions to establish aims, don't tell the coachee what to do;

Table 5.1   Coaching log (Example 1)

Objective	Situation in the beginning	Desired outcome	Target date
Improve the knowledge and use of collaborative tools	Coachee only organises audio conferencing meetings	Coachee must feel comfortable to moderate web conferencing meetings over distance, with online agendas	July 4th
Follow-up			
April 1st – coach presented the organisational tools and good practices; coachee to subscribe to web conferencing, download project monitoring template and organise practice meeting sessions with the coach. May 1st – coachee organises a weekly web conference with the local team (all in the same room), and they are comfortable with the tool. Coachee started using the template to monitor a local project. Tools to be deployed on a meeting over distance. June 1st – first meetings over distance did not work well, as coachee could not update the monitoring sheet and moderate the meeting at the same time. Suggestion is to have a local team member updating the spreadsheet, while coachee moderates the meeting. July 1st – the segregation of roles worked well, the meetings are finishing on time and covering all topics in the agenda.			

Table 5.2   Coaching log (Example 2)

Objective	Situation in the beginning	Desired outcome	Target date
Coachee must improve the relationship between the local team members and colleagues from different countries.	Around 40 per cent of tasks get delayed due to misunderstandings on the deliverables and dates	No tasks can get delayed for this reason	June 1st
Follow-up			
April 1st – coachee to evaluate the cultural differences between the local team members and other colleagues, and to understand the reasons for misunderstandings. May 1st – most reasons for misunderstandings are due to differences in 'uncertainty avoidance', as local team members tend to spend too much time on risk analysis, while other countries did not consider any time for this in the tasks duration estimates. Planning to be reviewed, as risk analysis can be performed before the start of the activity execution. June 1st – no tasks were delayed after the change in the planning. Other cultural differences were identified in a team building exercise, and coachee will now develop similar strategies to benefit from the cultural diversity.			

- ask questions that keep the attention of the coachee, and check on this regularly if you do not have visual contact;
- as the questions progress, increase the focus on the way forward;
- consider the current reality and cultural differences;
- good questions will make the coachees answer their own queries;
- reflect on the results and adjust the process;
- always generate options with participation from the coachee;
- together with the coachee, commit to a way forward;
- base the relationship on truth, openness and trust;
- focus on the coachees' beliefs, experiences and opinions.

Completing the global coaching process

When successful, the coaching process finishes once the coachee has achieved the objectives or has the confidence to achieve them independently. This can be tracked on the coaching log, which can also capture the coach recommendations on how the coachee can progress independently, by investigating additional sources of information, techniques and tools. As an example, when the contents of the coaching sessions are based on different chapters of

---

REAL-LIFE EXPERIENCE

'The first positive part of being a coachee and trying to progress on global project management knowledge, was to read about the coaching model, as this helped me to understand the coach strategies and approach. By sharing the model with me, the coach was inviting me to talk openly about my objectives as a coachee, which created a climate of confidence and willingness to reach my targets.

The advantage of having a regular meeting is the structuring of our thoughts and needs. Once a week, we took 1 hour to abstract ourselves from the stress of the project management activities, summarise the lessons learned and discuss how to use this learning to avoid future issues. In some periods of doubt about my performance and duties, the coach helped me to understand my roles and responsibilities on the project, and the limitations of the project management theory in real-world project situations.

The real-time update of the coaching log during the reviews was very helpful. This enabled us to regularly review the recurring actions and questions, allowing me to recall the main questions I had during the week in a summarised and efficient way.

This coaching session was also a very good opportunity to use each of the project management tools, for example, the financial spreadsheets and the global project binder, and learn 'tips and tricks' that are hardly available on documentation and training sessions. During these sessions, the coach also gave examples of his activities, explained how he solved different issues by the means of a creative PowerPoint Presentation or a humorous FAQ on the intranet pages. This helped me to understand how to use creativity and sense of humour to be successful on the job.

The open minded relationship and trust between the coach and me was the key success factor of this experience'

Marie-Paule Sottiaux
Global Project Manager

this book, the coach can build on the sources of information at the end of each chapter to provide this guidance. The coachees would then consult these additional sources to expand their knowledge on specific areas of interest.

A continuous follow-up of the coachee at the end of the process can help to detect if the guidance provided was followed and if corrections are needed. The process for this follow-up can also be defined in the last coaching session: the coach and coachee might establish together when they will meet again to review the evolution achieved, and if other people will be invited to observe the coachee during this period. These observers can provide feedback and other recommendations during the follow-up sessions.

YOUR LEARNING ON COACHING

Revisit the list or mindmap created at the beginning of this chapter. Would you deal with the challenges in a different way? Are you going to adapt your coaching style? What negative situations would be hard to avoid, despite the implementation of the five-step framework?

Now share your thoughts with other people, and read about their own experiences (www. GlobalProjectManagement.org).

Part I: Key concepts

- Global project managers must understand the definitions, dimensions and implications of culture on project management, in order to respect and use the cultural differences across various countries, improving project innovation and teamwork. The dimensions from Trompenaars and Hofstede can be used as a starting point, but the real experience of the global project team is a rich resource to be evaluated, documented and discussed.
- Global project managers must develop their leadership skills across borders, taking into account the cultural differences, language barriers and the lack of face-to-face contact. Traditional leadership theories and models must be adapted after an observation of their effects on people from different cultures.
- Global project managers need to establish trust among the key stakeholders from the project initiation, and include team building activities in the project plan. A trustworthy environment will improve motivation, innovation and performance, and the healthy relationships between team members will continue after the project closure. A global project team is only effective after trust is established among the key team members.
- Conflicts can lead to quality improvement when the project manager employs the right techniques, adopts constructive behaviour and considers the cultural differences as an important source of innovation. The inclusion of potential reasons for conflicts during the identification of risks and opportunities can facilitate the conflict management tasks during critical periods. The implementation of the Global Project Management Framework© can reduce the occurrence of conflicts, as the lack of face-to-face communication and wrong use of collaborative tools and techniques are among the main reasons for misunderstandings on global projects.
- It is possible to coach other project managers or team members over distance and obtain good results, by establishing a global context for the coaching sessions, agreeing on the objectives and strategies and correctly using the collaborative tools during the sessions. The coaching sessions can also be a good opportunity to practice the use of the methods and processes described by the Global Project Management Framework©.

Part I: Further reading

Hofstede, G. (2001) *Culture's Consequences: Comparing Values, Behaviours, Institutions, and Organizations Across Nations – second edition;*

Trompenaars, F. and Hampden-Turner, C. (2005) *Riding the Waves of Culture: Understanding Cultural Diversity in Business;*

Magala, S. (2005) *Cross-Cultural Competence*

These books are the starting point to understand how cross-cultural differences can affect the work environment and how to build on these differences to improve collaboration and creativity. These books focus on the academic foundation of cultural differences and provide a good theoretical background to cross-cultural studies.

Trompenaars, F. and Woolliams, P. (2003) *Business Across Cultures*

This book is the main reference to build cross-cultural awareness at the workplace, providing the subset of the results from the authors' studies that is directly applicable to the global organisations and their employees.

Rees, D. (2000) 'Managing culture' in *Gower Handbook of Project Management*

This chapter of the *Gower Handbook of Project Management* contains a framework for international project managers dealing with multicultural teams, also based on Hofstede and Trompenaars' dimensions.

Mead, R. (2004) *International Management: Cross-Cultural Dimensions;*

Mead, R. (2000) *Cases and Projects in International Management: Cross-Cultural Dimensions*

The first book provides a comprehensive view of the impact of cross-cultural relations in general management. The second book provides 21 case studies and seven projects, well suited to teachers and students of cross-cultural management.

Melkman, A. and Trotman, J. (2005) *Training International Managers: Designing, Deploying and Delivering Effective Training for Multi-Cultural Groups*

The authors developed an interesting framework and practical guidelines for the preparation of training sessions with multicultural groups, aiming to exchange experiences and leverage the cross-cultural understanding of international managers.

Morrison, T. and Conaway, W.A. (2006) *Kiss, Bow, or Shake Hands: The Bestselling Guide to Doing Business in More Than 60 Countries*

This book gives an overall view of different countries, with short hints on historical background, political context, cultural aspects and business etiquette. This type of information can be useful for a very basic understanding of the country, and help to start conversations. However, they are more powerful when combined with some of the previous sources.

Buchanan, D. and Huczynski, A. (1997) *Organizational Behaviour*

Mullins, LJ. (1996) *Management and Organisational Behaviour*

Hall, D. Jones, R. and Raffo, C. (1995) *Business Studies*

These books provide a comprehensive analysis of management and leadership skills and include detailed definitions of the main theories on leadership, motivation, conflict management and negotiation.

Cooper, D.J. (2003) *Leadership for Follower Commitment*

This book presents a detailed evaluation of the main skills and practices that can be applied to increase motivation and commitment in global environments.

Kostner, J. (1996) *Virtual Leadership*

This book provides practical recommendations to build leadership skills that will establish trust and motivate people working in distant locations.

Starr, J. (2003) *The Coaching Manual*

This book describes one form of coaching model in a detailed and practical level.

Part I: Interactive section

Share with other readers your general opinion on the people management skills applicable to global projects (www.GlobalProjectManagement.org):

- Do you know other cultural dimensions that are relevant to global project managers, not considered in Hofstede and Trompenaars' studies? What is your opinion on the results and usability of their dimensions?
- What are the leadership theories more accepted in your country? Are you aware of good theories defined and validated outside the Anglo-Saxon cultures?
- Do you believe that the management and leadership theories are valid across different countries, or should they be validated and expanded to consider the cultural dimensions?
- What topics not covered in this part could help to improve the effectiveness of global project teams?

Global Communication

Program and project managers spend most of their time communicating. In traditional project teams, you usually recognise the project manager as the one moving from one meeting room to another, rushing to the team members' desks to obtain information on the project activities and building informal networks around the coffee machine or during lunch time. Many project managers enjoy the contact with people and feel at ease performing these coordination activities. The communication flows naturally, the tasks get done and the projects are completed.

When these project managers are assigned to global projects, everything changes. Low budgets restrain them from travelling to the project locations and suddenly they spend a large portion of their days with a headset, making telephone calls and organising audio conferences. A typical day finishes after hundreds of e-mail exchanges and with at least a handful of unread e-mails for the next morning. The level of frustration increases when e-mail and voice mails are left unanswered and the tasks are not progressing as planned. The projects can be eventually completed, but are somewhat distant from the original cost, budget, quality and scope. Not to mention the customer satisfaction levels …

To avoid this situation, global project managers must know the communication channels between the stakeholders, define common rules and templates for communication over a distance and involve team members in defining a communication strategy. Different communication techniques may be deployed to increase the stakeholders' commitment level. Remote brainstorming techniques can gather ideas from team members across the globe, incorporating them into the project strategies and the product characteristics.

The chapters in this part provide a starting point for reflections on these processes and methods that can reduce the frustration of global project managers, and increase the probability that their projects achieve the targets.

6 *Stakeholders and Communication Channels*

According to the PMBOK® Guide, stakeholders are, 'persons and *organisations* such as *customers, sponsors, performing organisation* and the public, that are actively involved in the *project*, or whose interests may be positively or negatively affected by execution or completion of the project.' (PMI, 2004). The ICB defines stakeholders as, 'people or groups, who are interested in the performance and/or success of the project, or who are constrained by the project', preferring to employ the term 'interested parties' (IPMA, 2006).

For most projects, the project manager can increase the chances of success by correctly managing the stakeholders' needs, expectations and influence. The level of commitment of key stakeholders will determine the success or failure of certain projects which involve organisational change or have an important social, political, economical or environmental impact. Knowing the stakeholders' expectations and requirements is fundamental to define the quality standards and requirements for the project and the products or services to be delivered.

Project managers must know their stakeholders, understand the communication channels between them and develop a communication strategy to align the needs and expectations of the interested parties, using effective communication to improve their commitment level.

This chapter suggests a strategy to manage the stakeholders in global programs and projects, by identifying key interested parties, evaluating their attitudes to the project, analysing their positions, mapping the communication channels and increasing their level of commitment. The program and project managers will use this information in later project stages, when building a project communication strategy that effectively addresses the stakeholders' needs and expectations, to increase their commitment to the project success (see Chapter 8).

YOUR EXPERIENCE OF GLOBAL STAKEHOLDERS

Before reading this chapter, think about key stakeholders from previous or current projects. Were they supportive to the project? Did they make their resources available? Did they create positive or negative influence on other interested parties? How did you react to the negative behaviours?

Write on a list or mindmap the negative attitudes from certain stakeholders; how did you react, and how would you react to similar situations in the future? Make a separate list for negative stakeholders' attitudes you noticed that were effectively handled by other project managers, and how their reaction improved the commitment from interested parties that were opposing the project.

Identifying the global key stakeholders

The global project manager can refer to different sources to identify potential stakeholders, depending on the project type and on the availability of information. Examples of these sources of information are:

- **Senior Management** – the members of the steering committee, the project sponsor and people with a large working experience of the different organisations participating in the project can identify groups of people with interest in, or who are impacted by, the execution of the project.
- **Global team members, with local knowledge** – team members in different locations may know about local people or organisations who are interested in or constrained by the project.
- **Specialists** – external consultants or specialised team members usually have a deep understanding of organisations or people that may have a vested interest in the project.
- **Documentation** – press releases, newspapers, specialised magazines, research papers, the Internet and books can be a rich source of information for external parties that are affected by or interested in the project.
- **Organisational charts** – the map of the organisational structure from the partners, suppliers, customers and governmental entities involved in the project can serve as a checklist to ensure the completeness of the analysis.
- **Lessons learned** – success stories and failures from previous projects can provide recommendations for the stakeholders to analyse and manage.

The project manager can request that the team members located in different countries collect information from various sources, and organise a brainstorming session to compile the results into a stakeholder record, around pre-determined categories, some examples being:

- customers (internal and external) and end users;
- suppliers (internal and external);
- partners (internal and external) and sub-contractors;
- departments or employees;
- senior managers from different companies and countries;
- neighbours (physical and within the supply chain);
- resource providers (people, time, finance and other resources);
- governments, non-governmental organisations, regulatory agencies;
- opinion formers (media, commentators and trade unions).

To cover gaps in the information sources, the project manager can stimulate creative thinking by prompting the participants with questions like:

- Who will use the project deliverables?
- Who will need to adapt their working practices or processes during or after the project implementation?
- Who will provide resources to the project team?
- Who will benefit from the project outcomes?
- Who will be impacted by construction, noise, modified access routes or maintenance activities?
- Is anyone going to lobby against the project execution?

Knowing the global stakeholders

The project manager can build on the local knowledge of the participants of the brainstorming session to identify and document the stakeholders' characteristics that depend on their status and geographical location, and can determine their expected behaviour:

- What are the types and levels of political, social, economical or organisational power for each stakeholder?
- What is the influence level of each stakeholder? This can normally be represented by keywords (high or low) or by weighting scales.
- How the stakeholder fits in the different cultural dimensions? The dimensions evaluated in this book (Chapter 1) allied to the information provided by various team members on the different cultural patterns (Table 1.12 on page 35) can be helpful when managing the stakeholders' expectations and when defining the communication strategy. For example, different cultures have various levels of risk awareness and different perceptions on the level of detail required for planning documents. The team members must understand the cultural dimensions and patterns in advance, in order to be prepared for the brainstorming session, and to employ the stakeholder register during the project execution.

Analysing the global stakeholders

The next step in the global stakeholder management process consists of a detailed analysis of the stakeholders' attitudes to the project. Depending on the project size and complexity, this analysis can be performed in the same brainstorming session, in another session with the same team members or in additional sessions with smaller and focused teams, for example:

- local teams appraising the stakeholders located in their geographical areas;
- subject matter experts evaluating the impacts of the project deliverables on their areas;
- senior managers assessing the impact of organisational change initiatives.

The evaluation of power, influence and culture from the previous step can serve as a basis for this analysis, which aims to determine the level of knowledge and expected attitude towards the project and project team:

- What objectives does each stakeholder have in relation to the project strategies or deliverables? Are there 'hidden objectives'?
- What are the stakeholders' requirements? The project manager must translate all the stakeholder needs and expectations into prioritised requirements, which can affect the project objectives and strategies and determine quality requirements and standards.
- What position are the stakeholders likely to assume in the project, based on the relationship between their objectives and the project strategies and deliverables? As an example, the stakeholder position can be classified as ally, opposer or neutral. *Allies* agree with the need for the project and support the overall strategies, providing resources to the project and are usually available to promote the project benefits to other stakeholders. *Opposers* dissent from the project goals and disagree with the strategies, withholding resources from the project. *Neutral* stakeholders do not have a special interest in the project execution, but will not suffer from its completion, providing resources that will not affect their own activities and operations.

- What is the ideal position for the stakeholders in the project? While some stakeholders have a low influence level and can remain opposers, the project managers must change other stakeholders' position into neutral, or even to allies, to make sure the project will succeed. The next sections of this chapter discuss some strategies to improve the stakeholders' commitment.
- What positive or negative reactions is each stakeholder already making to the project? The stakeholders' attitudes can be visible in the early stages of projects, and the project manager must constantly monitor their reactions and update this information.
- What challenges or opportunities may the project team face when communicating with each of the stakeholders? The project manager can stimulate a proactive identification of possible reactions and behaviours, based on lessons learned and previous experiences, in order to be prepared for the stakeholder management and the definition of a communication strategy.
- What is the current knowledge level of each stakeholder? The knowledge level represents the amount of project information the stakeholders received by formal and informal communication, and range from full awareness to total ignorance. This information has direct repercussions on the position adopted by the stakeholders and is essential for the preparation of the global communication strategy of the project (see Chapter 8).

The reliability of this information will vary according to its sources: the initial investigation performed by the project team members, lessons learned from previous projects or project phases, or the organisation folklore. Thus, the project manager must include only factual data, completing and correcting the stakeholder record during all project phases in order to make it trustworthy. After this step, the stakeholder record contains confidential and sensitive information and cannot be placed on a public area of the project virtual room.

The stakeholder commitment framework

McElroy and Mills (2000) identified that stakeholders have different levels of commitment to projects (Figure 6.1), suggesting that communication is key to change this engagement level. Global project managers must understand how the proper use of different communication media over distance and across cultural borders can trigger these changes:

- **From ignorance to awareness** – project managers can gain a first level of commitment by creating a project virtual room and publishing the project information, key milestones and overall project performance. In many projects, most secondary stakeholders (low levels of power and influence) can remain at this level, and receive regular project updates by e-mail, or access the project virtual room when they require information.
- **Understanding** – project managers can create a good level of understanding on the project by organising local meetings in key locations and visiting key stakeholders at project onset, and by broadcasting regular updates during project execution.
- **Support** – the project team can obtain the support of key stakeholders by fostering debates and brainstorming over distance (see Chapter 10) for strategic discussions. Senior stakeholders can be invited to give feedback on the project communication strategy and to provide suggestions and steering on important decisions.
- **Involvement** – the key team members must be involved in the planning phase and in the preparation of important project components, such as the schedule and risk log. The

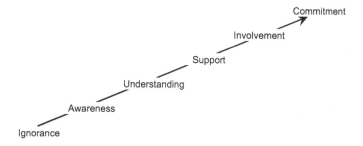

Figure 6.1   Levels of stakeholders' commitment (adapted from McElroy and Mills)

project manager must continue involving these team members in all important steps, when main changes occur and on problem-solving activities.

- **Commitment** – a consistent involvement of the project stakeholders in meetings and informal discussions will develop a high-level of commitment during project execution, simplifying the monitoring and control activities of the project manager. The commitment is often carried over to other projects, once the trust between the project manager and the stakeholders is established (see Chapter 3).

Defining strategies to change stakeholders' commitment levels

After the stakeholder analysis discussed previously, the register will contain the *current and desired stakeholder position*. According to the power, influence, cultural patterns, objectives, requirements, reactions, challenges and opportunities, the project manager can determine the strategic actions the project team can take for each stakeholder, in order to increase their knowledge level and move stakeholders to the desired position, thus increasing the success rate of the project. Based on all these aspects, the project team can decide on how to raise the effect of positive influences from key *allies*, how to reduce opposition from key *opposers* and how to enhance the influence of *neutral* stakeholders.

The project manager must evaluate the strategies according to their cost and the resources involved, compared to the importance and likelihood of achieving their goals.

REAL-LIFE EXPERIENCE

One senior executive decided to establish strong procedures to control resources and monitor the benefits produced by the projects executed by her division. She appointed a project manager to lead an organisational change initiative to create the new PMO department reporting to her (see Chapter 13), and establish a methodology to manage portfolios, programs and projects.

During the planning workshop for the new project, the team members noticed that three senior managers (all reporting to the senior executive and located in different countries) were unhappy with the project objectives, opposing the assignment of their human resources for the project execution. The project manager suggested evaluating the situation during the stakeholder analysis, before preparing the communications management plan.

The main outcomes of the brainstorming session for the three main *opposers* were:

- **Manager of the Asia-Pacific region** – high levels of power and influence, could not see the benefits of a PMO and was afraid of losing importance if some experienced project managers were transferred to the new department. Coming from a country with strong uncertainty avoidance culture (see page 27), the resistance to innovation of this manager was well known by many team members.

- **Manager of the Latin-America region** – medium level of power but highly influential, this manager also came from a strong uncertainty avoidance culture and was intrigued by the real reasons behind the creation of the new department, having heard rumours that the senior executive was unhappy with the results of recent projects coordinated by project managers in Latin-American countries.

- **Manager of the European region** – this manager would prefer to keep control of the PMO, as the original thoughts were to create a PMO department reporting to the European region, managing all important projects and the portfolio for the whole division. Coming from a short-term oriented culture (see page 28), this manager was struggling to see how a PMO director could work with team members across the three geographical regions.

Some project team members were suggesting that only regular face-to-face meetings with the three regional managers could increase their collaboration. However, the time and cost required for the travel could have a negative impact on the project schedule and budget. After performing a cost-benefit analysis, the project manager decided to organise regular meetings by video conferencing, nominating one local coordinator in every region and asking them to be present in the same room as the regional managers, trying to exert some influence and helping to moderate the meeting. Other suggestions took into consideration the cultural dimensions:

- A briefing on PMO concepts was provided to the regional managers in the first meeting, showing how the application of tight rules can standardise the project management practices and facilitate the demonstration of costs and benefits, while keeping the decision power of the regional managers. The two managers coming from strong uncertainty awareness cultures appreciated the briefing and started showing less resistance.

- A briefing on global project management challenges and strategies was provided to the regional managers in the same meeting, showing how the implementation of new working practices could allow effective work across borders. The European manager was very interested in seeing how these practices could work in reality.

- In the second meeting, the overall project plan was presented and approved by the participants. A detailed plan, specifying the participation required from project managers located in the different regions, was distributed 1 week before the meeting to all participants. This also improved the commitment of the managers coming from strong uncertainty awareness cultures.

- The following monthly meetings provided a report on the progress, the benefits already achieved and the short term targets for the next steps. The presentation included some quotes from different project managers on how the global project management practices were improving their work across cultures and time zones. A weekly update of the progress report presentation was posted to the project website, showing the same information items. This improved the commitment level from the manager with short-term oriented culture.

Completing the global stakeholder register

The project manager can then decide to have one-to-one interviews or informal discussions with key stakeholders in order to validate the information provided during the brainstorming sessions, to clarify conflicting standpoints of different team members and to obtain additional information. These interviews and discussions should be conducted face-to-face, mainly when the project manager is meeting a stakeholder for the first time.

The outcome of the analysis described in this chapter is a complete stakeholder register, which will be part of the communications management plan. The project manager can now define the process of maintaining the register, by specifying:

- The update frequency – determines how often to have meetings to review and update the stakeholder register.
- The ownership – defines who will monitor the changes on different items on the register (outside the regular meetings) and perform the updates.
- The confidentiality – controls who can have access to read the information on the stakeholder register.

The project team will employ the stakeholder register when planning the project communications (see Chapter 8), distributing project information and managing the stakeholders.

Global communication channels

The PMBOK® Guide suggests that, 'the project manager should consider the number of potential communication channels or paths as an indicator of the complexity of a project's communications' (PMI, 2004). The number of effective channels must be reduced by identifying the required communications for project success and creating clear guidelines.

The formula to calculate the total number of communication channels in a project is: 'n $(n – 1)/2$', where n is the number of stakeholders. In the example in Figure 6.2, there are six stakeholders, with a total of 15 communication channels: ($6 * (6 – 1)/2 = 15$).

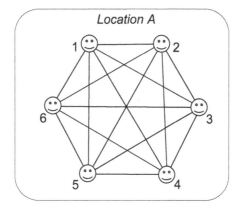

Figure 6.2   Communication channels in a traditional project

The number of potential channels crossing national borders will indicate the complexity level of communications on a global project. As stated in other parts of this book, the communication across borders is more complex, as there are natural barriers from cultures and time zones that can create misunderstandings. More preparation effort is then required for efficient communication. In Figure 6.3, the six stakeholders are distributed in two locations, and eight of the 15 channels are crossing country borders (represented by dashed lines).

The complexity of communications on this project tends to be higher than in the previous example (Figure 6.2). If the same six resources are distributed over four different locations, as shown in Figure 6.4, the number of communications across borders is increased to 13, on a total of 15 channels. The complexity of the communications is expected to be even higher in this case, as very few communications will benefit from the face-to-face contact.

The number of effective communication channels can be reduced by evaluating different project structures and implementing project coordination roles (see Chapter 11). As an example, considering again a project with six stakeholders distributed over two locations (Figure 6.5), the project manager (stakeholder number 6) can assign the team member 1 to coordinate all

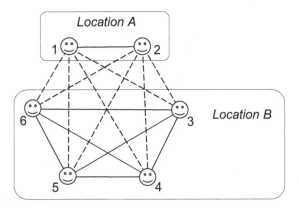

Figure 6.3   **Communication channels on a global project, two locations**

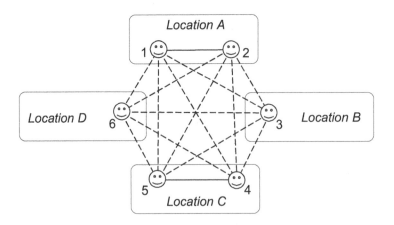

Figure 6.4   **Communication channels on a global project, multiple locations**

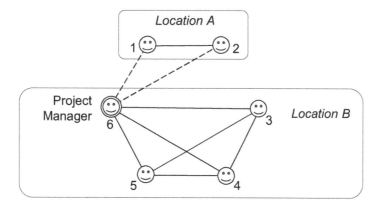

Figure 6.5   Reducing the number of virtual communication channels

activities on location A. The number of effective communication channels is reduced from 15 to nine, and the number of remote communications is reduced from eight to two.

Of course, this is theoretical as there are other factors to be considered and project teams are often more complex than this example. However, it shows the importance of understanding the communication channels, their impact on the project complexity and the importance of the recommendations in all chapters of this book to improve the communication across cultural borders.

YOUR LEARNING ON STAKEHOLDER ANALYSIS

Revisit the list or mindmap created at the beginning of this chapter. Would you handle opposers in a different way? How would you adapt your project communications strategy to improve commitment from key stakeholders? What stakeholders characteristics and attitudes will you note in your stakeholders record? How can you document the communication channels for medium to large projects?

Now share your thoughts with other people, and read about their own experiences (www. GlobalProjectManagement.org).

7 Meeting Rules and Templates

Global programs and projects often involve people from different organisational units and companies who have different standards, methodologies and tools for project management. These project managers might unite their efforts at the beginning of the project and define a common communication strategy for meetings, based on the standards of the organisation with the higher level of maturity or expertise in the project domain. In some situations, the standards are imposed by the organisation responsible for the overall project execution, which must provide training and coaching on the meeting practices to stakeholders from other companies, in order to foster their use and reduce misunderstandings.

This chapter provides a starting point for the definition of meeting rules and templates, which can be adapted to your organisation methods and practices and implemented in your global project or program.

Meeting types and communication media

Every meeting type requires the use of different communication means depending on the meeting format, frequency and audience. It is important to provide guidance to all global stakeholders on when to organise a meeting by audio, video or web conferencing. Clear rules can also be defined for occasions that require a face-to-face meeting. The guidance and rules will vary according to the company cultures, the familiarity of the team members with meetings over distance and the tools available to the project team. You can use the steps and examples below to develop a set of recommendations for your company:

- Organise a brainstorming session with your project coordinators and other global program and project managers (refer to Chapter 10). Start the session by identifying the major types

> **YOUR EXPERIENCE OF PROJECT MEETINGS**
>
> Before reading this chapter, think about recent meetings you moderated or attended with people in remote locations attending by audio, video or web conferencing. What were the main challenges faced by the meeting moderator? What were the strategies used to make the meetings effective? What were the problems that damaged the productivity of the meeting?
>
> On which occasions would you recommend organising a face-to-face meeting? When do you prefer to hold a video conference?
>
> Write on a list or mindmap the challenges and recommendations. Write on a separate list the problems and conflicts you experienced, and how you would avoid these negative situations in the future.

of meetings used for global projects, and classifying them according to categories such as the number of participants, the planned duration and the type of audience (project team members, senior managers, other stakeholders). Table 7.1 represents a possible outcome of this session.

- For every meeting type, brainstorm the positive and negative aspects of different communication media. Refer to Chapters 16–25 to obtain more information and complete the ideas generated by the brainstorming session.
- Prepare a summary of the positive and negative aspects, making a recommendation on the communication channels to use for each type of meeting. Table 7.2 shows a possible outcome of this exercise.
- Present the resulting recommendations to the global project team members and use them during the elaboration of the communications management plan (explained in Chapter 8).

Etiquette for cross-cultural meetings

Chapters 22 and 23 provide many guidelines on hosting and participating in meetings over a distance. You can use those recommendations to develop a 'meeting etiquette' protocol, with hints and tips applicable to your meetings. People from different companies and countries can have various viewpoints on what is acceptable during meetings. The points below provide some examples, you might review them during the project kick-off and when you notice that specific behaviours are creating misunderstandings or personal conflicts:

- develop rapport with your colleagues by using fun … but do not exaggerate;
- build rapport by starting the meetings with informal discussions … but know when to stop;
- get to the point: avoid spending too much time telling stories and providing detailed background;
- think about the audience: avoid starting detailed discussions with senior managers;
- know the audience: when the attendees are not responsible for strategies and decisions, cover these topics in a separate meeting;
- accept the different opinions, behaviours and values motivated by the variety of personalities and cultures, learn from the differences;
- respect the personal time: confirm with the audience their preferred times for meetings outside office hours, when the participants are in different time zones.

Online meeting templates

The project information is stored in a series of documents, tables, charts and databases prepared during project initiation, updated during project execution and controlling activities and archived for future use during project closure. The project records on companies applying the PMI PMBOK® Guide principles are the main inputs and outputs of the project management processes, some examples being:

- project charter, statement of work and scope statement
- project management plan
- project schedule

Table 7.1   Examples of meeting types

Meeting type	Number of participants	Duration	Audience	Moderators
Monitoring and control/regular follow-up meetings with coordinators	Fewer than five	Usually 1 hour or less	Local project coordinators	Project Manager
Monitoring and control/ regular follow-up meetings with key project team members	Between five and 15	Between 1 and 2 hours	Project team members	Local coordinators
Monitoring and control/ occasional meetings to resolve conflicts, discuss project risks, and so on	Fewer than five	Usually 1 hour or less	Project team members	Local coordinators
Workshops to prepare strategies and designs	Usually more than 15	Half-day to a week	Project team members	Local coordinators
Steering committees –regular meetings with the project sponsor group	Between five and ten	Usually 1 hour or less	Senior managers	Project Manager
Kick-off meetings	Usually more than fifteen	Half-day to a week	Project team members, some senior managers and local coordinators	Project Manager

Table 7.2   Communication media recommended for each meeting type

Meeting type	Local meetings	Audio conferencing	Video conferencing	Audio and web conferencing
Monitoring and control/regular follow-up meetings with coordinators	Only when all participants are in the same location	Audio conferencing alone should not be used, to avoid misunderstandings	Video conferencing can be used, however it limits the number of locations attending the same meeting, and may require additional time for preparation	**Recommended.** Brings the advantage of sharing documents on the screen and validates common understanding on the points being discussed
Monitoring and control/regular follow-up meetings with key project team members	Only when all participants are in the same location	Audio conferencing alone should not be used, to avoid misunderstandings	Video conferencing can be used, however it limits the number of locations attending the same meeting, and may require additional time for preparation	**Recommended.** Brings the advantage of sharing documents on the screen and validates common understanding on the points being discussed. For meetings with duration of 2 hours or more, a short break should allow the participants to improve their concentration

Table 7.2   *Concluded*

Meeting type	Local meetings	Audio conferencing	Video conferencing	Audio and web conferencing
Monitoring and control/ occasional meetings to resolve conflicts, to discuss project risks, and so on	**Recommended**. Face-to-face meetings can always help to resolve personal conflicts	Audio conferencing can be used when the conflicts are not motivated by personal reasons	**Recommended**. When face-to-face meetings are not possible, the visual contact can always help to resolve personal conflicts	Same as audio conferencing, with the added benefit of sharing visual images and presentations to improve the value of the messages being exchanged
Workshops to prepare strategies and designs	**Recommended**. Face-to-face meetings can improve the concentration when the duration is above 2 hours	**To be avoided**. Experience shows that participants lose focus on the meeting after 1 hour and start to 'multitask' (for example, read e-mails during the meeting)	**Use with caution**. Include short breaks after 90–120 minutes, to allow people to 'recharge their batteries'. The meeting coordinator must actively involve all participants from the different locations by asking questions and confirming understanding	**To be avoided**. Experience shows that participants lose focus on the meeting after 1 hour and start to 'multitask' (for example, read e-mails during the meeting)
Steering committees – regular meetings with the project sponsor group	The first meeting should be face-to-face, to allow the project manager to have an initial contact with all senior managers, and to establish a direct and open relationship with key members from the sponsor group	Audio conferencing alone should not be used, to avoid misunderstandings	Can be useful to keep the open relationship, perhaps alternating the meetings between video conferencing and audio and web conferencing	**Recommended**. Audio conferencing should be used in conjunction with web conferencing, to allow presentations of the meeting contents, graphics and pictures
Kick-off meetings	**Recommended**. Usually the first contact between team members happens during the kick-off meeting, and face-to-face contacts allied with team building events can establish informal relationships that will be beneficial for the project execution tasks	Audio conferencing should only be used during a kick-off meeting when the project complexity is low and all participants have already worked together on other projects	Video conferencing can be a good alternative when face-to-face meetings are not possible. The effectiveness will be reduced, as team building activities over video conferencing have limited effects	Audio and web conferencing should only be used during a kick-off meeting when the project complexity is low and all participants have already worked together on other projects. When the only material shared on the screen is a presentation or document, the web conferencing is not mandatory

- cost baseline
- change management log
- risk register
- issues log
- corrective actions log
- quality metrics, checklists and control measurements
- project organisation chart
- contracts
- meeting requests and minutes

Companies can prepare templates for all of the above items, or for a subset that is usually present in most of their projects. The practices and recommendations that follow are applicable only to the documents that are regularly updated during online meetings.

The major advantage of web conferencing and desktop-sharing facilities is the update of documents during the meetings, allowing collaboration from all meeting participants. There are many advantages in sharing these elements with the participants in real-time: validating common understanding of the points being tracked, prompt availability of the revised information and less effort and time to track all activities. The main challenge for the moderators is to make the updates quickly. You can prepare templates that can help the moderator tasks during online meetings. Common spreadsheet software tools and online databases provide all the automated functions, and all these suggestions use the risk register example (Figure 7.1):

- Use colours for a quick identification of different categories: the risks can be automatically coded in red, and opportunities in green (cells in the column 'risk or opportunity'). The cells in the columns 'probability' and 'impact' can use the red/amber/green colour code to differentiate between high/medium/low. The column 'weight' can also apply different colours to value ranges (for example, grey under 50 per cent, green between 50 per cent and 70 per cent, blue greater than 70 per cent).
- Use drop-down menus wherever possible to avoid typos, to speed-up typing and to ensure the integrity of the information. On the example in Figure 7.2, the choices for the column 'response' are limited, allowing an easy filter of all risks with response type 'accept', when preparing a report to senior management.
- Use automated filtering (Figure 7.3) to select only the entries applicable to particular meetings. For example, you can select only the top ten risks, the risks with high impact or only the opportunities. This also allows the team members to select only the entries that are assigned to them.
- Include legends and explanations on the available fields and entries (Figure 7.4), to ensure the use is consistent across different meetings and meeting moderators.
- Depending on the project structure (see Chapter 11), add one column to identify the location, team or company, to allow the local coordinators to filter all and only the lines assigned to their teams.
- Define rules for local coordinators and project team members to update the entries assigned to them outside the meetings, considering that other people may need to be aware when entries in the register are updated.

Nr.	Situation analysis	Risk or Opportunity	Trigger	Impact	Owner	Level	Prob.	Impact	Weight	Rank	Response Type	Response Strategy	Response cost and time impact
1	Technical problems on the new devices	Risk	Installation of new devices	- Warehouses can be unavailable during the outage	M. Souza	Project team	M	H	89%	1	Mtigate (prob.)	Move the test systems to the new devices earlier and perform validation tests	20 workdays required to perform testing, adding one extra week to project schedule
2	Technical problems on the new devices	Risk	Installation of new devices	- Time is required to solve the problems, impacting the project schedule	J. Sato	Project team	M	M	67%	3	Mtigate (impact)	Install the units 2 weeks earlier, allowing time for testing and problem solving	Higher cost (+500k Euros): purchase devices from another seller that has all units in stock
3	Users may not be available to validate the new system	Risk	Test phase	- Increased number of technical problems impacting the production line	T. Hammar	Project management	L	H	78%	2	Transfer	Outsource the testing activities	- Estimated cost : 50K Euros - 20 Workdays to be added for the project team to define tests scripts in more details
4	If new computers are in place, design activities can use new 3D software and finish earlier	Opportunity	Design phase	- Project schedule	S. Petit	Project management	M	M	67%	3	Enhance (prob.)	Proposal will be made to Senior Management, with cost and impact assessment	- Estimated cost: 25k Euros - Savings on workdays: 20k Euros - Reduction on schedule: 3 weeks
5													

Figure 7.1   Example of a project risk register

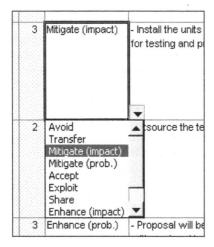

Figure 7.2   Example of drop-down menus

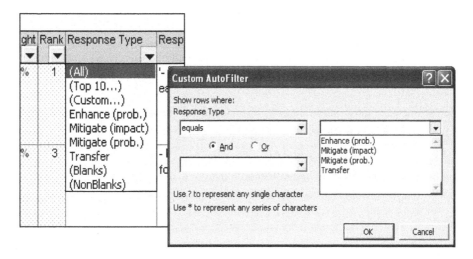

Figure 7.3   Example of automatic filtering

	Response types	
RISK	**Avoid**	e.g. changing project plan to eliminate risk
	Transfer	Other project or department accepts to provide a response and take ownership
	Mitigate (impact)	Reduce consequences of an adverse risk event
	Mitigate (prob.)	Reduce probabilities of an adverse risk event
	Accept	No changes to project plan or architecture will be made, ideally a contingency plan should be prepared and executed if the risk occur
OPPORTUNITY	**Exploit**	e.g. changing project plan to ensure opportunity will happen
	Share	Other project or department accepts to provide a response and share the opportunity benefits
	Enhance (impact)	Enhance consequences of an opportunity event, if it happens
	Enhance (prob.)	Enhance probability of an opportunity event to happen
	Accept	No changes to project plan or architecture will be made, ideally a contingency plan should be prepared and executed if the risk occur

Figure 7.4   Example of legends to define available entries and their meaning

REAL-LIFE EXPERIENCE

The project knowledge base can take diverse forms, and a good project management information system will provide a repository for all project records. Online collaborative tools also provide databases and tables that can be adapted to satisfy the project requirements. For projects with a smaller team, or involving different organisations that cannot have access to the same online repository, one simple and good solution is to develop a 'global project binder'. The global project binder is one spreadsheet serving as the knowledge database for the whole project, containing most of the information created during project initiation and planning, and required during the project execution, monitoring and controlling. The main phases to develop a global project binder in a global company are:

- Development – a group of experienced project managers can bring together the different tools and documents used in their projects, and learned from project management training and books. They can use the format of the project risk register as a model (Figure 7.1), and include the information items from their tools and documents that are required for most projects.

- Improvement – all project managers must commit to deploy this first version of the global project binder in all new projects, and meet regularly to exchange experiences. They can adapt the global project binder to the revised requirements, and publish new releases in the organisational repository of tools and templates.

- Maturity – once the global project binder is validated by the whole company, and widely accepted within the project management community, it can be converted to an online version, in the format of a set of tables and databases, or imbedded in a Project Management Information System.

Some examples of information that can be included on the global project binder:

- change record (Figure 7.5)
- meeting minutes (Figure 7.6)
- communication requirements matrix (Figure 8.2 on page 104)
- global communication matrix (Figure 8.3 on page 106)

Visual information

During presentations, brainstorming sessions, risk identification and problem-solving meetings, use as many visual elements as possible. If you have a list of structures being changed in different phases, make drawings to show the overall picture. It is easier to prepare the drawings in advance than to draw them during the meeting. Preparation is worth the effort.

REAL-LIFE EXPERIENCE

A pharmaceutical company started a project to upgrade two plants situated in different locations. The project manager received the following project description from the sponsor, in order to prepare a presentation to the newly assembled project team:

- There are currently two plants using the old production line, Berlin (line A) and Tokyo (line X). Both are connected to the old versions of the warehouse systems.

Nr.	Date of change	Description of change	Impact analysis				Comments	Status
			Scope	Time-frame	Costs			
1	27-Dec-06	Additional 5 factories will be migrated to new system	Factories A,B,C,D,E will be in scope	Go-live will be postponed by 4 weeks (customer decision) to allow preparation for the extra factories	Additional 200.000 EUR will be required to pay for the increased disk space	Steering Committee will raise this point in a meeting with the customer on the 3rd Jan	S.C. informed
2								
3								

Figure 7.5   Global Project Binder – Change record

Date	Type	Attendees	Excused	Agenda	Key points
01-Jan	Weekly technical meeting	Surname, Name; Surname, Name	Surname, Name; Surname, Name	- Review status of technical activities	- Informations items - Decisions items - Other points not covered in the Actions and Issues, Risks, change logs.

Figure 7.6   Global Project Binder - Meeting minutes record

- The objective of the first project phase will be to document all functions and volumes of the old systems.

- The second phase will implement two new production lines (B and Y), connected to the central warehouse system, and validate that these new lines can replace the existing ones, for the duration of the outage required by phase III.

- The third phase will replace the equipment on production lines A and X, and connect them to the central warehouse system, retiring the old equipment.

The project manager decided to transform the above information into a graphic representation of the three-step approach (Figure 7.7). The one-page slide was used during a 1-hour meeting that presented the project to the team members, considering major threats and opportunities, and identifying the main cross-dependencies with other projects and with the production activities.

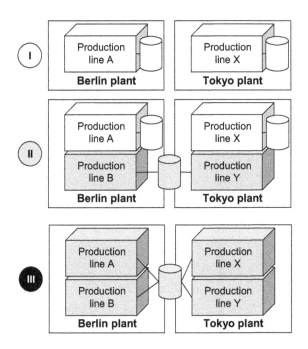

Figure 7.7   Graphic representation of project phases

YOUR LEARNING ON PROJECT MEETINGS

Revisit the list or mindmap created at the beginning of this chapter. Would you handle the negative situations in a different way? What problems and conflicts would be hard to avoid, despite the use of common practices and meeting etiquette? What are the advantages and disadvantages of having a common set of meeting recommendations and practices? What are the positive and negative aspects of using visual information to avoid misunderstandings during web and video conferences that involve people with different native languages?

Now share your thoughts with other people, and read about their own experiences (www. GlobalProjectManagement.org).

8 *Global Communication Strategy*

The early development of a good communication strategy can reduce misunderstandings between stakeholders from different country and company cultures communicating over distance. The main interested parties must work together to define this strategy, creating the project communications management plan. This chapter suggests three main steps to prepare a global communication strategy, by:

- identifying the types of information to be communicated;
- gathering the communication requirements from key stakeholders;
- determining how the communication will effectively happen.

Defining the types of project information

As a first step, you need to identify the project information that must be part of the communications plan, with the help of the project team members and other key stakeholders. The information items can be grouped into broad categories, which will vary according to the knowledge area, the project complexity and the type of organisation. These are some examples of information categories that are applicable to most projects:

- **Project Management Plan** – the heart of the project information, containing the detailed project definition that will serve as the main source of information for the project execution and control activities.
- **Project status** – the project managers and coordinators must produce project performance statistics, which compare the current costs, schedule, customer satisfaction levels and quality measurements with the approved baseline.
- **Project records** – different project records keep track of the elements that may affect the project performance, such as issues, risk and changes.

YOUR EXPERIENCE OF PROJECT COMMUNICATION

Before reading this chapter, think about the communication practices in previous or current projects. How did you know if all stakeholders received the information they needed during the project? Did you formalise their requirements at the beginning of the project? Did you verify that the information was exchanged according to their requirements? Did all team members know their roles in the preparation and distribution of information?

Write on a list or mindmap the communication problems, how you solved them and how you would react to similar situations in the future. Make a separate list of project communication success stories, which you are likely to repeat in the future.

- **Status of the work packages** – the work package owners maintain a status report for their activities, normally in a level of detail that allows the project team members to understand their tasks, and the project manager to link related events (issues and risks) that occurred in different activities.
- **Project organisation** – the global project manager is responsible for the definition of the project organisation chart, combined with clear roles and responsibilities for team members coming from different organisations and locations.
- **Logistics** – the project team members collect useful information on office locations, travel guidelines and other basic knowledge for the stakeholders who are travelling across countries and working abroad.
- **Standards and templates** – the project team members must define a set of document templates that will form the project knowledge repository. They can also produce guidelines instructing the project office or other team members to collect the project information and to update the documents in the repository. This will avoid project team members located in different countries or working for different organisations using various document formats with inconsistent information structures.

You can organise a brainstorming session with the main interested parties to decide on the information categories required by the project and to provide more details on the contents and formats of the project knowledge base. One possible outcome of this exercise is shown in Figure 8.1.

Identifying the stakeholders' requirements

After the main project knowledge components are identified, you need to analyse the stakeholders' information requirements. One possible way is the preparation of a communication requirements matrix (see Figure 8.2) describing the relationship between the stakeholders (listed in the matrix columns) and the information items (represented in the rows). In each cell of the matrix, describe how the stakeholder contributes to the project communication, by:

- preparing the information, alone or together with other stakeholders;
- informing other stakeholders;
- receiving and analysing the information;
- reviewing or approving the information before distribution;
- archiving or deleting the information or documentation.

You must prepare the requirements matrix during the communications planning activities, keeping in mind the strategies to change the stakeholder commitment level (see Chapter 6). The investment of time and resources on knowledge generation and distribution must be measured against the value they produce to the project. Thus, the project team must avoid producing information not specified in the communications requirements matrix, except if this is requested via the formal change control process. In this case, the communications requirements matrix must reflect the change and its impact on all stakeholders. This will bring the added value of providing the new information to a larger community of stakeholders, increasing their level of commitment to the project goals and strategies.

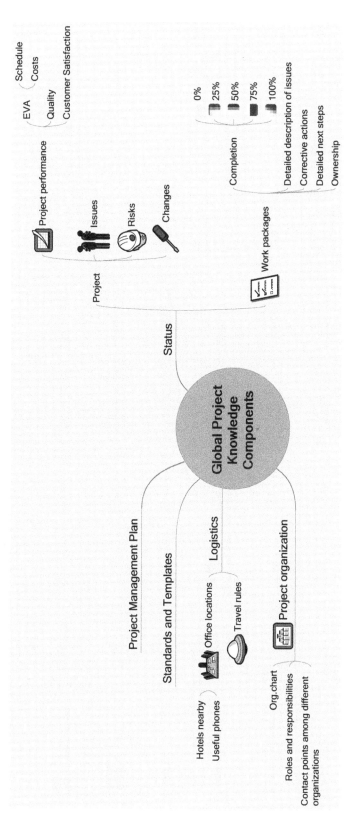

Figure 8.1   Examples of global project knowledge components

Stakeholder / Information	SP Sponsor	SC Steering committee	PM Project Manager	PC Project Coordinators	TM Team Members	C Customers	S Suppliers	P Partners
Project status	Informed by PM	Informed by PM	Prepare with PC	Prepare with PM	Informed by PM	Partially informed by PM (select relevant information)	Partially informed by PM (select relevant information)	Partially informed by PM (select relevant information)
Work package status	n/a	n/a	Informed by PC	Prepare with TM, inform PM	Prepare with PC	n/a	n/a	n/a
Project organization	Provide input to PM & Approve	Provide input to PM & Approve	Prepare with PC Review with SP & SC	Prepare with PM	Informed by PM	Partially informed by PM (exclude confidential information)	Partially informed by PM (exclude confidential information)	Partially informed by PM (exclude confidential information)
Logistics	Informed by PM	Informed by PM	Prepare with PC	Prepare with PM	Informed by PM	n/a	n/a	n/a
Standards and Templates	n/a	n/a	Prepare with PC	Prepare with PM	Informed by PM	n/a	n/a	n/a
Project Management Plan	Informed by PM	Informed by PM	Prepare with PC	Prepare with PM	Prepare with PM	Partially informed by PM (exclude confidential information)	Partially informed by PM (exclude confidential information)	Partially informed by PM (exclude confidential information)

Figure 8.2   Example of a communication requirements matrix

Define a global communication matrix

In the third component of the global communications management plan, you will define the format of each communication, its frequency and participants, by using all the information discussed in the previous chapters:

- **Meeting types and communication media** – start your communication matrix with the main meeting types and communication media you have used in previous, similar projects. During the lessons-learned sessions, identify other types of meetings that can increase the level of commitment of key stakeholders. Review Chapter 7 when preparing this list, to identify the information distribution patterns to be used during the project (especially Tables 7.1 and 7.2).
- **The project knowledge base** – use the standard established by your company for the project knowledge base. If there is no standard available, define one for your project, using the recommendations from Chapter 7.
- **Online meeting templates** – all documents on the communication matrix must be adapted for online meetings, promoting the use of online conferencing by allowing a quick capture of the discussions and decisions.
- **The advantages of using visual information** – consider publishing charts and dashboards with a visual status of your project, and use the same information during the status meetings. This can reduce the time required by the stakeholders to understand the message being transmitted. You can also shorten the preparation time by using the project knowledge base to produce charts automatically with the project performance information. Visual information can help to obtain buy-in from stakeholders that are not available to participate in regular meetings, allowing them to learn the status of the project at a glance.
- **The global communication channels** – as discussed in Chapter 6, all communication flowing across borders requires careful planning and the application of the principles specified across various chapters of the Global Project Management Framework©. The number of remote communication channels can also be reduced by assigning the roles of local coordinator to local team members.
- **The stakeholder register** – when determining the format and technology of communications and meetings, take all elements on the register into consideration, mainly power, influence, reactions, challenges, opportunities, knowledge level and cultural patterns.
- **Cultural aspects** – when preparing executive reports to specific-oriented stakeholders, start with an executive summary. On the other hand, people from diffuse-oriented cultures will appreciate having the executive summary at the end (see page 31).

Although the format of the communication matrix can vary, you can use a spreadsheet (see example on Figure 8.3) with the same line and column headers as the communication requirements matrix shown in Figure 8.2. The contents of each cell might show the *frequency* of the information distribution (reflecting the amount of information the stakeholders must receive in order to keep or increase their levels of commitment), the communication *medium* (based on the recommendations in Chapters 16–25) and information on *confidentiality and security*, when applicable.

Stakeholder / Information	SP Sponsor	SC Steering committee	PM Project Manager	PC Project Coordinators	TM Team Members	C Customers	S Suppliers	P Partners
Project status preparation	n/a	n/a	**Monthly** web-conferencing	**Monthly** web-conferencing	n/a	**Quarterly** web-conferencing	**Quarterly** web-conferencing	**Quarterly** web-conferencing
Project status meeting	**Monthly** meeting face-to-face	**Monthly** face-to-face or video-conference	**Monthly** face-to-face or video-conference	n/a	Informed by PM	n/a	n/a	n/a
Project status publishing	**On demand** Access the project virtual room	**On demand** Access the project virtual room	**Monthly** Publish on the project virtual room	**On demand** Access the project virtual room	**On demand** Access the project virtual room	**On demand** Access the project virtual room, public area	**On demand** Access the project virtual room, public area	**On demand** Access the project virtual room, public area
Work package status preparation	n/a	n/a	n/a	**Weekly** face-to-face	**Weekly** face-to-face	n/a	n/a	n/a
Work package status information	n/a	n/a	**Weekly** web-conferencing	**Weekly** web-conferencing	n/a	n/a	n/a	n/a
Project organization	**On demand** Access the project virtual room	**On demand** Access the project virtual room	**On changes** Publish on the project virtual room	**On demand** Access the project virtual room	**On demand** Access the project virtual room	**On demand** Access the project virtual room, public area	**On demand** Access the project virtual room, public area	**On demand** Access the project virtual room, public area
Logistics	**On demand** Access the project virtual room	**On demand** Access the project virtual room	**On changes** Publish on the project virtual room	**On changes** Publish on the project virtual room	**On demand** Access the project virtual room	n/a	n/a	n/a
Standards and Templates	n/a	n/a	**On changes** Publish on the project virtual room	**On changes** Publish on the project virtual room	**On demand** Access the project virtual room	n/a	n/a	n/a
Project Management Plan preparation	n/a	n/a	**During planning** face-to-face or video-conference	**During planning** face-to-face or video-conference	**During planning** face-to-face or video-conference	n/a	n/a	n/a
Project Management Plan updates	n/a	n/a	**Monthly** web-conferencing	**Monthly** web-conferencing	**Monthly** web-conferencing	n/a	n/a	n/a
Project Management Plan publishing	**On demand** Access the project virtual room	**On demand** Access the project virtual room	**On changes** Publish on the project virtual room	**On changes** Publish on the project virtual room	**On demand** Access the project virtual room	**On demand** Access the project virtual room, public area	**On demand** Access the project virtual room, public area	**On demand** Access the project virtual room, public area

Figure 8.3   **Example of a global communication matrix**

REAL-LIFE EXPERIENCE

During the planning phase of a top priority project involving four different companies in several locations across the globe, the project managers defined a global communication strategy that satisfied the main requirements of the key stakeholders. When the project implementation started, the team members from the supplier company were struggling with the aggressive schedule, and working very hard to commit to the agreed delivery dates. The project communication strategy was not followed, and the other three companies (the customer and two technology partners) started to suffer from the poor quality of information. The main symptoms were:

- Deliverables were completed on time, but the other parties only received the information afterwards, with impact to their own activities and to the availability of resources.

- Some deliverables were not completed on time, and the other parties were not informed of the main causes, the impacts on schedule and costs and the new estimated dates.

- Meetings were repeatedly cancelled without warning, or key participants did not attend, increasing frustration and loss of time.

- The levels of customer satisfaction and trust among the three partners were very low.

A team of specialised project managers performed an assessment of the situation and recommended the immediate assignment of project coordinators. Their main role was to learn and follow the project communication strategy, adapting the frequency and format of meetings when required.

The project finished on time, and the level of customer satisfaction was very high between the assessment and project closure. This showed, to all participants, the importance of following the project communication strategy, adapting it to new requirements and planning for resources to execute the strategy. The time required to collect information, process the data, build the project knowledge and attend meetings must be built into the project plan and included in the resource estimates.

YOUR LEARNING ON PROJECT COMMUNICATION

Revisit the list or mindmap created at the beginning of this chapter. Would you define a communication strategy for your project in a different way? How would you adapt your project communications strategy to improve commitment from key stakeholders? How can you use your success stories to improve the quality of the communication strategy in future projects?

Now share your thoughts with other people, and read about their own experiences (www. GlobalProjectManagement.org).

9 *Global Communication Techniques*

Chapters 7 and 8 covered in detail the set-up of tools and templates to streamline communication on global projects, and the definition of the communication guidelines during project initiation and planning. This chapter will present the main forms of communication that global program and project managers can use for information *collection*, *distribution* and *exchange* during the project execution, monitoring and controlling activities.

This chapter consolidates the knowledge presented previously and establishes a link between the practices in this book and the communication techniques from project management references such as the PMBOK® Guide, the ICB, and PRINCE2®.

Collecting information from the global team members

The different locations and organisations participating in a global project can have diverse methods and tools to gather information about time, cost and project performance. The program or project office may need to define manual or automated processes to combine the information available in different formats, to produce consolidated reports and performance summaries. This is not an easy task, and sometimes it is not even possible to find similar information items across various time tracking and financial systems.

Global projects will benefit from a standard method, to be used by all project team members, when recording the time spent for each work package and when reporting the cost items. This will simplify the consolidation of the project cost and time tracking information, and the preparation of Earned Value Analysis reports, or other control and monitoring tools. At project onset, the program or project manager must involve the project office team, and other team members that have knowledge in the different systems and tools, in order to agree on a common method for the duration of the project. This will be a challenge for projects

---

YOUR EXPERIENCE OF COMMUNICATION TECHNIQUES

Think about the communication techniques you have used when managing programs and projects. Were you always able to collect the required project information? What types of barriers did you face? Did you provide timely information on project performance to the interested parties? What communication media did you use? How much information did your team members exchange during your checkpoint meetings? What are the main differences between local and global projects?

Write on a list or mindmap the challenges and barriers you faced when collecting, distributing and exchanging project information with your team members. Make a separate list of success stories on communication gathering, publishing and exchanging that you are likely to repeat in the future.

involving people from different organisations, but can resolve many issues when addressed early.

The same considerations are required for other processes and tools used to collect performance information (for example, quality and customer satisfaction). The implementation of automated project management information systems (see Chapters 20 and 25) may bring many benefits to global projects. During project execution, these systems can help the project manager, or project office members, to collect project information, by:

- providing a central place where project team members can store all project documentation;
- allowing the use of electronic forms, where the project team members will enter information on project milestones and deliverables in a structured and standardised format;
- providing databases that will store this information and will be available for queries by different stakeholders;
- integrating with other office software suites, and prompting team members to enter information on due actions, issues and risk items.

Online meetings are another important source of project information. The meeting moderator can use databases or spreadsheets and prompt team members for the status of their activities, issues and risks, updating the project schedule or other records during the meeting. This will increase the level of commitment from key project team members, by allowing them to:

- voice their concerns on specific actions or issues;
- participate in the risk assessment;
- identify the impact of change on all project elements;
- coordinate the activities of their local colleagues and represent them during meetings.

Distributing information to the global stakeholders

Project managers or project office administrators can use software packages to structure and summarise the project performance data, in formats that include spreadsheets, graphics and colour-coded presentations. The information can be presented during project status meetings, but also be available on the project website. The web format can provide the information to a larger audience, and use hyperlinks to structure the information according to the requirements of different stakeholders. One possible approach is the preparation of a project dashboard, published on the home page of the project virtual room, with the following structure:

- **Level 1 – overall status**: in one web page, present the actual status and the evolution of the main relevant project performance items over time. This will satisfy the requirements of stakeholders who need to have an understanding of the project progress, but who are not interested in detailed information. Figure 9.1 shows an example of a project dashboard that allows the interested parties to monitor project status by presenting a summary of the project schedule, performance of work (using Earned Value Analysis technique), scope, risks, issues and quality.
- **Level 2 – detailed analysis and list of additional references**: depending on the audience, more explanation will be required for a complete understanding of the charts and acronyms. As illustrated in Figure 9.2, the main dashboard page can provide hyperlinks

REAL-LIFE EXPERIENCE

A valuable source of information on intangible performance items is the lessons-learned process, which focuses on identifying project successes and failures. A lessons-learned process in global projects aims to develop recommendations and guidelines to improve the project team behaviour and processes, increasing the success of future project phases or other projects, usually including:

- face-to-face lessons-learned sessions during closing of project phases;
- online sessions at completion of key deliverables;
- items of status meeting agendas;
- web surveys.

Lessons-learned sessions are always good occasions to promote team building, and electronic mindmap tools are very useful to increase the collaboration and foster knowledge exchange, mainly when these meetings are organised by web or video conferencing (see Chapter 10). Some examples of items that can be prompted by the moderators of lessons-learned sessions of global projects are:

- Are the project team members taking cultural aspects into consideration when communicating with stakeholders from your area? Or do you have any recommendations to avoid misunderstandings in the future?
- Are the meetings being organised at convenient times for your locations, or is there any change required to make your participation easier?
- Do you receive answers to your questions in a timely manner? Or are there any delays that could be avoided by a different attitude when using asynchronous communication?
- Do you see different procedures being used by team members from diverse organisations? Are there any benefits in deploying a standard procedure in these cases?
- Do you have any suggestions for the improvement of company good practices on global project management?

to a second level of information, containing a detailed analysis on the project knowledge, and providing a link to other documents that contain more details on specific items. As an example, this level can expand the Earned Value Analysis charts into indexes and forecasts, with enough explanations to make all stakeholders understand the project status.

- **Level 3 – detailed information**: the last level of information will be the documents that were used as a basis when producing the summaries on the previous levels. As an example, auditors can access the project cost documentation, and the spreadsheets used to calculate the Earned Value Analysis indexes, to review the data, validate the formulas and understand the reasons for deviations.

Other methods of project information distribution are presented in other chapters of this book:

- project meetings (Chapters 22 and 23)
- electronic databases (Chapter 24)
- electronic communication and conferencing tools (Chapters 17, 18, 22 and 23)
- project management information systems (Chapter 20)

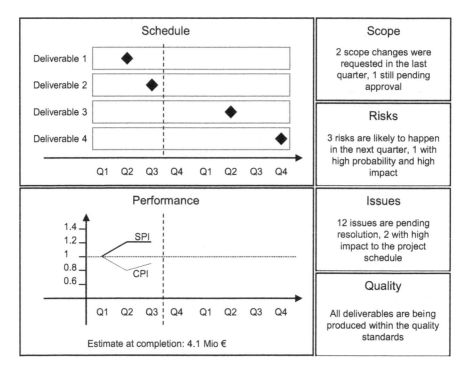

Figure 9.1   Example of a project dashboard – main page

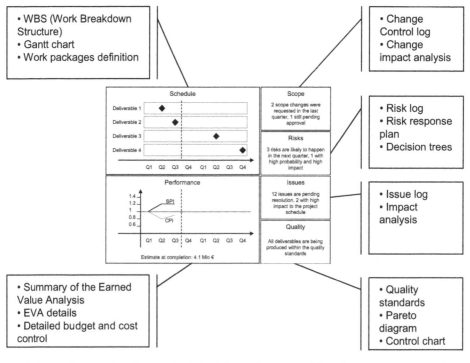

Figure 9.2   Example of a project dashboard – second level pages

Exchanging project information

Good checkpoint meetings use video or web conferencing technologies to validate understanding, as described in Chapters 17, 18, 22 and 23. These review meetings will be fundamental during critical periods, usually in the weeks or months leading up to the completion of major deliverables. However, these periods will be very busy for most team members, who will appreciate spending most of their time concentrating on their jobs, and not wasting time on meetings. Good preparation and coordination are fundamental so that every minute of the meeting adds value to all the team members, increasing the collaboration level and ensuring a common awareness of the whole team on the project status and the cross-dependencies between their activities. Therefore, all the team members participating in these sessions should be familiar with the recommendations in Chapter 23, to achieve a high level of productivity during meetings.

As discussed in Chapter 7, global project managers can benefit from the use of a Global Project Binder to hold most of the information generated by all project management tasks. The status review meetings can share the global project binder with all meeting participants, using online collaboration tools, reviewing and updating the main information items. Project websites that are easy to update can be another alternative to exchange the project information, by alternating asynchronous and synchronous communication media.

When the project is performing well and the team is composed of motivated and independent people, the meeting will not check on the status of each action or issue. Each team member should update the database directly when their activities are completed, or inform the project manager in the case of exceptions (for example, when the target dates cannot be met). For these project teams, the meeting will be an occasion to get together and review if the recent updates on the project items create any impact not foreseen by individual project members, usually on tasks outside their knowledge domain. Reality shows that many project teams still require the status meetings to get more information updates on each work package, as the team members may not take full ownership of their actions, issues and risks, may not update the project records and may not keep the project managers, coordinators or project office administrators informed. In this case, the meeting will take longer and impact the productivity of the team members. Alternatively, one project team member (usually the project office administrator) will own the project records, and have short status review meetings with individual coordinators or team members before the status review meetings. The project manager will need to monitor the effectiveness of the team meetings and adapt the project organisation and the meeting agendas to obtain the optimal ratio of meeting duration and number of items discussed.

The agenda of the checkpoint meetings can include discussions on:

- **Stakeholders** – introduce new members to the project team, inform the team members of important changes on the stakeholder register and identify the impact of these changes on the activities from different project team members. Decide if these changes generate issues that affect the project and if separate meetings or task forces will be required to prepare a strategy for the corrective actions. In the same way, identify whether these changes add new risks to the project. Discuss the impact of these changes on the project organisation chart and roles and responsibilities matrix.
- **Communication** – inform the team members of changes to the global communication matrix, and confirm if the project team members require inclusion in the distribution chain of new types of project information. Inform the team members of important changes to the structure of the project web site.

- **Assumptions** – detect if the assumptions made in early project phases were valid or incorrect. Discuss the impact of incorrect assumptions on the project schedule, costs and risks.
- **Project schedule** – review the progress of activities and the impacts of delays on the project schedule. Identify if important changes have occurred that require approval from other stakeholders. Decide if these changes generate issues or risks that must be evaluated in more detail. In this case, identify which project team members will be required for this evaluation, and who will own the corrective action.
- **Issues and corrective actions** – review the latest status of the main issues and their corrective actions, and discuss the impact of critical actions that are still open after the target resolution date. Decide on the best method to obtain the appropriate resolution: a change in the action ownership, escalation to line managers, assigning more resources for its resolution or making a change to the project schedule.
- **Risks and Opportunities** – review the status of the risks that have past or imminent trigger dates, reviewing the appropriateness of their response strategies and impacts on the project. Review major changes of the estimated levels of probability and impact.
- **Changes** – review the changes requested or approved since the last status meeting, and discuss their impact on scope, schedule or cost. Ask the team members whether they are aware of unofficial or imminent change requests that need to be formalised.
- **Quality** – review the overall results from control measurements, and discuss how the recommended corrective or preventive actions can be implemented, and if they generate a change to the project.
- **Procurement** – review changes on sellers, contracts and other procurement items that have an impact on the activities of various project team members.
- **Meeting log (meeting minutes)** – before closing the session, review the main decisions taken during the meeting, and other important points not captured in the previous items of the agenda.

In large programs and projects, separate status review meetings are required to cover points owned by different groups, organisations or organisational units. As an example, a complex program might have one status meeting for each major project, and one consolidated status meeting with all project managers to cover the items that have an impact on the different projects or on the whole program.

The items on the agenda refer to information in different sections of the global project binder (for example, the discussion on stakeholders may generate entries on the risk register or the issues register). Thus, the format of the Global Project Binder or project web site will need to provide a good level of flexibility, for the meeting moderator to switch from one section to another, while keeping the meeting momentum.

REAL-LIFE EXPERIENCE

The meeting agenda and the duration of each discussion item will vary according to the project type, duration, criticality and the project phase. Figure 9.3 gives some examples of the variations on the same project, for status meetings during project start (top left chart), during periods of intensive preparation of critical deliverables (top right chart), on periods after the implementation of these deliverables (bottom left chart), and on the periods leading to the project closure (bottom right chart). Each sector on the chart represents the meeting agenda items explained before, and even if the durations are for illustrative purposes only, the meeting moderator might fix targets in advance, in order to control the meeting duration.

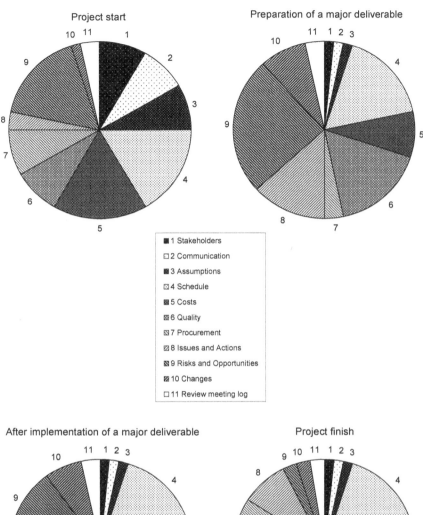

Figure 9.3   **Examples of different patterns of project status meetings**

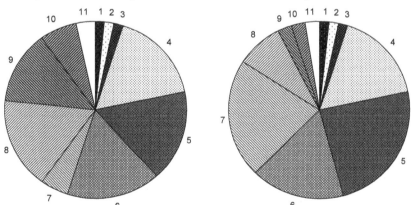

YOUR LEARNING ON GLOBAL COMMUNICATION TECHNIQUES

Revisit the list or mindmap created at the beginning of this chapter. Would you collect, produce, distribute or exchange information in a different way? Share your thoughts with other people, and read about their own experiences (www.GlobalProjectManagement.org).

10 *Global Creativity*

Projects are undertaken to create *unique* deliverables. This uniqueness requires the global project team members to unite their creative minds and design new products, define new services and build innovative strategies. People from different cultures may see constraints and opportunities from various angles before finding together a strategy that takes into account the different standpoints. Brainstorming techniques can be deployed to gather, structure and consolidate these different ideas into a creative solution.

While traditional brainstorming methods use white-boards, flip-charts and stickers for idea generation and consolidation, global project managers must adopt novel coordination styles and employ remote software tools to achieve similar results. This chapter covers two different formats for idea generation on global teams, and suggests the use of software tools that can stimulate creativity over distance.

Project management processes and creativity

Depending on the project type, complexity and area of application, creativity can be required for the execution of every project activity during the whole project life cycle. As a general rule, global project managers must consider if the organisation of brainstorming sessions on the following occasions would add value to the project outcomes:

- development of project charter and preliminary scope;
- preparation of all components of the project management plan;
- definition and preparation of the scope planning and the WBS (Work Breakdown Structure);
- activity definition and schedule development;
- estimating (resource, duration and costs);
- risk identification, risk response planning, qualitative and quantitative risk analysis;
- selection of sellers;

YOUR EXPERIENCE OF GLOBAL CREATIVITY

Before reading this chapter, think about some situations that required creative thinking from a group of people. Were they located in the same room for a brainstorming session? What challenges did you face, and how did you deal with them? What additional challenges do you think you would face, if they were sitting in different countries, and coming from different cultural backgrounds? How would you deal with this new situation?

Write on a list or mindmap the positive aspects of the brainstorming sessions you have participated in recently. Write on a separate list the challenges you faced, and how you would deal with them in the future.

- when the project team must consult a group of specialists (for topics related to specific knowledge domains) or local groups (for topics related to political, economic, social, technological, cultural or legal aspects of specific regions or countries).

There are two different ways to stimulate creativity and foster the exchange of ideas in global projects. The program or project manager can make a choice depending on the type of ideas being exchanged and the location of the team members. The *online* brainstorming method is recommended for most cases, but requires all team members to be connected at the same time, during the whole session. The *asynchronous* brainstorming method is the alternative to be used when the team members are in different time zones without possibility for a shared time, or on special occasions when the project manager prefers to omit the identity of the participants. The use and applicability of these two techniques will now be discussed in more detail.

Online brainstorming sessions

The first coordination style for idea generation is 'online brainstorming', which consists of people spread over different locations participating in a brainstorming session through interactive video or imaging tools. The project manager acts as a coach, stimulating creativity, organising ideas and moderating the meeting. Good preparation and coordination will produce excellent results, despite the distance between team members. The four-step approach described below provides you with guidance on how to prepare and conduct online brainstorming sessions:

STEP 1 – PREPARE THE MEETING

Select the appropriate media to use during your session (usually video conferencing or a mix of audio and web conferencing), using the information provided in Chapters 22 and 23. Schedule the session by sending a 'meeting request' as illustrated in Table 10.1, specifying:

- the goals of the brainstorming session and what is expected from attendees (meeting subject, background and objectives);
- the preparation tasks to be performed by the team members to learn more about the topic being discussed (meeting preparation);
- the main categories of ideas to be collected, when you know them in advance. As an example, if the brainstorming aims to collect environmental risks and opportunities to the project, ask the participants to think in advance about political, economical, social and technological aspects (meeting agenda);
- the meeting logistics, such as the locations, dial-in numbers for audio conferencing and links to web conferencing facilities.

When organising the first sessions with a global project team, make individual phone calls to discuss the session informally, to confirm that all attendees have the same understanding of the meeting objectives and to ensure they know what is expected from them.

Table 10.1   Example of meeting request for an online brainstorming session

Subject	Project X - Brainstorming on environmental risks and opportunities
Background	• The project X will implement distributed offices for round-the-clock operations and help desk • To build from previous experiences on similar projects, we need to identify all environmental risks that can have negative impacts on the project implementation, and prepare mitigation strategies. At the same time, we will identify some opportunities that can enhance the project benefits
Objectives	Identify environmental risks and opportunities that may affect project X
Preparation	1) Read the preliminary report on the social, political and economic environments on countries A, B and C (*link to the document in the project virtual room*) 2) Search for lessons learned from previous projects, collecting risks that may be relevant to project X 3) Use the change log and issues log from these projects and note down if these can be applicable to project X 4) Ask your local colleagues about their previous experiences on similar projects, and note down identified risks and issues that can also be applicable to project X 5) Speak to the local experts and obtain a list of potential threats to the implementation of project X
Agenda	• Risks related to the social and political situations of the countries A, B and C • Risks related to the economic instability of country A • Opportunities related to the good economic prospects of country B • Risks related to the poor technological infrastructure of country B • Opportunities that can exist for using the new technological developments of country C • Other risks and opportunities
Logistics	Identification session: Monday – May 21st, 2007 10:00–12:00 CET Review session: Wednesday – May 23rd, 2007 10:00–12:00 CET Mitigation session: Friday – May 25th, 2007 10:00–12:00 CET A offices, room 7654 B offices, room 321 The participants that cannot be in the above offices must dial-in from locations with internet access, as the use of web conferencing is mandatory
Audio conference details	A: (nn) 234 5678 B: (nnn) 234 567 C: (nn) 3456 7890 PIN: 9123456
Web conferencing details	www.my-web-conferencing.com/12345678/join.htm

STEP 2 – MODERATE THE MEETING

The online session can benefit from the basic brainstorming principles, which must be reiterated to all participants at the beginning of the session:

- no ideas will be discarded, all opinions can be valuable in the later stages;
- the participants should build on each others ideas, and mix different points to bring up new suggestions;
- quantity is more important than quality during the data collection step.

There are many different ways to capture the ideas using very common software tools. As illustrated in Table 10-2, one simple spreadsheet can be created and shared with other participants by the use of web or video conferencing. The brainstorming moderator can add each idea in a different cell, optionally grouping the related topics in the same columns.

Another approach is the use of mindmapping techniques, which are a good way of gathering ideas in a semi-structured format. The meeting moderator can group similar ideas, link related topics and note down the criticisms or evaluations coming spontaneously from the participants. Even if this is not allowed in pure brainstorming sessions, practice shows that meeting moderators can briefly capture the first reactions to the ideas being generated, without allowing deep discussions to take place. This feedback will be a starting point for the later steps of detailed analysis. The main advantages of mindmapping are the following:

- time saved by noting and reading only relevant words;
- the use of 'Basic Ordering Ideas' (key concepts) allows participants to work in a naturally structured way and saves time when searching the mindmap for ideas;
- key concepts are easily discernible, and juxtaposed in time and space, thus improving creativity and recall;
- the association between key words is clear;
- mindmaps are visually stimulating, helping the team to remember the main topics and find them on the diagram;
- mindmaps shared across the project locations ensure that every member understands the viewpoints of other participants, and completes them with their own opinions;
- the collaboration level of the group can increase after a mindmapping session including all individual contributions;
- mindmaps can also function as meeting minutes;
- visual cues can help non-native speakers to see the ideas in context.

Buzan (2006) identified some of these benefits, and defined the mindmap laws and recommendations to increase the mental precision, creativity, power and freedom of the participants. Based on his guidelines, the following suggestions can increase participation and effectiveness of mindmapping sessions over distance:

- Develop a positive mental attitude before starting the session. Keep in mind the different cultural mindsets of the participants when doing this. Remember that people from higher power-distance cultures can have difficulty in expressing their opinions in the presence of their local managers. A mix of people from higher and lower uncertainty avoidance cultures will result in different opinions on the level of innovation and risk acceptance. Consult Chapter 1 and consider organising the 360° analysis of the cultural dimensions before the brainstorming session.
- Nominate a 'scribe' to take notes of all suggestions in the mindmap.

Table 10.2   Example of a brainstorming spreadsheet for the identification of risks and opportunities

	Legal	Socio-cultural	Political	Economic	Technological
1	[OPPORTUNITY] Forecasted taxation changes in country B can be favourable to local employees	[R] Known rivalries between nationals of countries A and B might impact collaboration	[R] If the relations between countries A and B deteriorate after elections, work permits for knowledge exchange sessions may be hard to obtain	[R] Inflation rates in country A can increase if X party wins elections. Decrease on quality of life can impact motivation	[R] Quality of local equipment in country B is below company standards
2	[RISK] Competitors may access company software, as the intellectual property laws on countries B and C are weak			[R] If the demand for local workers in country C expands, the salary levels could raise, increasing the operational costs	[O] Highly-skilled technical support is easily available in countries A and B
3	[O] Nationalisation laws in country C are likely to be revoked, making it easier to expand the existing offices				[O] Company offices in country C are near the local university
4					

- Nominate a 'moderator' to stimulate ideas from everyone in the meeting, organising 'virtual round tables' (by naming each participant and requesting their opinions) to start the session or when the number of ideas slow down.
- Use emphasis, by adding images, icons, colours and different types and sizes of fonts, shapes and lines.
- Use association with arrows, links, colours and codes.
- Be clear, using few key words per node.
- Use hierarchy and numerical order.
- When navigating large mindmaps using software screens, make sure that all participants have a clear view of the position of the ideas in the overall context, by announcing operations like expanding/contracting branches, zooming and scrolling.

Figure 10.1 provides an example of mindmap captured during a risk identification session. Note that all risks were identified, but only some impacts were considered as they appeared spontaneously during the session.

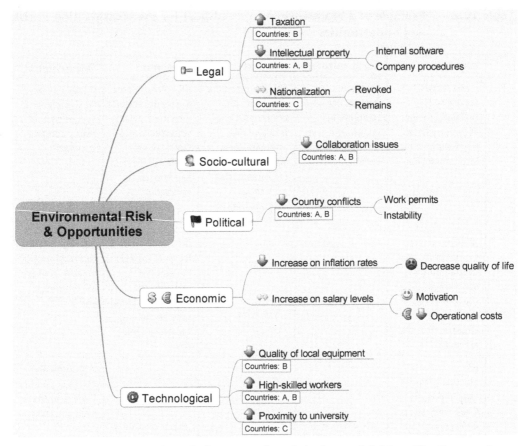

Figure 10.1   Example of a mindmap produced during a risk identification session

STEP 3 – FOLLOW-UP THE MATURATION OF THE RESULTS

The participants in the online brainstorming session are usually representing their local teams. It is important to have them validating the points with their colleagues and reviewing other sources of information, adding to the existing collection of ideas. The main activities in this phase are:

- Ask participants to organise review sessions with other colleagues from the same location or from the same knowledge area. Offer help to be a scribe or moderator of these sessions, or make yourself available for coaching if they want to learn the mindmapping technique.
- Ask participants to confront the ideas already collected with other sources (books, research papers, specialised magazines, external advisers, lessons-learned).
- During risk management activities, the participants can add information to be used in future qualitative and quantitative risk analysis and risk response planning. For example, you can describe every risk in terms of 'cause-and-effect', and then detail the possible outcomes. For other types of idea-gathering, the participants can capture any kind of information in a format that can help in later phases.

Figure 10.2 provides an example of a mindmap branch detailed during a local brainstorming session.

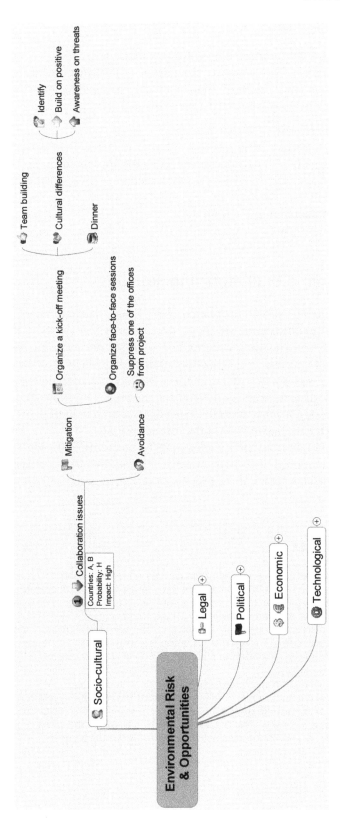

Figure 10.2   Example of a mindmap branch detailed during a local session of risk analysis

STEP 4 – CONSOLIDATE RESULTS

The various local sessions will produce different individual results, adding details from local knowledge and from subject matter experts. The global project manager will then need to consolidate all of these outcomes, adding complementary ideas and noting down conflicting views that require decisions. The main activities for this step are:

- consolidate all ideas generated on step 3;
- organise a meeting to review the results and to agree on a recommendation;
- convert the mindmap into a project document, using the appropriate project management diagrams and templates (refer to Figure 10.3 for a section of the risk list generated by the previous examples);
- distribute the recommendations for approval;
- organise a final review session.

Limitations of online brainstorming sessions

Many global projects involve people in different time zones, making it hard for the team to find shared time for brainstorming sessions, which usually last for more than a couple of hours. One negative consequence is the exclusion of remote team members from the creative discussions. This can create a feeling of segregation that will destroy the collaboration environment. The same segregation can also happen when the team members have various levels of fluency in the common language used during the project meetings. People who have more difficulty in expressing themselves in this language will tend to limit their collaboration, and this will certainly create a biased view of the team decisions.

Another limitation comes from the need for a precise recording of the ideas coming from the session. If the information is not noted correctly or is captured with a distorted meaning, it cannot be used for the later stages of the process, or can be a source for misunderstandings and conflicts.

REAL-LIFE EXPERIENCE

The cultural differences between team members can also create contentious issues. When attending audio conferences and the microphone is in mute, it is not uncommon to hear people in the room making negative comments about people from other companies and countries. The project is already in a critical phase, there is no time for a 'cultural awareness workshop', the milestones start to slip, and the 'search the guilty' mentality starts to surface. The first step in this type of situation is always to remind people of the problem with generalisations, discussed in Chapter 1. However, how often will this solve the problem?

You still have two alternatives. The first is to have different brainstorming sessions with each company or location, and consolidate the ideas in such a way that their origin will not be associated with one or other party. The outcomes are usually worth the effort. The second alternative is to try the 'asynchronous brainstorming' discussed on page 49.

Nr.	Situation analysis	R/O	Trigger	Impact	Owner	Level	Prob.	Impact	Weight	Rank	Response Type	Response Strategy	Response cost and time impact
1	Collaboration issues may happen between nationals of countries A and B	Risk	Activity 10.25.2	Impact on schedule (tasks may get delayed) and quality of deliverables involving both teams	M. Souza	Project team	H	H	100%	1	Mitigate (prob.)	1) Mitigate probability by organizing a kick-off meeting, with team building exercises that identify cultural differences, determine how to build on the positive differences (that increase creativity), and raise an awareness on both teams of the differences that may impact the teamwork. Conclude the activity by a dinner to build the relationship among the participants. 2) Mitigate probability of problems by organizing regular face-to-face sessions.	Cost (1 working day for 10 people + travel for 5 people) x 5 face-to-face sessions. Time 6 working days to be added to project schedule (no impact on the project end date)
2													
3													
4													
5													
6													
7													
8													
9													

Figure 10.3   Example of one entry on the 'Risk and opportunities list' prepared after the brainstorming session

Asynchronous brainstorming

Asynchronous brainstorming can be a good alternative to make the team members participate in all project activities, independently of their languages, locations or time zones. As the team members involved in the process will not know who is adopting a given position, the consensus can be developed without the direct influence of certain groups or individuals. The project manager (or a specialised moderator) consolidates all the information, organises translations, stimulates creativity, monitors the answers and controls the quality of the ideas.

One approach is the Delphi technique. It is especially applicable to risk management, scope management and other processes that need to collect opinions from specialists in order to make a strategic decision. The anatomy of a Delphi session is as follows:

- The participants are selected according to their knowledge on specific domains or countries.
- The moderator presents a series of assumptions to the participants. Some examples are a list of identified risks, suggested response strategies, technical issues or work packages.
- The participants vote on these alternatives, giving their evaluations on the probability and impact of risks, costs and appropriateness of the response strategies, potential solutions for the technical issues, estimated costs or duration of work packages.
- The moderator gathers and combines all the evaluations, presenting the results individually to all participants for their review.
- The participants can then approve some of the decisions, and voice their comments and disagreements on other points.
- The moderator will again collect this feedback, incorporating the comments into the results, and submit them again to the same panel.
- The moderator can then repeat this cycle until an acceptable level of consensus is reached.

The three rules for successful Delphi exercises in global projects are:

- The participants must not have face-to-face contact – different communication media can be used, including e-mails, chat and knowledge-sharing tools, which can allow time for reflection before giving comments, and time to reflect on the comments from others participants before reacting.
- The identities of the participants must remain anonymous – usually the knowledge-sharing tools allow the creation of voting lists and questionnaires that do not reveal the identity of the people participating. Having e-mails sent only to the moderator is another approach to follow this rule.
- The monitor of a Delphi exercise must build consensus among the participants – good analytic skills are required for the session moderator, who also needs to be impartial and aware of the cultural differences between team members.

YOUR LEARNING ON GLOBAL CREATIVITY

Revisit the list or mindmap created at the beginning of this chapter. Would you organise creativity sessions in a different way? What challenges might you face during online and asynchronous brainstorming sessions?

Now share your thoughts with other people, and read about their own experiences (www.GlobalProjectManagement.org).

Part II: Key concepts

- Global program and project managers need to manage the stakeholders' needs, expectations and influence, and increase their commitment level, by identifying the different parties involved or interested in the project execution, evaluating their attitudes and positions to the project, and mapping the different communication channels that require special attention.
- The establishment of standard rules and templates can increase the effectiveness of meetings over distance. The rules must consider the use of communication tools and techniques, the differences in culture and language, and the need for preparation. The templates need to facilitate the update of project information during the meetings, saving on all team members' time and effort, and promoting mutual understanding.
- Program and project managers must define the communication strategy during the planning activities, by identifying the types of information that will be exchanged during the project, analysing the stakeholders' requirements and defining how the communication can improve the commitment from the key interested parties.
- The program and project managers, the project coordinators and the team members must master the global communication skills required to collect project performance data, distribute project information and to exchange knowledge during all project activities.
- Brainstorming techniques can also work over a distance, to allow all team members to participate in creative thinking and team decision-making sessions. Online sessions can share mindmaps or spreadsheets through video or web conferencing, to collect and share the ideas. Offline sessions can maximise the participation of team members in different time zones, native languages and cultures.

Part II: Further reading

McElroy, B. and and Mills, C. (2000) 'Managing stakeholders' in *Gower Handbook of Project Management*

This chapter of the Gower Handbook presents a comprehensive strategy to identify and manage stakeholders by evaluating and satisfying their communication requirements.

Haywood, M. (1998) *Managing Virtual Teams*

This book provides recommendations on the establishment of project communication rules oriented to virtual teams.

Buzan, T. (2006) *The Ultimate Book of Mind Maps*

This book is a complete introduction to the mindmapping technique, with a step-by-step guide and many examples of mindmaps for personal and professional use. See also the author's website for an online initiation and other references (www.mind-mapping.co.uk).

Part II: Interactive section

Share with other readers your opinion of communication skills, techniques, tools and templates, using the online discussion groups (www.GlobalProjectManagement.org):

- Are you planning to define standard templates to be used by all programs and projects in your organisation? Should these templates be slightly adapted by the various program and project managers to fit their own needs? Or have you experienced problems with centralised and standardised approaches, preferring to leave the program and project managers free to create and use their own formats for project documents?
- Do you believe in the use of communication to change the commitment levels of global stakeholders? To what extent can internal politics and social networking be more important than communication?
- Have you identified pros and cons of mindmapping applied to project management? Do you have some mindmap examples to share and get opinions on how to improve them? Would you recommend any mindmapping software to other readers, based on your own experience?
- Do you have any experience with creativity sessions over a distance, using other methods, such as 'system envisioning'?

 *Global Organisations*

When organisations start coalitions that span country borders, or projects that require cooperation between subsidiary companies or divisions across the globe, they must consider the impact on their organisational cultures and structures. The program and project structures must be adapted to the way the human resources are distributed, considering the optimal communication between team members. Once the structure is defined, the team must be put in place, through international recruitment and selection of global program and project managers, project coordinators and team members, building project teams with the right skill set and an optimal disposition of resources. Global project offices can be created to support these global initiatives, helping to set up the project teams, and supplying program and project management services worldwide.

The chapters in Part III discuss the above topics in more detail, and also make suggestions to international companies on how they can support a global project management culture. The closing chapter shows how organisations can collaborate with other companies across borders, preparing their processes and methods to develop solid partnerships, and have a smooth integration of their employees within networked projects.

11 *Global Project Structure*

International projects can be structured in different ways, depending on the project size, complexity, types, organisational structures and the creation of work packages according to functional or regional criteria. The maturity level of the organisation on global project management and the level of experience of the project manager, project coordinators and team members on global projects are also key factors when choosing between the different project structures.

This chapter shows some examples of these basic structures, keeping in mind that experienced project managers will often apply a combination of them according to the organisational culture and the availability of resources. Some organisations may prefer to have mainly collocated teams and opt for the structures with local coordinators, while others prefer to employ virtual teams and can opt for the centralised structure. The first group of organisations can have difficulty in finding resources available in the right location, and can use expatriation and temporary assignments to fill their requirements (see 'internal recruitment', on Chapter 12). The second group will employ the right resources in any possible company location, and need to have a high maturity in project management and worldwide adoption of the Global Project Management Framework©.

Centralised project management

In the first form of project structure (Figure 11.1), all team members report directly to the project manager, who performs most of the coordination and control tasks using collaborative tools (described in Chapters 16–25). The projects can have a centralised form when the level

---

YOUR EXPERIENCE OF GLOBAL PROJECT ORGANISATIONS

In your previous global projects, were the team members grouped by their functional activity or according to the project task or phase? Did they report to a local project coordinator who helped the project manager to organise local activities? How many organisations were involved in the project execution tasks?

What were the main challenges for each type of project structure? How did the project managers react to these challenges?

Write on a list or mindmap the types of project structures you are familiar with from previous experiences. For each type, define when they should be used, their main benefits and challenges, and the best way to react to the potential problems, improving the effectiveness of program and project managers. Complete the mindmap as you read this chapter, including the new types of project structure, and noting their main challenges and benefits for your situation.

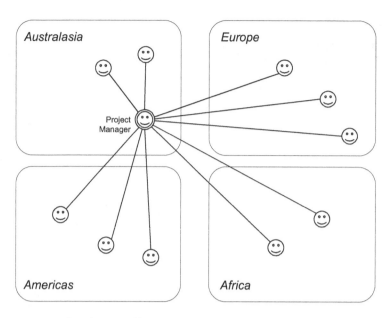

Figure 11.1   Example of centralised structure

of complexity of the coordination activities is relatively low, or when other forms are not applicable. Some examples:

- When the size and complexity of the project are small enough to allow effective coordination over distance.
- When the dispersion degree is high among team members and the size of each local team does not justify assigning local coordinators.
- When the team members working in different locations are familiar with collaborative tools and different cultures, and like to work independently – having a proven record of delivering their tasks on time without close coordination.
- When the use of other structures is not possible because local coordinators are not available.

    Some recommendations to project managers working with centralised project teams are:

- to train all team members on the collaborative tools, cultural differences and all other areas discussed in this book;
- to study and apply the good practices on global team leadership and the other topics covered by Chapters 1–10;
- to identify team members with good communication and coordination skills, who can work as local coordinators on future projects (allowing the use of the project structures described in the next sections).

Distributed project management, with local coordinators

This is the recommended structure for most global projects. All or most of the team members report to local coordinators, who are responsible for the planning and execution of sub-projects or work packages, depending on the project complexity (Figure 11.2). In other situations,

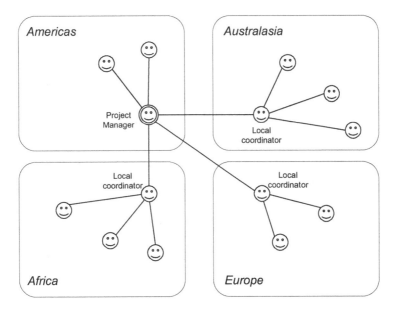

Figure 11.2   Example of distributed structure

REAL-LIFE EXPERIENCE

Some examples of distributed projects with local coordinators are:

- A project implementing a new Enterprise Resource Planning system (ERP) requires the participation of financial specialists in Czech Republic, the research and development team in Switzerland, the IT department in the USA, the service management specialists in five different Asian countries and the ERP development team in Brazil. In the first project phase, a core project team can unite people from all these countries in the same location, in order to define the project strategies, produce a detailed plan and define all deliverables with clear roles and responsibilities. Afterwards, each of these teams can perform their own tasks, communicating over distance. The local coordinators might have periodic meetings to review the status of all activities and validate that the whole project team is following the project strategies and guidelines, and working towards the project mission.

- A project developing a new product can split the work into two components: the team located in Germany can build the prototype of component A, while the Australian team develops component B. At the end of the prototyping phase, the Mexican team integrates both components into the final product, collaborating over distance with the Australian and German teams to correct problems and adapt the prototypes when required.

- A project implementing an integrated global warehouse system can have a development team located in the UK together with the project manager, and the implementation teams in different locations: the French team being responsible for the implementation in South European countries, the Dutch team for the North European countries and the German team for the Eastern European area.

In all these examples, the local coordinators in the different countries must stay in close contact with each other, monitoring the communication between team members in different locations, controlling the progress against the plan and paying special attention to the execution of local tasks that have dependencies on activities executed by teams in other locations.

each local team receives a detailed definition of their scope of work and performs their tasks autonomously. Key team members can be involved in a detailed definition of the interfaces between tasks performed by different teams, and between the deliverables produced by different teams. The need for communication over distance may be reduced to the monitoring and control performed by the project manager, and to the follow-up meetings among all local coordinators. This avoids misunderstandings and reduces the amount of work outside office hours when the teams work in different time zones. Some situations when global projects can benefit from distributed structures are:

- when the international companies are organised using local competence centres, and most work packages group the activities from a functional perspective;
- when competencies are distributed and every location can develop a complete component of the final product;
- when a cultural or geographical proximity to the final customers is important.

Project managers with distributed teams will need to perform coaching, training and organise meetings over distance with a limited number of local coordinators, while these will manage their own teams without the barriers created by different languages, time zones, cultures and distance. All knowledge and practices for global project management will be implemented and employed by the project manager and local coordinators. The local team members will learn these practices by participating in the meetings, using the project collaboration devices and attending the cultural workshops.

Distributed project management, with functional coordinators

This is the recommended structure when the complexity or size of the work packages demands a group of knowledgeable people coordinated by experienced or specialised coordinators, all in different locations (Figure 11.3). Some examples are:

- when organisations allocate people to projects based on their knowledge and availability, not their location;
- when companies are organised on functional competence centres, and each work package includes many cross-functional activities;
- when competencies are distributed across locations, and the project work packages are grouped on a functional perspective;

REAL-LIFE EXPERIENCE

Some examples of distributed projects with functional coordinators are:

- One project requiring that specialists from Germany and Australia work together to develop a new software version, with the test teams located in Germany, Mexico and India. In parallel, web developers, located in Germany, Australia and India, prepare a website to launch the marketing campaign in three languages, with different graphical concepts adapted to the local cultures.

- Another project implementing this new software version in a global company may require testers from the UK, France and Netherlands to work together and validate the new functions by simulating the activities of their regional customers.

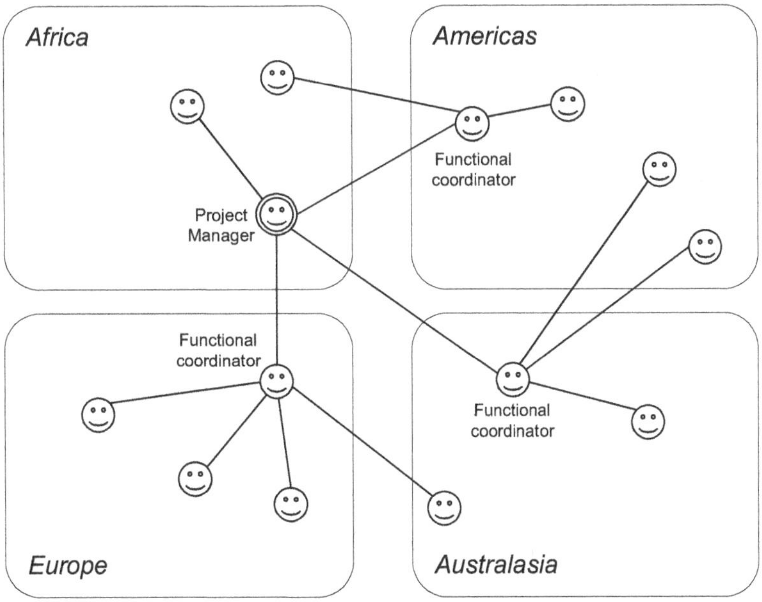

Figure 11.3   Example of distributed-functional structure

• when the project team must include team members close to the customers or key stakeholders.

There is an important difference between the two distributed structures. The functional coordinators working with team members in different countries must receive training and coaching in global communication and collaboration tools, and transfer this knowledge to all distributed team members. Most meetings happen over distance and must avoid the barriers created by the different languages, time zones, cultures and distance. The project manager, local coordinators and most team members must learn and employ the knowledge and practices in the Global Project Management Framework©.

Round-the-clock project management

Organisations with a high level of maturity on their processes can deploy specialised teams strategically located around the globe to reduce the time to complete the deliverables, or to implement them in customers dispersed geographically. The communication methods among the different teams and project managers must be clearly defined and understood by all parties, the level of integration and teamwork must be extremely high, usually with a global work authorisation system in place. The benefits achieved by global organisations are often worth the effort in setting up this structure, which is very similar to distributed project management. The main difference is the high degree of independence of the project managers, which makes them share the responsibilities of updating the project records, preparing presentations to the stakeholders and taking strategic decisions (Figure 11.4).

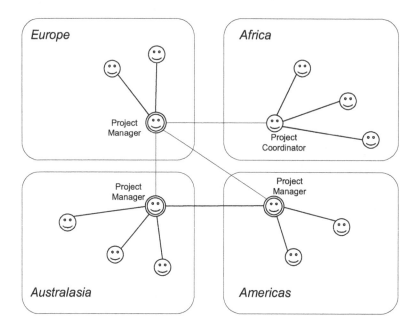

Figure 11.4   Example of round-the-clock structure

REAL-LIFE EXPERIENCE

A global company can start a project to perform a series of weekly system migrations, each involving a different set of systems, knowledge areas and complexities, with durations of 20–30 hours. The German team will prepare and start the work during their office hours. At the end of their working day, they will transfer the activities to the Mexican team, who will monitor the migrations during their working hours and then attend a status check meeting with the Australian team. The Australian team will make sure the activities finish correctly and inform the German team – already back to their next working day – which will verify the operation and execute the final steps. On the remaining days of the week, the three teams can continue working in shifts to complete the documentation, to inform the customers and to prepare the future activities.

There can be three global project managers located in the different countries, alternating the ownership of the project management processes, and monitoring the execution of the activities, paying special attention to the status check meetings and the quality of the information being transferred at the end of each work period. Usually, as the team maturity develops, the need for coordination and monitoring will decrease, requiring the project managers to manage by exception, communicating mainly when problems and conflicts appear.

Project management global network

This is another variant of distributed project management, when the local coordinators work for different organisations. This is the usual structure of projects that employ outsourcing, offshoring and out-tasking strategies for the execution of certain work packages or activities (Figure 11.5). The added challenge of this structure is the need for the project manager to understand and

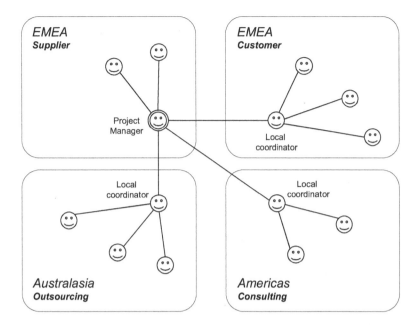

Figure 11.5   Example of project network structure

synchronise different organisational cultures and country cultures in the same project.

This type of project organisation is very common, and often the main reason for project failures involving different companies around the globe. Chapter 15 evaluates the challenges of this situation in more detail, providing recommendations for project managers to improve the collaboration level and the effectiveness of their project teams.

REAL-LIFE EXPERIENCE

Consider a project involving teams from four companies, which must work in a coordinated manner to execute the project activities. A typical sequence of events is:

- At first, the local coordinators from the four companies may assume that their counterparts employ similar structures, processes and tools.

- After they realise the existence of completely different structures, processes and tools, some coordinators may try to impose their own project management toolkit as a standard for the project. During this period, different practices are employed at the same time, confusing the team members that work on various work packages coordinated in different ways.

- After many conflicts and issues impact the project schedule, cost and quality, the coordinators can finally obtain an agreement on the way to move forward or …

- Another project failure is likely to happen!

YOUR LEARNING ON GLOBAL PROJECT ORGANISATIONS

Revisit the list or mindmap created at the beginning of this module. Would you structure your future global projects in a different way? Did you identify a type of project structure that was not mentioned in this chapter? What additional benefits can this structure bring to global projects? What are the main challenges and benefits of each type of structure to your global project?

Share your thoughts with other people, and read about their own experiences (www. GlobalProjectManagement.org).

12 *Selection of International Human Resources*

On some occasions, the allocation of people to the project team will be based on the availability of resources, and the influence of key stakeholders or partner companies. The project managers may evaluate the previous experience of the team members on global projects, organising training and coaching to avoid clashes between different personalities and cultures, avoiding negative conflicts and increasing the productivity and team spirit. The recommendations in Chapters 1–10 provide a solid foundation for this process. On other occasions, the selection of the project team will be one of the first responsibilities of a project manager, consisting of internal or external recruitment based on the project needs.

Chapter 11 provided examples of global project structures that can serve as a basis for the preparation of human resource planning. International organisations can develop a standard process to follow when preparing resource plans and allocating qualified people to work on global project teams. This chapter aims to provide a better understanding of the selection criteria for global project managers, coordinators and team members, and suggests a process to recruit, select and train people around the globe. This information will help international companies and global project managers to appoint the right team members independently of their current or future locations.

This chapter does not present a complete set of recommendations for the recruitment and selection of new employees, and assumes that your organisation already has a process in place to recruit internal candidates and hire new employees. As in other parts of the book,

---

YOUR EXPERIENCE Of THE SELECTION OF INTERNATIONAL HUMAN RESOURCES

Suppose you are a program manager and need to hire one global project manager to be based in a different location to you. What main skills would you expect from the best candidate? Which of these skills would be equally applicable to a new team member?

What methods would you use to identify potential candidates? Would you prefer someone already based in the new location? Or would you suggest one of your local colleagues to be transferred to that location?

How would you interview the candidates? Would you prefer to have face-to-face or telephone interviews?

Write on a list or mindmap the skills required for global team members and project managers. On a separate list, write the methods you would apply to identify and interview the candidates, defining their main advantages and challenges. When you read this chapter, complete your mindmap with the knowledge you acquire and can apply to future recruitment and selection processes.

this chapter shows only the specific knowledge applicable to global programs and projects, allowing you to adapt your existing recruitment and selection processes.

Global team members' skills

Technical skills and specialisations are not the only elements to consider when evaluating potential team members to work on global projects. Previous research on project management identified that team members must have a set of 'global skills' to work effectively on global projects (Majchrzak and Malhotra, 2003; Turetken and Jain, 2004). These global skills involve the ability to work remotely and openness to other company and country cultures, being summarised as follows:

- **Global communication** – the ability to communicate over distance (or the willingness to develop such competence) is an important factor in determining which team members will be effective on global projects, since most of the communications with the project manager and colleague team members will be made over distance. Good listening skills are an example of this ability, like rephrasing the sentences being said to confirm understanding (reflective listening) and showing a true interest in the topic being presented by the speaker, by asking more questions and clarifying meanings (active listening).
- **Global experience** – some team members will have already worked in different countries, on other global projects or with other team members over distance. These people will tend to require less coaching on the communication skills, and may also bring new ideas on how to improve the existing tools and procedures, based on their previous experiences.
- **Global thinking** – the team members involved in creative tasks will usually need to consider different cultural or geographic standpoints when identifying risks, preparing quality assessments or when designing the deliverables. These team members will like the intellectual stimulation and the diverse opinions from a cross-cultural environment and might also provide coaching on global creativity to less experienced colleagues during brainstorming sessions (see Chapter 10).
- **Culture awareness** – the team members that are familiar with the organisational and country cultures involved in the project may also have fewer requirements for training and coaching, and are less likely to generate conflicts. They tend to feel more comfortable than other people when working with a mix of different ethics, standards, policies or working practices.
- **Technical capabilities** – people who have proven capabilities on the use of office suites and other software tools will tend to learn quickly how to deploy and use the collaborative tools (described in Chapters 16–25). The team members who demonstrate a very good understanding of these tools might then be very useful in providing coaching and training to other team members.
- **Self-discipline** – people working in different locations to the project managers must have a working discipline that allows them to work independently, with a reduced need for supervision. They must also be willing to work according to the established processes, rules and responsibilities. When little is known about the self-discipline of a team member, frequent monitoring must occur at the beginning to ensure that the rules are being followed correctly, with corrective actions taken in the case of deviation.
- **High personal confidence** – the team members will work effectively over distance when they are confident that their skills and capabilities allow them to act independently

on their work packages or activities. The project manager or a senior specialist must compensate low levels of confidence by using a formal method of coaching or mentoring (see Chapter 5).

- **Tolerance for ambiguity** – some degree of ambiguity is often present in global projects, despite all efforts from the project manager and the team members to define clear roles and responsibilities and detailed work packages. The global team members must know how to resolve the problems created by this uncertainty, by clarifying the roles and responsibilities, patiently investigating the reasons for the lack of definition, volunteering to participate on the activity execution and suggesting corrective actions to avoid impact on the project.

- **Self-motivation** – some people are naturally motivated, according to their career orientation, relocation aspiration and working preferences. These team members will tend to collaborate for the success of the project, with a reduced need for detailed supervision, and without requiring specific motivation instruments. When some key team members are lacking motivation, a specific process can be deployed (see Chapter 2).

- **Self-efficacy** – the team members that show a good performance track record, by completing their actions on time with the expected quality level or providing reasonable explanations for deviations, will increase the trust from remote project managers, coordinators or colleagues. When the performance is not within the expected limits, the project managers or coordinators might perform a follow-up of the deliverables, and work together with the team members to correct the deviations and avoid future occurrences of the same problem.

- **Good organisation** – the team members who have good organisation skills will thrive on global projects. They usually establish a prioritised 'to-do' list linked to the project schedule and issues log, organise their time to perform the activities on the global projects without conflicts with daily or local activities and inform the project manager in case of potential deviations, risks or issues. Global project managers must provide coaching on organisation skills to team members that are not performing some of the actions above, to improve their productivity and avoid impacts on the project.

- **Concentration** – team members working away from the main company building (home workers or people located in small satellite offices) must have a higher level of concentration to avoid disruption from other colleagues or family members. Otherwise, they may require coaching from another remote colleague or the project manager on possible alternatives to increase their level of participation in the project activities. Some situations might require that these team members move to a different location for the duration of the project.

- **Reduced social interaction** – the remote team members will also have less opportunity for social contact with the project manager and other stakeholders working on the same project. When social interaction is an important element that motivates specific team members, they might develop new relationships with local colleagues working in the same location but on other projects, or consider a temporary relocation to another office that contains a group of project team members.

- **Openness and flexibility** – the team members who are open to working with people from other cultures and located in different countries will enjoy the experience of participating in a global project. They may even help to identify, avoid or resolve conflicts between other team members. Intercultural training is required for the team members who show resistance or discomfort when working with diverse cultures (see Chapter 1).

Global program and project managers' skills

Professionals who occupy program or project management positions need to master most of the global skills identified previously, in order to provide coaching and mentoring to the distributed team members. In addition, they must have a specific set of skills for effective coordination, monitoring and control of the project work packages over distance. These skills are covered in detail by other chapters of this book, and can be summarised as:

- understanding of the cultural differences and ability to build on them to improve the teamwork, creativity and innovation levels (Chapter 1);
- proven leadership when working with virtual team members (Chapter 2);
- trustworthiness (Chapter 3);
- openness to understand and manage conflicts involving different cultures (Chapter 4);
- coaching and mentoring of remote team members (Chapter 5);
- excellent communication skills and techniques (Chapters 6–10);
- experience in coordinating meetings using audio, video and web conferencing (Chapters 21–23);
- familiarity with knowledge sharing and PMS tools (Chapters 24 and 25).

The level of global skills required will depend on their functions and the types of project structure, as presented in Chapter 11:

- Project managers in centralised structures (Figure 11.1) – these project managers must develop a high level of global skills, as most of their activities involve communication crossing country borders – including project monitoring, coaching, conflict management and team leadership.
- Local coordinators working on distributed projects (see example in Figure 11.2) – the local coordinators can spend most of their time coordinating the team members at their locations, but a certain amount of communication with other coordinators and the project manager might happen across borders.
- Functional coordinators on distributed projects (see Figure 11.3) – these functions will need a higher level of global skills, as most of their activities will involve team members in other locations.
- Project managers on distributed projects (Figure 11.2 and Figure 11.3) – these functions will require good global skills, to perform the management of the project coordinators and the monitoring and control of their work packages.
- Project managers working in round-the-clock structures (Figure 11.4) – they will need excellent skills for asynchronous communication and an excellent discipline to deploy and follow processes.
- Project managers working on global project networks (Figure 11.5) – as well as all the skills from the above categories, these professionals will need to understand and accept different company cultures, processes and tools.

Recruitment

JOB DESCRIPTION

The recruitment process starts with the preparation of a job description. The job description outlines the major responsibilities of each team member or project manager, the specification of the professional experience and skills required by their roles, the potential sources of candidates, reporting positions, salary and grade levels (Hannagan, 1995). For global projects, the job description can also specify one or more desired locations, and include the global skills identified in the previous sections of this chapter.

The level of global skills will depend on the project structure (see Chapter 11). As an example, the project manager can opt for hiring one programmer with strong technical knowledge, to execute well-defined tasks under supervision of a local coordinator. In this case, the global skills may not even be part of the job description. On other occasions, the same project manager will prefer to hire a less specialised programmer, with solid communication skills, to work in a remote office near to the customer. In this case, remote coaching can be provided by a more experienced programmer, to build the required technical skills.

The job description for people working on global projects may also specify the required availability to work outside office hours (when working with offices in different time zones), the frequency and type of travel involved, ideal language skills and previous cross-cultural experiences.

When hiring project managers, you might wish to specify which qualifications are required from the candidates, according to your organisation standards (see Chapter 13, Table 13.1). Examples of professional certifications are the PMP® (see www.pmi.org), PRINCE2® (www.prince2.org.uk) and IPMA (see www.ipma.ch and www.apm.org.uk).

INTERNAL RECRUITMENT

When the job description is ready, you can start looking inside your company to fill the position. The ideal candidates can be in one of the desired locations, or in a different country.

When the ideal candidates are not based in the desired location, you have two options. You may redesign your project structure, and appoint the persons to work on your project remotely. In this case, you might revisit the global skills required in the original job position and identify if the candidates have the required skills or are in a position to acquire them during the initial project phases. Local employees can bring advantages to the project when an acute cultural understanding or local knowledge is important for their functions, or when their personal networks and relations with local stakeholders can bring benefits to the project.

When remote working is not possible, the second alternative is to start a *relocation* or *expatriation* process. A relocation process usually consists of a permanent transfer of the employee to a new location. The expatriation process usually maintains the work base of the employee, transferring the employee to a new country only for the duration of the project. Both may require a lengthy procedure to adapt or reformulate the job contract, to evaluate the company support in searching for a new house and moving household goods, and to take into consideration the relocation of family members. The advantages may be the specialisation of the employee, a reduced time for training on the project duties and the existence of a personal network with other team members performing complementary activities.

EXTERNAL RECRUITMENT

Keegan and Turner (2000) identified that most companies prefer to recruit people via 'headhunting' agencies, personal contacts or local universities. Online business-oriented networking sites are helping project managers to expand their network of contacts beyond their cities and companies, and are allowing them to recruit people through recommendation of peers around the globe. These networking platforms have various levels of affiliation in different countries and some provide the user with a choice of languages, which is especially useful for global projects. The project manager, or the person responsible for the recruitment process, can search for potential employees by accessing their direct contacts and the people who are connected to them, having the opportunity of asking people they already trust to provide references and recommendations. Some examples of these network sites are LinkedIn (www.linkedin.com), Ryze (www.ryze.com), XING (www.xing.com) and Viaduc (www.viaduc.com).

Another frequent method suggested by Keegan and Turner to select new employees is, 'the hiring of personnel on project trials and work experiences.' New employees can start working on back-filling positions dedicated to non-project activities or simple projects, before being assigned to more important project tasks. New project managers can be assigned to local projects and become more familiar with the corporate culture, the project management methodologies, techniques and tools used by the organisation. During this trial period, their technical and global skills can be evaluated and improved, before they are assigned to global projects.

Selection

PREPARATION FOR THE INTERVIEWS

After identifying the potential candidates, you must start the interviewing process. The first step is to prepare the interviews, not only to allow a fair comparison between the candidates, but also because some interviews may be performed over the telephone or using video conferencing. Like other meetings over distance, effective interviews require good preparation.

REAL-LIFE EXPERIENCE (PART I)

An international company decided to hire a new global project manager. The manager of the project management team wrote a job description (see Table 12.1) and contacted the human resources department to consider internal recruitment, as well as asking different recruitment agencies to identify external candidates interested in the assignment and to supply their resumes.

The job description was compared to the resumes received, to ascertain the candidates' skills and to decide which ones would be retained for a screening phase. After reviewing more than 20 resumes and selecting nine applicants for interview, it was identified that only one of the candidates lived near to the desired location. All other candidates were based in other countries.

The manager was now ready to start the interviews, but the cost of travelling to the different locations, or to bring them to the project location, was too high. How to perform the interviews?

Table 12.1   Example of a job description

Job title	Global project manager
Major responsibilities	Manage a global outsourcing project (budget of 4 Mio Euros) with 40–50 team members distributed across two European countries and one corporate office in Asia
Experience required	5–10 years experience in global program and project management
Ideal skills	• Excellent project management skills (must possess PMP qualification or IPMA level B) • Excellent meeting management skills • Good presentation skills
Global skills	The candidate must possess global communication skills; demonstrate self-confidence, discipline, good organisation and cultural awareness. The ideal candidate will have lived and worked in different countries, and speak fluent English and French
Job location	Nyon, Switzerland
Availability	• The candidate must be available to adapt their working hours to other time zones, when meeting with team members in South-America and Asia. • The position requires frequent travel (2 weeks per month), including many long-distance trips to Asia and South-America

Start by identifying the main phases of the interview. You can start each interview with an 'ice-breaker' phase, by asking questions that make the candidate comfortable and get a first idea of how well the candidate gets prepared to participate in such an important meeting. A second phase can ask 'traditional' questions that obtain more information on the candidate's background, current position and motivations to work on the project.

An important phase of the interview consists of asking situational questions. By using current or previous global experiences mentioned in the first phases, the candidate can be asked to explain their roles and responsibilities on the projects, present the project status and describe the items in the agendas of recent review meetings and steering committee meetings. When interviewing project managers, their answers will show the methods they use to manage their projects, and may allow you to evaluate how well they employ their certifications in real-life situations. For other team members, their answers may provide an understanding of their level of participation on project meetings, and you might ask other types of questions that evaluate their knowledge on specific specialisation areas.

Another phase of the interview might contain questions to evaluate how well the candidate dealt with cultural diversity in the past, by asking for examples of conflicting situations, problem-solving activities, negotiation processes, coaching, leadership and personal relationships. You can also ask for the main challenges faced by global project managers and team members, and question how they would deal with difficult situations involving people from different cultures.

The closing phase of the interview usually consists of confirming the availability and interest of the candidates to start working in the new position, providing them with more information on their main tasks, roles and responsibilities and telling them more about the next steps.

After deciding how to structure your interview, prepare a guide with the main questions to be asked in each phase, allowing space for you to note the answers during the meetings. By doing this, all the interviews will follow the same format and sequence, allowing for a quick comparison between different candidates.

Before proceeding with the selection process, consult your human resources department to understand local hiring practices and procedures and equal opportunities legislations.

WHAT MEDIUM FOR THE INTERVIEWS?

Experienced interviewers may recommend face-to-face meetings, to detect how the candidates present themselves and have a better feeling of their communication styles and presentation skills. However, global project managers and team members may spend most of their time communicating across borders, using audio conferencing, e-mail, the telephone and other collaborative tools. Therefore, it is helpful to divide the interview process into two steps. The first step can be a preliminary screening, conducted over distance, to ascertain that their competencies match their resumes, and to identify their communication skills over

---

REAL-LIFE EXPERIENCE (PART II)

The manager decided to divide the selection process into two major steps: a screening interview over the telephone and a detailed interview with a panel composed of project managers in different locations.

To be prepared for the selection process, the manager created a list of the candidates, including their locations and the evaluations from the panel at the different stages of the process (see Table 12.2).

The manager prepared for the interviews by creating a template of the main phases and the questions to be asked, leaving space for the answers (see Figure 12.1 and Figure 12.2).

During the screening interviews over the telephone, some candidates were eliminated as their experience level was not sufficient or their communication skills over a distance were not suitable for a global project manager. Four candidates were retained for the panel interviews.

As three candidates were currently based in the same country, the manager organised face-to-face interviews at a corporate location in that area and decided to make the trip to meet them, organising a video conference with other project managers who remained at the project location. The fourth candidate lived near to the project location, and the situation was then inversed: the manager organised a face-to-face interview with participation from the members of the panel, all in their home base. One member of the panel on an assignment abroad participated in the meeting via video conferencing.

The members of the panel remained the same throughout the full process and gathered after the last interview to make a decision. After the selected candidate was hired and started working, they concluded that a mix of telephone with face-to-face and video interviews worked very well, approving this method for future recruitment and selection processes.

When asked for feedback on the method, the new project manager said that the questions were asked naturally, without intimidating the interviewee or giving the impression of a formalised process.

Table 12.2   Example of an interview control sheet

Candidate name	Base location	Evaluation				
		Telephone interview	Panel member 1	Panel member 2	Panel member 3	Manager
A.B.	London, UK	Good communication and global skills	Candidate provided valid examples of previous cultural experiences, but does not demonstrate solid project management skills	Candidate did not demonstrate working knowledge of the PMP concepts	Candidate has good presentation and communication skills	**Not hire**: candidate does not possess solid project management skills
C.D.	Reading, UK	Good experience on global projects and communication skills	Candidate provided confusing explanations and examples of previous experiences	Candidate did not demonstrate working knowledge of the IPMA concepts	Candidate has good presentation and communication skills	**Not hire**: communication skills are good on face-to-face contact, but not sufficient for meetings over a distance
E.F.	Lausanne, Switzerland	Good experience on global projects, fluent in French and English	Candidate provided convincing explanations and examples of previous experience as a project manager	Candidate has shown working knowledge of the project management processes	Candidate has acceptable presentation and communication skills	**Hire!** (training and coaching required on presentation and communication skills)
G.H.	Surrey, UK	Good knowledge of project management methods and techniques	The experience of this candidate on global projects is not sufficient	Candidate has shown working knowledge of the project management processes	Candidate has acceptable presentation and communication skills	**Not hire**: Good project manager but lacks working experience on global projects
I.J.	London, UK	Poor communication skills, lack of experience on large global projects	-	-	-	**Not hire**:

Phone interview

Objectives
- Detect if the candidates are good project managers, able to handle situations out of their basic knowledge area
- Detect their knowledge of main processes and areas (formal and informal)
- Detect their ability to communicate in a short period of time, on the phone
- Detect if they are not 'too senior' to deal with technical people
- Detect their ability to work on global projects
- Detect their interest in the position

I Icebreakers

Did you get the conference call easily? Can you hear us without problems?

Are you in a location where you can talk freely?

Is this your first interview over the phone, or are you familiar with this?

Do you normally have meetings on the phone, over distance?

Do you know about our company?

II Traditional

Describe (in 1 minute) your current position and your main responsibilities.

Why did you decide to move to a new position?

Before being a project manager, what do you consider to be your main knowledge area and skills?

What was your first project outside your technical background? Please comment on it [challenges, good and bad aspects]

III Culture-fit

When you consider people who have worked closely with you on previous projects, what culture was especially different to yours, and how did you handle this?

IV Situational

What is the main project you are managing today?

Imagine we are new senior managers in your company interested in your project. Can you summarise the major items of your original business case in no more than 5 minutes? [detect which items below were spontaneously mentioned]

Objective:

Scope:

Deliverables:

Budget:

Schedule:

Main risks and mitigations?

Stakeholders: How many areas and people involved ?

Other:

Imagine we are new senior managers in your company interested in the current status of your project. How well is your project going, can you summarise the major items of your last steering committee meeting, in no more than 5 minutes? [detect which items below were spontaneously mentioned]

Cost control:

Schedule control:

Quality control:

Risk Monitoring and Control:

Other points:

How would you summarise the above in a couple of sentences, to inform your team members of the project status and obtain their buy-in for the next period?

V Availability and interest

Do you have problems with frequent business travel abroad?

Do you have any problems adapting your working time to the project stakeholders across the globe? (having meetings in early mornings, lunch time, evenings)

Are you still interested in this position, considering the challenges of cross-cultural project management?

Next steps

Our comments

Figure 12.1   Example of a preparation sheet for a telephone interview

Face-to-face interview

Objectives :
- Detect how efficiently the candidates can express themselves in face-to-face meetings
- Confirm the skills identified in the previous interviews
- Confirm their interest in the position

I Icebreakers

Did you have a nice flight, when did you arrive?

Did you have any problem in finding the office?

II Traditional

What are your greatest strengths?

What are your main weaknesses?

Why do you enjoy being a project manager?

What are your preferred communication methods: formal written, informal oral, ... when do you feel more comfortable?

When would you apply these different methods?

III Situational - Project Management

If you were fully responsible for initiating and completing the outsourcing project that is starting now, what are the main questions you would ask me, so that you could prepare the initial project documentation?

Objective:

Scope:

Deliverables:

Budget:

Schedule:

Main risks and mitigations?

Stakeholders: How many areas and people involved?

Other:

What would be the main documents you would use during the planning phase ?

WBS

Schedule

Network diagrams

Resource planning

Cost planning

Risk planning

Procurement planning

Communications planning

Quality planning

[for the documents not mentioned spontaneously, ask if they are familiar with them, to describe the last time they used them]

Figure 12.2   Example of a preparation sheet for a face-to-face interview

What would be the main tools you would use to control your project ?

  Cost control:

  Schedule control:

  Earned value:

  Quality control:

  Risk Monitoring and Control:

  Stakeholder management:

  Other points:

[for the tools not mentioned spontaneously, ask if they are familiar with them, to describe the last time they used them]

IV Situational - Global Projects

  What are the main challenges you have faced in projects with people located in different countries?

  How to address these challenges?

  What are the main challenges you have faced when working with people from different native languages?

  How to address these challenges?

  What are the main challenges you have faced when working with people from different cultures and traditions?

  How to address these challenges?

  What are the main challenges you faced when working with people from different time zones?

  How to address these challenges?

  Other challenges in global projects?

  How to address these challenges?

V Availability and interest

  Are you still interested in the project management position? When can you start?

  Do you have any questions?

Figure 12.2   *Concluded*

the telephone or video conferencing equipment. This will allow the elimination of the less qualified candidates, while reducing the effort of travel, organisation of meeting rooms and other logistic arrangements.

The second step can be conducted by an interview panel, with some members in the same location as the interviewee, and others attending the meeting by telephone or video conferencing. The group of people sharing the same physical space with the candidate can observe the body language and the local presentation and communication skills, while the members attending via the telephone will measure how effectively the candidate can convey a message over a distance.

The members of the interview panel can share their impressions on each candidate after the interview is finished, and decide together on their selection or to restart the process with another candidate.

Induction and training

After the right candidates are selected for their new positions, an induction session can inform them of the project mission, objectives, strategies and other elements that may be available depending on the stage of project planning or execution. The new project managers and team members will also benefit from knowing the locations of the team members and other key stakeholders, the cultures involved in the project and key legal, political, social, economic and environmental aspects that may influence their roles in the project.

Depending on the assessment between their current and desired global skills, training sessions on the Global Project Management Framework© can be beneficial (see Chapter 14), complemented by coaching from more experienced project managers or team members (see Chapter 5).

YOUR LEARNING ON THE SELECTION OF INTERNATIONAL HUMAN RESOURCES

Revisit the list or mindmap created at the beginning of this module. What additional skills you would require from global project managers and team members? What methods would you use to recruit and select new project managers and team members across borders?

Now share your thoughts with other people, and read about their own experiences (www.GlobalProjectManagement.org).

13 *Global Program and Project Offices*

Many international companies and partnerships aim to implement a worldwide standard for program and project management practices, and to align the methods and procedures of different companies, countries and organisational units working on the same program or project. Program and project offices can achieve these goals. This chapter reviews the different definitions and objectives of project and program offices, and the main services they provide to foster innovation and improve the effectiveness of global programs and projects.

Defining project offices

Many companies and authors use the term project office and its derivatives to mean different things:

- The concept of a Project Support Office (PSO) is one of a central pool of skilled resources to provide the roles of Project Support, such as clerical support, configuration librarians and possibly PRINCE2® consultants to individual projects. (…) A PSO provides continuity of standards across all projects. The office can be the centre of expertise in the PRINCE2® method, any software packages used (such as planning and control software), configuration management and the quality review technique. (OGC, 2002).
- A Project Management Office (PMO) is an organisational unit to centralise and coordinate the management of projects under its domain. (…) A PMO oversees the management of projects, programs, or a combination of both. (…) The PMO focuses on the coordinated planning, prioritisation and execution of projects and subprojects that are tied to the parent organisation's or client's overall business objectives. (PMI, 2004).
- The Project Management Office (PMO) (…) is the department or group that defines and maintains the standards of processes, generally related to project management, within the organisation. The PMO strives to standardise and introduce economies of repetition in the execution of projects. The PMO is the source of documentation, guidance and metrics on the practice of project management and execution (www.wikipedia.org).

This chapter employs the generic term '*project offices*', the meaning of which can encompass the three definitions above:

- A project office is an organisational unit composed of skilled professionals in project and program management, which centralises, coordinates and oversees the management of portfolios, programs and projects in its domain. The project offices also define and maintain project management standards and methodologies, and are the keepers of the project documentation, templates and metrics.

The project offices interact with all hierarchy levels of the company in different ways. Figure 13.1 illustrates the relationship between the organisational project office and four

YOUR EXPERIENCE OF PROJECT OFFICES

In your organisation, is there a department that performs the functions of a PMO? Is it formalised as a project or program management office? What are the main contributions of this department to improving the communication and collaboration on global projects? Do you see the need for improvements in the PMO role for global projects?

Have you worked on large projects and programs that established a dedicated team of people fulfilling project office functions? Did they promote the use of collaborative tools and online meetings? Did they use online databases, project websites and other communication techniques?

Write on a list or mindmap the positive contributions of the project offices to global projects, and the services they provided to the program and project managers. Make a separate list for the improvements they can make in the promotion and use of collaborative tools, and the services they could provide to improve the effectiveness of program and project managers.

groups of stakeholders: the executive board, the program and project managers, the team members and the customers. The next sections will define the two main categories and types of project offices (Project Management Offices and Project Support Offices), and describe the exchange of information and the main services provided to these stakeholders (illustrated by the arrows in Figure 13.1).

Program or Project Management Offices (PMO)

The PMO is a permanent team directly linked to the organisational structure, coordinating the management of the portfolios, programs and projects of one company or organisational unit. The PMO team members can be distributed across various countries (Global PMO). Different types of PMO exist in international companies, depending on their hierarchical position and the main functions provided to the organisation: corporate, regional, functional and outsourced.

- Corporate PMO (Figure 13.2) – this type of project office provides portfolio management functions for the whole organisation and focuses on collecting program and project information to establish priorities, allocate resources and decide on project initiation, continuation or termination. These decisions are taken together with the company executive board, in order to align the program and project execution to the corporate strategies.
- Regional PMO (Figure 13.2) – international companies can opt to combine the administration, prioritisation and 'stage gate' decisions for various global projects and programs according to their geographical locations. The regional PMO will perform these activities for a logical cluster of countries, grouped by different criteria such as geographical regions (for example, Americas or Asia-Pacific), cultural affinities (for example, Germanic, Arabic or Anglo-Saxon) or languages (for example, Spanish, Portuguese or English). The regional PMO can be subordinated to a corporate PMO, to regional directors, or both.
- Functional PMO (Figure 13.2) – the functional PMO centralises the administration, prioritisation and stage gates decisions for strategic projects and programs executed under

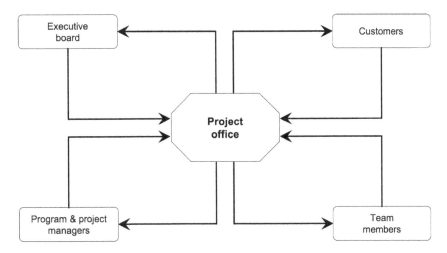

Figure 13.1   Project office and the stakeholders

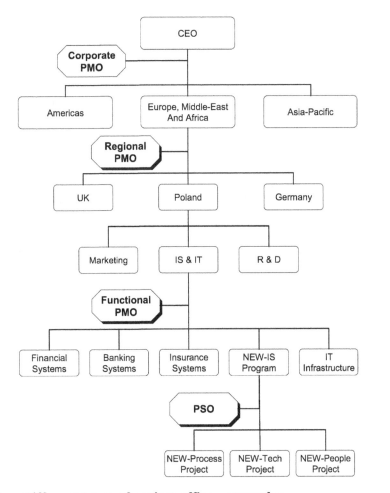

Figure 13.2   Different types of project office – examples

the responsibility of one functional area or division. The organisation can have one functional PMO for each core department such as Information Systems, Marketing and Research and Development. The functional PMO can be subordinated to a corporate PMO, to functional directors, or both.

- Outsourced PMO (Figure 13.3) – a novel form of PMO consists of specialised companies providing services to smaller organisations that wish to benefit from the advantages of a centralised project office, with specialised individuals and reduced costs. Usually this form of PMO will focus on performing program and project management activities and providing consolidated information on the progress and status of the organisation's programs, projects and portfolios.

Program or Project Support Offices (PSO)

The project support office is a team directly linked to the program or project organisation (see Figure 13.2), providing support to the program and project managers on the use of tools, techniques, templates, reporting and knowledge management. The program or project life span will determine the duration of the PSO. When attached to global programs and projects, the PSO can contain team members from the different organisations and countries (global PSO), to align processes, tools, methods and templates, and to facilitate the exchange of information across the various knowledge bases. This will also simplify the organisation of meetings using different calendar systems and locations, and the collection of information from team members located in different places (see Figure 13.4).

Features of global project offices

Global organisations can create project management offices to implement strategic control, balancing the centralisation and decentralisation needs of global projects and programs. Different subsidiaries and departments around the globe can propose different initiatives to the global PMO. Instead of defining the strategy, the global PMO will promote decentralisation and review, make suggestions, approve, coordinate, provide support and allocate resources to these initiatives. The centralisation of knowledge will help to track the timescale, budget, quality and customer satisfaction levels of projects in different countries, and to manage the cross-dependencies between various local initiatives, global projects and global programs.

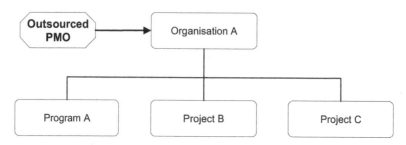

Figure 13.3   Different types of project office – outsourced PMO

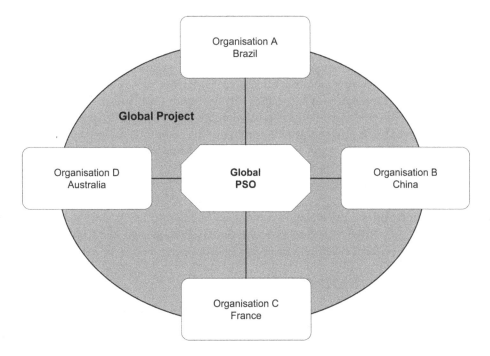

Figure 13.4   Different types of project office – global PSO

The main categories of services provided by the global project offices to local subsidiaries and other departments will now be described in more detail: knowledge management, management of portfolios, management of programs and projects and support to program and project managers.

PROJECT KNOWLEDGE MANAGEMENT SERVICES

- **Central lessons-learned database** – global projects can benefit from past experiences of project teams that worked with the same countries, cultures, stakeholders or customers. The PMO can own the database and make sure that all project teams use and update the lessons-learned information.
- **Centralised configuration management** – the PMO and PSO can make sure that the product configurations are consistent across various countries and organisations, by understanding the different policies and systems.
- **Centralised risk repository** – the PSO can ensure all risks are tracked and followed-up correctly by the global team members; the PMO can make sure the risks are managed consistently across the organisation, and escalate 'top ten' risks for executive information and actions.
- **Centralised repository of project issues** – the PSO can confirm that all issues are tracked and followed-up on time by the global team members; the PMO can ascertain that the issues are managed consistently across the organisation, and escalate 'top ten' issues for executive information and actions.
- **Centralised repository of quality standards** – the PMO and PSO can provide information for quality control processes and collect their results, making sure that the

quality level is maintained within corporate standards for project deliverables executed by different companies and locations around the globe.

- **Project reporting** – the PSO can produce the reports on the project metrics and progress, adapting them to other organisational unit formats, organising translations into local languages and converting amounts to different currencies.
- **Information distribution** – the PSO can distribute information such as the project performance metrics, risks, issues, achievements and changes to the stakeholders in various organisations and countries according to the project communications plan.
- **Scheduling database** – the PSO can track the actual activity durations and the use of contingencies, classifying this information according to the company or country that executed each task, and working together with the PMO to make this information available for future projects.
- **Project dictionary** – the global PSO can maintain a project dictionary that will help the stakeholders to translate the project terminologies to their own methods and standards. The PMO can perform the same task at an organisational or departmental level.

PORTFOLIO MANAGEMENT SERVICES

- **Identification and categorisation of portfolio components** – the corporate PMO can monitor new projects and programs being initiated in different organisational units and countries, and include them in the portfolio if they satisfy basic criteria such as geographical span, size and importance.
- **Evaluation and selection of components** – the corporate PMO might evaluate the new initiatives and consolidate the information required by the decision-making process. The PMO can make recommendations to the executive managers or portfolio review board, who decide upon the prioritisation, acceptance or rejection of the programs and projects. The establishment of a corporate PMO to manage the portfolio helps to keep the mix of components aligned to the organisational strategy, by taking impartial decisions regarding programs and projects being requested by different countries or organisational units.
- **Prioritisation, balancing and allocation of resources** – the corporate PMO can use the program and project characteristics (such as funding, risk level, return on investment and duration) to constantly monitor and revise the execution priorities. A project ranking can influence the allocation of resources, and may also determine the suspension or termination of certain programs and projects. The corporate PMO has the additional benefit of taking impartial decisions, based on objective evaluations such as cost-benefit analysis, with disregard to favouring individual countries or organisational units involved or interested in the project execution. The allocation of cross-functional and distributed team members to the corporate PMO can facilitate the communication with these stakeholders, and increase the trust on the prioritisation criteria.
- **Portfolio reporting** – the corporate PMO can collect the performance indicators from the various programs and projects, preparing consolidated reports that will inform the executive management of the overall performance of the portfolio, allowing strategic decisions that may affect the individual components. Examples of information to be produced are project workload, health status, strategic opportunities and risks. The corporate PMO can organise translations between different languages and convert the monetary amounts to different currencies, when presenting the information to stakeholders across the globe.

PROGRAM AND PROJECT MANAGEMENT SERVICES

- **Program management** – the regional, functional and outsourced PMOs can be responsible for the management of strategic or complex programs, executed or sponsored by their organisational units, and for making sure the benefits realisation is attained. As an example, companies can group global program managers in the PMO, and give them responsibility for specific types of global programs.
- **Project management** – the regional, functional and outsourced PMO can be responsible for the management of strategic or complex projects executed or sponsored by their organisational units. When a project is initiated, the PMO can apply pre-defined selection criteria (such as cross-functional participation, costs, duration or risk level) to determine if a project manager from the PMO is required, or if the assignment of a project manager from the functional teams is recommended.
- **Project recovery** – when high deviations to project scope, cost, time, quality or customer satisfaction are foreseen, the PMO can assign a senior project manager to assess and recover the project. For example, a global PMO might identify that the reason for delays, conflicts and deviations is the poor communication between team members in different countries, and recommend a skilled project manager to provide coaching on the Global Project Management Framework©. The PMO can also take over the management of a project during long absences of the project manager.

SUPPORT TO PROGRAM AND PROJECT MANAGERS

- **Monitoring and health checks** – the PMO can track the evolution of project metrics, and recommend remediation actions when critical variations are foreseen. The PMO can also perform health checks to assess the correct use of methodologies and global project management good practices, recommending the project managers to follow coaching or training sessions to correct the deviations.
- **Coaching and mentoring** – the PMO can provide coaching and mentoring over distance (see Chapter 5), on project management methodologies, soft skills and the Global Project Management Framework©.
- **Training** – a corporate or regional PMO can organise external training sessions to leverage the project management skills from different organisational units and countries. A corporate PMO is also well placed for the coordination of internal training sessions on the company methodologies and good practices, fostering their adoption by all projects of the organisation.
- **Establishing a career path** – the corporate PMO can establish a career path for program and project managers, linking the professional experience, training and credentials with the complexity and size of the initiatives (see Table 13.1).
- **Corporate project management methodology, good practices and standards** – the corporate PMO can investigate different methods, methodologies, good practices and standards from departments and external organisations across the globe, and consolidate them into a uniform set of corporate policies and processes (see 'Develop and promote a global project management methodology' on page 167). The outsourced PMO can bring the same advantage to smaller companies, by deploying a standard set of methods with some adjustments to the organisational or country culture. The methods and standards should be adaptable and flexible in order to facilitate collaboration with organisations using a different set of practices.

Table 13.1   Example of a career path for program and project management

Professional Experience	Recommended Training	Recommended Certification[1]	Project Complexity	Budget
1–3 years	Core project management modules	PMI CAPM®, OGC PRINCE2® Foundation or IPMA Level D	Small (local project team < 10 people, no external parties)	< 1 Mio EUR
3–5 years	Quality, risk and procurement	PMI PMP®, OGC PRINCE2® Practitioner or IPMA Level C	Medium (local project team > 10 people)	1–4 Mio EUR
5+ years	Global Project Management Framework©	IPMA Level B	High (global project team)	> 4 Mio EUR
7+ years	Program management	PMI PgMP℠, OGC MSP practitioner or IPMA Level A	Programs and portfolios	n/a

1   Usually organisations choose one type of certification; this example shows both PMI, OGC and IPMA for comparisons only. See www.pmi.org, www.ogc.gov.uk and www.ipma.ch for more information.

- **Specific project management methodology, good practices and standards** – the functional PMO can develop a set of policies and processes that are particular to their specific knowledge areas, which should complement (and not replace) the corporate standards. These practices must be understood and adopted by (or adapted to) customers, suppliers and partners involved in the project.
- **Global project management good practices and standards** – the corporate PMO can guide the implementation of the Global Project Management Framework© in different organisational units across functions, regions and countries. The functional and regional PMOs can adapt the framework, by validating if the practices and recommendations comply with local cultures, ethics and rules, and making suggestions based on their own experience with global project management from different cultural and functional perspectives.
- **Collaborative tools and techniques** – the PMO can coordinate the implementation of the collaborative technologies (suggested by the chapters in part IV), the dissemination and publishing of the guidelines (prepared using the chapters in part V), champion their use and adoption, and provide support to other project and program managers. The corporate PMO can coordinate the deployment of standard tools across different departments, countries and regions, streamlining the communication across borders.
- **Project management tools and techniques** – the corporate, functional and regional PMO can provide examples and support to foster the use and adoption of software tools, methods and procedures for standard estimating, planning and control.
- **Project management maturity** – the PMO can coordinate the implementation of strategic programs to evaluate and increase the organisation maturity on project management. Examples of maturity models are the CMMI (Capability Maturity Model Integration, see www.sei.cmu.edu), OPM3™ (Organisational Project Management Maturity Model, see www.pmi.org) and PMMM (Project Management Maturity Model, see Kerzner, 2005).

REAL-LIFE EXPERIENCE

'PMO? What is this exactly? What are you offering? And to whom?

As the founder and leader of a global functional PMO, I faced these questions many times. They reflect the key challenges when setting up a PMO: its definition and positioning.

When supervising a project office team of 20 professionals, and a portfolio containing more than 100 programs and projects distributed all over the world, my experience shows two critical factors for a successful PMO implementation: the definition of a clear identity for the PMO and its positioning within the organisation.

The PMO level (Enterprise PMO, regional PMO, functional PMO) will depend on the kind of sponsorship obtained. The PMO must be positioned according to its mission and to the key stakeholders addressed. One common mistake is to address all the stakeholders at once (senior executives, program managers, project managers, project team members and customers) and to implement all different types of services (knowledge management, support to project managers and management of portfolios, programs and projects).

In my case, the main issue was the lack of visibility and governance of the IT function. The sponsors were naturally the CIO and the CFO, interested in controlling the IT expenditures worldwide. The main PMO audience was therefore the senior management, and a top-down implementation was the natural choice.

After positioning the PMO, we created a Project Management Board, and defined a clear set of services focused on Program and Portfolio Management: identification and categorisation of projects, authorisation or rejection of initiatives, project prioritisation and resource assignment, project balancing (local versus global), support to global budget calculation, project review at go/no-go gates, cross functional and strategic alignment.

As pre-requisites to perform these tasks, it was necessary to put in place the project management standards, methodology and global tools to share the project status worldwide and powerful systems to support document management and collaboration. We have built these foundations without losing our focus: our main stakeholder was – in this specific case – the executive management and not the project managers or their team. Our PMO is not perceived as an operational or administrative function, but it is clearly positioned as a strategic organisation, being the guardian of the IT alignment with the business strategy and supporting a continuous improvement approach.'

Yannick Jolliet, Strategic PMO and Governance Office Director

YOUR LEARNING ON GLOBAL PROJECT OFFICES

Revisit the list or mindmap created at the beginning of this chapter. Would you recommend any changes to the structure of the PMOs across your company? Would you recommend your company to implement a PMO? What benefits can a PMO provide to your company, to global program and project manager and to the international team members? How could you measure these benefits during the implementation of a PMO to show the return on investment?

Now share your thoughts with other people, and read about their own experiences (www. GlobalProjectManagement.org).

14 *Organisational Support*

Program managers, project managers and project office members alone cannot improve the effectiveness of global projects. Global organisations must adapt their processes, policies and procedures to cope with the new challenges faced by international project teams. Senior executives must adapt their leadership styles and act as role models for the implementation of new methods and tools. This chapter suggests that global organisations should build an emotional intelligence culture, promote work-life balance for employees around the globe, value the employees independently of their locations, promote the use of collaborative tools and methods, develop a global project management methodology and establish international performance appraisal systems, reward policies and training schemes.

Build emotional intelligence

Emotional intelligence (EI) can be defined as, 'the capacity to reason about emotions in order to enhance thinking' and includes the abilities to perceive emotions, to use emotions to facilitate thought, to understand emotions and emotional knowledge, and to promote intellectual growth by managing emotions (Mayer, Caruso and Salovey, 1999).

Global program and project managers will face different challenges in using EI skills. As discussed in other chapters of this book, people from different cultures can have diverse ways to express the same emotion: attitudes and expressions that are common in one country can look peculiar in another one. The perception of other people's reactions is harder without face-to-face contact, requiring dedication and advanced interpersonal skills. However, the advantages of perceiving emotions correctly are worth the effort. Even in busy project periods, or outside your working hours, you may need to dedicate time for one-to-one discussions over the telephone and audio conferencing (see 'Neutral versus affective' on page 31 and 'Motivation' on page 46). In these discussions, you can better perceive the emotions of distant team members and interpret them to decide on the best communication strategies and

---

HOW YOUR ORGANISATION SUPPORTS GLOBAL PROJECTS

Do you believe that your organisation provides full support to global program and project managers, by understanding their main challenges and contributing to their success? Are your organisational policies, processes and culture adapted to the global project requirements? Are there equal opportunities for employees in different countries? Do senior executives provide a role model for management, leadership and communication across borders?

Write on a list or mindmap the positive contributions of the organisational policies, processes and procedures to the effectiveness of global programs and projects. Make a separate list for the changes you could implement to improve the organisational support to global projects.

methods to convey the project goals and strategies. You need to manage your emotions and negotiate with tact, attracting the attention of colleagues in other locations toward the project deliverables and fostering creative thinking.

Employees that deal with communications across borders must develop the understanding and use of EI behaviours and skills. International organisations can create an atmosphere where these behaviours are valued, and promote EI in the workplace, by:

- **Assessing the organisation's needs on EI** – determine the level of emotional competencies required by different job positions in your company, such as program managers, project managers, project coordinators, team managers and specialised workers. Evaluate how often they deal with diversity, conflicts and stress, how important teamwork is for their effectiveness and how acute their leadership skills must be.
- **Preparing an EI development plan** – investigate what different forms of EI courses and 'soft skills' training are available near to your main locations, and analyse how well they fit the levels of competencies you have identified for the different job positions.
- **Increasing the EI awareness** – organisations can also include information on EI on their website, directed to different types of audiences, like academic papers, newspaper and magazine articles.
- **Measuring EI levels** – managers and supervisors can evaluate EI levels from their subordinates, by using the competencies required for their job positions, discussing strengths and weaknesses individually with each employee, and determining with them their training and coaching requirements.

REAL-LIFE EXPERIENCE

Tactful project managers can recognise that team members from certain locations react positively to humour, and show examples of ironic situations faced by previous projects before starting a risk analysis session. This can change the attitude from 'there is no risk here' into 'mistakes can happen', improving the outcomes of a risk identification session. Global project managers also need to detect emotions in e-mails, which are sometimes considered a very cold communication medium. One project manager complained to a program manager that certain team members located across the ocean never replied to the meeting requests, never attended meetings or sent excuses. How could they be so impolite?

On the same evening, the program manager called one of these team members, a long-time acquaintance from a previous work assignment, and had an informal conversation about life and recent projects. After some laughs and complaints about the excess working hours, the name of the project manager came up naturally, and the program manager heard the following comment, 'oh, the lady that keeps booking meetings with me after 6pm? That's so impolite I don't even bother answering her requests.'

The lack of answer can have many different meanings. People can be very busy, disorganised when dealing with incoming messages, or simply prefer to concentrate on their work rather than on e-mails. However, very often this silence means 'upset', and requires more investigation, either directly with the people involved or by asking someone in your network that may know the other person better, as in the case above. To solve the problem, the project manager called the team member the evening after and agreed on acceptable times for future meetings.

A second point in this case is the reaction of the team member. In most cultures, this would be considered inappropriate and extremely impolite. It is the equivalent of ignoring a colleague that crosses you in the corridor and asks you a question. The team member above should also learn about EI, to understand how others can interpret their acts.

- **Improving EI** – organise the training sessions identified in the development plans. Make employees across the globe conscious of how the expression of their feelings and their emotional responses can affect the collaboration of other team members. People in job positions that involve management and communications must also know how to interpret emotions – or the lack of responses – and find the appropriate attitude to solve the problem in the interests of their goals and objectives.
- **Considering EI in evaluations and promotions** – managers and supervisors must evaluate employees according to the EI competencies identified for their job positions, and provide them with feedback on their strengths and areas needing improvement. Promotions can also consider the EI skills, to determine if the employee is suitable to change into a leadership position, or to identify whether additional training is required before the person assumes a project management role.
- **Leading by example** – senior managers and directors can be the first to follow the training sessions, and participate actively in the explanations about EI to other employees.

Promote work-life balance

One of the main motivational problems faced by international organisations is a feeling from employees that their work routines are damaging their personal lives and reducing the amount of time they can spend with their families or in leisure activities. Some people can also feel uncomfortable about receiving business telephone calls outside office hours, when the criticality of the matter does not justify a need for immediate action. People working on global projects have an increased probability of facing the situations above, due to the differences in culture and time zones.

Global organisations can keep up the motivation level of employees working across cultures and time zones by:

- **Promoting the use of home offices** – employees may feel more comfortable in taking telephone calls and participating in meetings outside office hours if they can spend part of their daytime working from home. This can help them to avoid traffic jams and experience other home-office advantages.
- **Creating flexitime working schemes** – employees can chose their working hours according to pre-established rules and depending on the amount of time required by synchronous collaborative sessions or meetings with colleagues in different time zones.

REAL-LIFE EXPERIENCE

Certain cultures may consider lunchtime as 'normal business hours' for meetings and non-important telephone discussions, while others see the lunch hour as an essential break to increase concentration in the afternoon, and use the opportunity for social contacts and personal networking. The differences in time zones can act unfavourably on both sides: one individual working in Geneva that faces a dilemma in order to complete the product specifications by 4pm CET may have problems in making a telephone call to a colleague in Sydney at 2am EST. If the telephone call is not made, the specifications may not be ready on time, delaying the project activities. And if the colleague in Sydney does not understand, 'how the specifications were not clear enough already', the incident may damage the relationship.

- **Offering special remuneration and bonus packages** – employees working skewed hours (frequent early mornings or late evenings) can be compensated by a different pay scheme to their colleagues who work normal hours, as well as the correct application of overtime compensation rules.
- **Offering compensation days** – employees can compensate their late evenings and early mornings by taking some holiday, additional to their statutory holiday period.
- **Discouraging travel** – stimulate the use of audio, web and video conferencing facilities in all company offices (see below), and define rules for meetings involving people from different locations (see the section 'Meeting types and communication media' on page 91). As an example, all employees must know when face-to-face meetings are required or how to achieve a similar effectiveness by using remote communication tools, with coaching from managers, experienced project managers and supervisors.
- **Balancing travel needs** – when different teams must have regular face-to-face meetings, stimulate a rotation of the meeting location, or chose 'neutral' locations that are equidistant to the company offices.
- **Listening to the employees** – organise anonymous surveys and focus groups to understand how employees see their work-life balance, and how they think the company can make improvements in this area.
- **Leading by example** – company executives can follow similar practices to the employees, promoting an organisation where the work-life balance is equal across different hierarchical levels, job positions and corporate offices.

Value the human resources

Organisations must pay attention to differences across corporate offices, and avoid some employees losing motivation by feeling that they are undervalued in comparison to their colleagues in other locations. Some examples of human resources policies that can reduce the likelihood of negative comparisons are:

- **Equal opportunities** – employees must have the same opportunity for work-related needs such as career development, personal growth, training, working conditions and health and safety. A careful balance must be sought between corporate headquarters and remote locations. When diverse laws and regulations force the use of different company policies, employees must receive information and support from management to understand these differences, and be involved in discussions to compensate the discrepancies or find alternative solutions.
- **Pay equity** – the analysis of equal opportunities must also consider the salary levels, taking into the account the cost-of-living in different countries.
- **International assignments** – companies can create programs of short- and long-term assignments for employees to work in different locations for a period of time. These missions must involve intensive work by the employee with local people, allowing social integration and building networks. Job rotation can also be part of a development program, which gives employees the opportunity to learn about cultural diversity before being promoted to global program and project managers.

Promote the use of collaborative tools

International organisations must promote the use of collaborative tools at all hierarchical levels, understanding the advantages of collaborative working to improve work efficiency, reduce travel costs and increase job morale. Companies must support the costs associated with the implementation of hardware, software and training in all locations, aiming to develop collaborative standards and practices that are equally deployed across most corporate offices. As well as the recommendations in this book (see Chapters 16–25), two further corporate practices can foster the adoption of collaborative working standards across borders:

- **Showing the example** – employees at corporate headquarters and corporate executives can be included in the pilot implementation of new techniques and tools on global project management. This gives them more credibility when trying to implement these practices in other locations, and is likely to increase the adoption levels of employees in different countries.
- **Monitoring the adoption** – senior executives can assess the adoption level of the collaborative tools when using the project websites to look for project information, when participating in online project status meetings and when getting information on the 'top ten' project risks and issues. When most of the events affecting a project are created by remote communication, collaboration across countries and cultural differences, the PMO or PSO must be assigned to assess the use of the Global Project Management Framework© (see 'Program and project management services' and 'Support to program and project managers' on page 159).

Develop and promote a global project management methodology

International organisations must streamline and standardise their processes to ensure that team members located in different countries can collaborate using compatible methods, techniques and procedures. Project management is one of the areas that can benefit most from this standardisation, as global projects require that team members located in different offices work together to achieve their common goals and objectives, or participate in related activities that demand synchronisation, interaction and the exchange of information. These organisations can develop a global methodology in project management by:

- **Forming a global team** – a task force can be created to develop the methodology. Ideally, this activity will be under the responsibility of a corporate PMO (see page 153). The team must integrate experienced project managers from different countries in order to take different practices into account and consider various standpoints when taking decisions. Include at least one team member with experience or interest in collaborative tools, to make sure that innovative forms of communication and documentation will be imbedded in the methodology.
- **Investigating current methodologies** – different departments and locations can already have practices and methods in place, at different stages of development and implementation. Their strengths can be evaluated and integrated into the new methodology, increasing the adoption from locations that are already using advanced practices. When integration is not possible, training on the new methodologies can include a 'migration

path' that uses analogies with their existing methods, practices and templates, facilitating the adoption of the new processes.

- **Defining a global methodology** – the new methodology must be defined and published on a website that is accessible from all locations. The global team must consider the translation of the methods, documents and templates to local languages if this increases the adoption level. The methodology must be adaptable and flexible in order to increase the adoption by departments using specialised methodologies linked to their domains, and to facilitate the collaboration with organisations using a different set of practices.
- **Promoting the methodology** – different project offices (PMOs and PSOs) can promote the methodology by providing training sessions, coaching, support and templates. Project managers working for PMOs must be the first to use the methodology on their own projects, setting an example to other project managers. Program managers must also reinforce the use of the methodology with project managers under their supervision.

Establish 360G performance appraisals

In functional organisations, each employee has only one hierarchical superior: the functional manager. This type of organisation usually employs traditional performance appraisals to plan the employee's training and developments (see Figure 14.1). The appraisals are based exclusively on the feedback of the functional managers, and can also serve as the basis for promotional and pay decisions. Some organisations also involve the subordinates in the evaluations of the functional managers (upward feedback).

In matrix organisations, each employee reports to a functional manager, while spending a certain amount of time working under the responsibility and coordination of program and project managers. This type of organisation can employ traditional performance appraisals and request the feedback of both functional and project managers (see Figure 14.2). The compilation of the assessments from different managers can evaluate the employee's performance on different occasions, such as routine work and project-related tasks. When the assessment of project-related tasks receives the same weight as routine work tasks on the performance appraisal systems, the employees will have a higher level of motivation to work on projects, and to excel on project-related activities. These organisations can request that

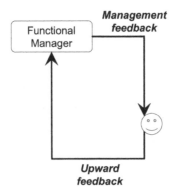

Figure 14.1   Traditional performance appraisal in functional organisations

team members provide upward feedback for the evaluation of their project managers, who usually do not have direct reports.

Functional and matrix organisations can also organise 360-degree reviews, adding the feedback of colleagues, customers and suppliers to the evaluations from functional managers, project managers and direct reports (see Figure 14.3). Instead of quantitative ratings, the assessment might include a qualitative appreciation of the employee's strengths and qualities, suggestions for skills improvement and career development recommendations.

While the evaluation systems above include only the assessments of local superiors and peers, they offer an additional challenge to global projects: the employees may show more dedication to the work supervised by local managers. Team members will have a higher level of motivation to work on global projects when the feedback received from stakeholders in different locations has the same weight as the opinion of local managers and peers on the performance appraisal systems. A global 360-degree feedback system (360G performance

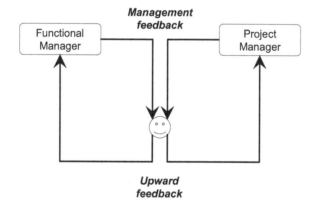

Figure 14.2   Traditional performance appraisal in matrix organisations

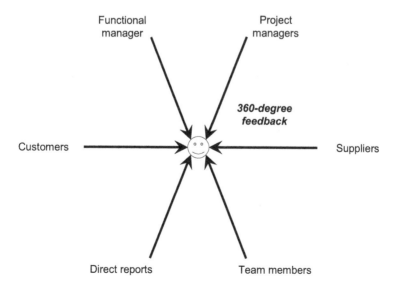

Figure 14.3   360-degree performance appraisal

appraisal©) requests that project coordinators, other team members, customers and senior managers from different countries provide recommendations for improvement on communication and leadership skills over distance and across cultures (see Figure 14.4). The 360G performance appraisal evaluates the employees from different angles and detects points for improvement on the skills and techniques discussed in other chapters of this book.

International organisations can standardise their performance evaluation systems around the globe using the 360G performance appraisal model, in order to promote equal evaluations and opportunities for the employees working in different countries and locations. Employees on short-term assignments in other countries might also benefit from a standardised system that integrates their managers' evaluation with the assessment of their local supervisors and project managers. These global performance appraisal systems need to flexible enough to consider different local policies, rules and cultures when applying the results into promotions and pay decisions. Global stakeholders can provide their feedback by using free-form e-mails or text-document appraisals. More advanced systems can allow the use of online surveys with structured questions, which can evaluate the employees' job-related skills and performance, as well as the global project management knowledge and practices, such as:

- cross-cultural skills
- team leadership skills
- conflict management techniques and skills
- coaching techniques and skills
- global communication tools, methods and skills
- level of participation in knowledge-sharing initiatives
- level of participation in global creativity sessions
- compliance with corporate policies and procedures
- use of the right tools and techniques when working over distance.

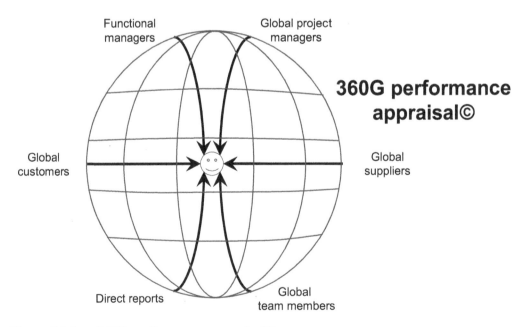

Figure 14.4   360G performance appraisal©

Establish a global rewards policy

Allied to global performance appraisal systems, organisations must establish fair and consistent reward processes across different countries and locations. Financial rewards must consider the recommendations on 'pay equity' and avoid discriminations across locations (see page 166). Non-financial rewards can provide additional motivation by recognising the contribution of each individual in the team to the project achievements.

Companies can foster teamwork and collaboration by promoting group rewards instead of praising personal achievements, however this topic is subject to cultural differences. As suggested by Trompenaars and Hampden-Turner (2005), high-performing individuals from communitarian cultures may prefer that the whole team is rewarded, in order to obtain more respect and reinforce group cohesion. In more individualistic countries, the competition among individuals is more common and can have a higher impact on motivation. Every corporate office can define the optimal mix between personal and group rewards based on their country cultures. However, global projects will probably have a mix of team members from individualistic and communitarian countries, and need to adopt a uniform rule. Organisations can inspire team spirit by rewarding the whole project team in recognition of outstanding teamwork and after the achievement of key milestones. When awarding specific individuals for heroic exploits and exceptional triumphs, non-financial rewards can increase their motivation while minimising competition, some examples being:

- more responsibility on future projects;
- participation in projects with higher complexity;
- participation in new challenging ventures;
- participation in or coordination of strategic initiatives;
- opportunities for intellectual growth;
- team recognition awards (publishing news on a corporate website).

Implement a corporate training scheme

International companies can implement a training scheme to increase the awareness of program managers, project managers and team members on the various topics covered by the Global Project Management Framework©, such as communication techniques and tools over distance, cultural diversity, leadership skills, trust building, conflict resolution, coaching and brainstorming. Other examples of training areas that can increase the effectiveness of global project teams are networking, relationship building, negotiation and other domain-related skills such as procurement, legal and finance.

The training sessions on the Global Project Management Framework© can bring together employees from various locations, improving the learning experience with cultural exchanges, discussions of real-life experiences, analysis of techniques and tools used in different countries, and comparing the effectiveness of the new methods and tools on different situations.

HOW YOUR ORGANISATION MIGHT SUPPORT GLOBAL PROJECTS

Revisit the list or mindmap created at the beginning of this chapter. Would you add any new suggestions for your organisation to improve the effectiveness of global programs and projects? What topics from this chapter would be beneficial to your organisation? What recommendations do not fit in your organisational culture? Would you be motivated and able to conduct an organisational change initiative to implement new learning?

Now share your thoughts with other people, and read about their own experiences (www. GlobalProjectManagement.org).

15 *Global Collaborative Networks*

Many organisations form strategic alliances and partnerships to access specific markets, to obtain capital resources or sponsorship, or to share R&D and manufacturing skills. Very often, the relationship is sealed around a group of programs or projects. A seamless exchange of information is essential for these initiatives to be successful. This chapter describes the characteristics that define these collaborative networks, discusses the main challenges presented by these forms of relationship, suggests a strategy to achieve effective collaboration and makes recommendations to kick-off the partnership and to concentrate on the interfaces during the project execution.

Collaborative networks: a project-centred approach

Castells (2000) suggests that organisations are evolving from multinational enterprises to international networks, which include large corporations and a series of small and medium business, each in a different country and organisational culture, all with a shared mission to be achieved within a limited timeframe. These networks can aggregate the main suppliers, producers and customers with their sub-contractors and service providers, and are strongly reliant on the cooperation among different individuals and on the communication between the computer networks. Program and project managers have the responsibility of driving these networks towards their common mission, by coordinating the collaboration and communication activities, and managing the sharing of interests between the common objective and the goals of the individual companies.

Figure 15.1 exemplifies this concept, by showing a 'new product development' project coordinated by a producer company, including team members from the customer, one outsourcing company and one offshore services provider (represented by the dark-grey

---

YOUR EXPERIENCE OF COLLABORATIVE NETWORKS

Have you been involved in programs and projects that were part of a collaborative network, when different organisations had a common target and united forces to achieve it? What were the main benefits achieved by this form of collaboration? What were the main challenges the program and project managers faced in this situation? Did they employ conciliating methods and techniques to get all team members working in the same direction? How did they reconcile different tools and processes during the project execution?

Write on a list or mindmap the benefits and challenges of collaborative networks, noting down the strategies adopted by the program and project managers, and your opinion on the outcomes of these strategies. Make a separate list for the recommendations you would make for programs and project managers working on a collaborative network in the future.

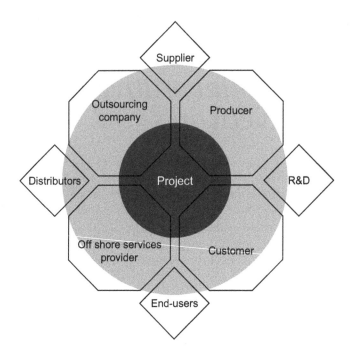

Figure 15.1   Project-centred collaborative network

circle). These team members will collaborate during the product development and liaise with stakeholders from suppliers, R&D, distributors and the end-users (represented by the light-grey circle).

Understand the challenges

When managing a program or project that is part of a project-centred collaborative network, you must understand the main challenges that may exist in such a relationship. You can organise a brainstorming session to gather ideas from more experienced program or project managers, from senior executives that had previous experiences with the companies and individuals participating in the network and from consultants that are specialised in outsourcing and offshoring initiatives in your domain of expertise. Some examples of these challenges are:

- **Different interests** – each company can be joining the network with hidden interests, forcing their views during project meetings or working implicitly towards them. The program and project managers need to evaluate these interests in advance of every conflicting situation and be prepared to negotiate at every occasion (see Chapter 4).
- **Different corporate cultures** – each company has a different view on risk awareness, decision making, motivation, rewards, conflict management, leadership styles and hierarchical structures. The project manager must consider these differences when preparing the stakeholder analysis (see Chapter 6) and defining the project communication strategy (discussed in Chapter 8).
- **Different maturity levels on project management** – while some companies value project management and have established solid methodologies on how to manage and work

on projects, other organisations still 'improvise' and compensate the lack of competencies on project management with hard work. The project manager must investigate which companies in the network have the higher levels of maturity, by evaluating lessons-learned databases and involving project managers from all companies in the project initiation and planning. The project manager can also organise presentations and coaching on project management skills to the team members coming from organisations with lower maturity levels.

- **Different maturity levels on processes and procedures** – some companies can be process-oriented, with clear procedures that allow effective communication across different teams executing complementary tasks. The team members from these companies might adapt quickly to working within a global project team when all components agree to use the same processes and procedures. Other companies can run in a more informal environment, requiring face-to-face discussions to synchronise different work packages. The project managers may need to convince the stakeholders of these companies to use the new procedures, by showing them the benefits of shared practices and processes to the effectiveness of communication on global projects (see Chapter 7).
- **Different collaborative tools and communication techniques** – the various companies in the network can have their own set of collaborative systems, using different software providers, and choosing to implement and customise the tools in diverse ways. Some companies may not even have a good knowledge level of these systems, employing only e-mails and audio conferencing for cooperation across borders. The project managers will need to identify the different collaborative tools in advance, and determine the standards to be adopted during the project, to satisfy the collaboration requirements (see Chapters 16–25).
- **The challenges of global projects** – all challenges from global projects apply to the collaborative networks, requiring the application of the Global Project Management Framework©. The project manager can use the framework to obtain agreement from the different companies that a set of good practices is required, and apply the learning from the different modules during the whole project, from initiation to completion.

Define a collaboration strategy

After evaluating the challenges that are applicable to your situation and considering how to address each of them, you need to define an inter-organisational collaboration strategy, by:

- Defining the mission in specific and clear terms that can be accepted by all parties.
- Identifying the need for standardisation of organisational practices and policies, taking into account the capability of the different organisations to adapt to the new standard.
- Defining the desired maturity on project management and the required level of details of process definition, conciliating the project requirements and the abilities of different organisations.
- Defining the collaborative tools and the modules of the Global Project Management Framework© that are essential for effective cooperation, and fixing a target date for the development and implementation of the tools, methods and good practices across all teams working on the project.

Initiate the collaboration

You can organise a 'collaboration kick-off session' to put the strategy in place. This session can include the program managers and project managers coordinating different initiatives in the same collaborative network, sharing the main outcomes with key stakeholders from the companies in the network.

The items in the kick-off session need to address the challenges you identified, and cover all topics you specified in the collaboration strategy. The agenda can include the following points:

- establish the purpose of the programs and projects;
- prepare a team charter;
- define roles and responsibilities;
- agree on common and flexible systems, structures, policies, tools and methods;
- define a shared goal for the different companies to work as a team, reducing the influences and differences from organisational and country borders;
- understand the different organisations' values and styles;
- identify the need for different training and coaching sessions on the new techniques, processes, tools, methods and good practices;
- Have lunch breaks, team dinner events and other social activities that allow relationship building and the creation of informal networks.

Monitor the interfaces

Once you have defined a core set of practices, tools and directions together with the representatives from the other companies, you need to define the group of people who

---

REAL-LIFE EXPERIENCE

'When my company decided to entirely outsource its worldwide network and telecommunications operations, I was assigned to manage a large project to implement a Service Management organisation across 70+ countries. The project team was distributed all around the world, and included many different cultures and languages.

We obviously started by setting up a collaborative space to share documents and to support asynchronous discussions. We then put in place clear communication rules and mechanisms (for example, meeting frequency, formal versus informal communication and real time messaging).

Because of the 24x7 nature of our operations, the key was to manage seamlessly the project across the different time zones. We needed to manage efficiently our project knowledge and foster collaboration among the various team members. A good example was the capacity to transfer effectively open items, potential risks or actual issues from a project team member based in Kuala Lumpur to another colleague in St-Petersburg or in Toronto.

This experience highlighted to me how an effective management of project knowledge and a good usage of collaborations tools was essential to the success of a complex global project.'

Yannick Jolliet, Strategic PMO and Governance Office Director

will make sure that the agreements are respected by all parties. When deviations are found, the group must get together and analyse the reasons and potential alternatives. This group must concentrate on the interfaces, which are the communications between people across organisational borders and the data exchange between different corporate information systems. The roles assigned to this group must be part of a charter assigning clear responsibilities. Some examples of activities under the responsibility of the 'monitoring team' are:

- track progress towards the program and project missions, and identify activities and behaviours that go against these directions;
- make sure that the collaborative tools are being employed according to the communication strategy;
- monitor the use of the shared processes and practices as agreed during the kick-off session;
- monitor the effectiveness of the training and coaching sessions, and recommend additional educational sessions or guidelines;
- fine tune business processes that involve different companies.

Companies can opt for selecting local agents (persons or partnership firms) to perform a link between the foreign and local cultures, and optimising the network processing, by applying the following criteria (adapted from Sennara and Hartman, 2002):

- experience on project environments;
- a proven track record of experience in the project's knowledge area;
- respect and trust from at least one organisation in the project;
- openness for understanding of the foreign cultures;
- existence of a strong network in the local country, helping to identify and analyse the project stakeholders;
- alignment with foreign corporate values.

YOUR LEARNING ON GLOBAL COMMUNICATION TECHNIQUES

Revisit the list or mindmap created at the beginning of this module. Would you make a different set of recommendations to programs and project managers working on a collaborative network? Which recommendations in this chapter may be applicable to your environment, when working with other companies?

Now share your thoughts with other people, and read about their own experiences (www. GlobalProjectManagement.org).

Part III: Key concepts

- Programs and projects can be structured in different ways, according to the level of maturity on global project management, and the dispersion of specialised team members. Mature organisations can deploy centralised project teams with a high level of dispersion, to make use of highly specialised team members working in their home locations. Programs and projects involving team members from regional or functional competency centres may prefer a distributed structure, assigning more responsibility to local coordinators. Some organisations can benefit from teams in different time zones executing the project activities 'round-the-clock', coordinated by local project managers. A project-centred partnership can combine the efforts of various project managers, each coordinating the activities of their organisations.

- In order to recruit and select team members from different countries to work in a global project team, organisations must identify the coordination and communication skills required for each role. The recruitment process can make use of internal job posting, personal references and networking or external agencies. The interviewing process can occur via telephones and video conferencing, if the questions and evaluation method are well defined in advance.
- International organisations must provide support to global project teams, by promoting EI, work-life balance, collaborative tools, a global project management methodology and 360G performance appraisals.
- Project offices can provide benefits to international companies and global projects, by fulfilling different requirements: knowledge management services, the management of portfolios, programs and projects, and support to program and project managers. Project Management Offices (PMOs) are permanent organisations overseeing programs and projects at corporate, regional or functional level. Project Support Offices (PSOs) are attached to large programs or projects, providing support to the team members on the use of tools, techniques, templates, reporting and knowledge management.
- Organisations forming strategic alliances and partnerships around a group of programs or projects must avoid underestimating the challenges created by the diversity of standards, methods and corporate cultures. A collaboration strategy must be defined early in the partnering process, and implemented during a kick-off meeting. The different partners must monitor the level of collaboration and knowledge exchange during the whole program or project, correcting deviations as they appear.

Part III: Further reading

Andersen, E. (2000) 'Managing organization – structure and responsibilities' in *Gower Handbook of Project Management*

This chapter of the Gower handbook presents different alternatives for the relationship between the project and its parent organisation (external structures) and for the internal project structures.

Keegan, A. and Turner, R. (2000) 'Managing human resources in the project-based organization' in *Gower Handbook of Project Management*

The authors discuss the selection processes in project-based firms, in comparison to hierarchical, line management organisations.

IPMA – International Project Management Association (2006) *IPMA Competence Baseline*

The IPMA Competence Baseline (ICB) provides a comprehensive list of competencies required by project managers, and can be used as a basis for the list of project management skills required from the candidates.

Merlier, P. and Jolliet, Y. (2006) *Mettre en place un Project Management Office: du rêve à la réalité*

This presentation provides a real-life experience that consolidates the learning from the implementation of a global PMO in an international enterprise.

Kendall, G.I. and Rollins, S.C. (2003) *Advanced Project Portfolio Management and the PMO*

This book is a very comprehensive source of information to companies considering the implementation of a PMO, providing recommendations on the main functions, benefits and building steps.

www.eiconsortium.org

The Consortium for Research on Emotional Intelligence in Organizations publishes research findings and practical guidelines on emotional intelligence. Of particular interest to global organisations are the 'good practices guidelines' and the 'business case for EI'.

Mayer, J.D., Caruso, D. and Salovey, P. (1999) *Emotional Intelligence Meets Traditional Standards for an Intelligence*;

Goleman, D. (1996) *Emotional Intelligence*

These sources provide a comprehensive understanding of emotional intelligence, showing how they can help global program and project managers to perceive the emotions expressed by team members from different cultures.

Haywood, M. (1998) *Managing Virtual Teams*

This book provides clear guidelines to implement a telecommuting program, covering a range of needs from technical to legal requirements.

Part III: Interactive section

Share with other readers your general opinion on the organisational strategies and support applicable to global projects (www.GlobalProjectManagement.org):

- How important is the type of project structure to the success of a project? Should the structures adapt to the location of resources, or the other way round?
- Do you agree with the use of telephone and video conferencing for interviewing candidates to work on your project? What other alternatives are there to select global resources?
- Do you see clear benefits of the implementation of a PMO or PSO? What can be the negative side of these structures?
- How important is the organisational support for the motivation and effectiveness of a project team? What other types of support can be provided by your organisation, not covered in this book?

IV *Implementation of Collaborative Tools*

The chapters in this part provide strategies to implement collaborative tools in your company and make them available to all project team members around the globe.

At the beginning, you need to determine which types of tools are required in your company to foster collaboration on global projects. You can refer to the introduction sections in each chapter to understand the main objectives and advantages of the different technologies.

For each type of collaborative tool, there are different recommendations to evaluate the software and hardware solutions available in the market, to implement the solutions, write documentation and analyse the implementations afterwards, in order to detect areas for improvement. You can obtain a list of the various solution providers from the web companion (www.GlobalProjectManagement.org) to identify which systems to evaluate.

As well as the tools described in this chapter, other technologies are available to improve the productivity of global projects. The boxes 'real-life technologies' provide some examples and web references with more information, replacing the 'real-life experience' sections. The Global Project Management Framework© is built using a modular approach, allowing a future expansion to include other equipment used at your company, or future collaborative tools. The process to select and deploy these new technologies can then follow a similar pattern to the following chapters.

16 *Basic Infrastructures*

Before considering the implementation of new collaborative technologies, it is useful to investigate the current status of the basic communication infrastructure and spend some time identifying potential improvements in documentation, user directories and integration with other companies. This chapter covers these activities for basic infrastructure components such as telephones, e-mail and remote access.

Basic technologies

Telephones and e-mail are the basic tools for remote communication, available in most organisations. Global project team members must be able to quickly locate the contact details of their colleagues working in other locations or in different companies. Some companies provide a global telephone and e-mail directory, including all contact details and a picture of every employee. Projects crossing company borders will benefit from a similar database of contacts, maintained by the project office. A nice way to implement this is to use the project virtual room, as discussed in Chapter 19.

Wireless computers, home connections and webmail are also very important in global projects, motivated by the different time zones and amount of travel, which will require people to access e-mails from home, hotels, airports and offices outside the corporate networks. Companies must develop secure and user friendly procedures, in a format that can allow their use outside the office.

The number of international conversations may also justify the deployment of Internet telephony (also called Voice over Internet Protocol – VoIP). Besides important reduction of costs, there are functional advantages: the telephone calls routed to the VoIP phone can be received anywhere in the world, allowing team members to keep the same telephone number

---

BASIC INFRASTRUCTURE IN YOUR ORGANISATION

Do you have any difficulties in finding the e-mail addresses and telephone numbers of other project team members? How often do you face problems with low-quality equipment in meeting rooms that disturb telephone discussions? How long does it take to connect to the office from home, hotels or airports? Is it easy to reserve a meeting room or working desk at the different project locations? What other issues do you face regularly, due to the lack of equipment or the absence of documentations and procedures?

Write on a list or mindmap the weak points in your organisation's infrastructure. For each point, make a recommendation based on your current knowledge of the area. While you read this chapter, complete your mindmap with the knowledge you acquire, with suggestions to improve the basic infrastructure in your organisation.

when working in different locations. VoIP telephones can also simplify the connection to other technologies, such as video or audio conferencing, having one set of integrated media to share voice, images and desktop applications. The integration of VoIP telephones with other hardware and software components can help to streamline communication, allowing you to answer one e-mail message by using the telephone, with a simple click.

Good communication devices must be available in all conference rooms, to allow one group of people working in the same location to sit together when meeting via audio conference with distant colleagues. Among the many benefits of this approach are the use of visual cues to reinforce opinions among the project team members in the same room, the creation of a social rapport and the possibility of staying in the room after the meeting to distribute tasks assigned to the team, to hold informal discussions and team events. There are different types of telephone equipment available for these situations, and special care must be taken to ensure the devices are adapted to the room size and the average number of people. The microphones must be placed in a way that allows all participants to be heard equally. For some important meetings, it may be appropriate for some people to travel to the meeting venue in order to be together and benefit from the advantages of physical proximity.

For individuals who communicate regularly on the telephone, headsets can improve comfort and the sound quality, also leaving the hands free to write meeting minutes, to operate applications being shared during the meeting or simply to take notes.

International workers are increasingly adopting the practice of sending text over mobile telephones (SMS technology) for professional use. The messages should not contain any sensitive material and global project managers must investigate and inform their team members about the electronic communication compliancy laws of other countries and companies, when working together in a collaborative network.

Wireless handheld devices (such as Personal Digital Assistants, BlackBerries and Smartphones) and wireless networking can also be deployed to attain ubiquitous connectivity, but cultural aspects must be taken into account for their deployment. While exchanging e-mails on Saturday evenings may be considered acceptable in some countries, in others it can show a lack of respect for private life.

Evaluating the current situation

Now you can assess the level of implementation and documentation of the basic technologies in your company or project. The checklist in Table 16.1 provides a template to identify the opinion of global project team members on the quality level of the existing technologies and on the availability of information about other colleagues. This list is not exhaustive and should be completed with the information in the mindmap you created at the beginning of this chapter, and adapted to your company needs.

Implementing changes

You need to consider the basic technology required for effective collaboration over distance, and satisfy the needs identified on the assessment. You can prepare an action plan to address each of the items identified as critical (responses 'disagree' and 'strongly disagree'), and to implement some of the suggestions provided by the global team members in the last question.

Table 16.1   Survey to identify efficiency of e-mail, telephones and remote access

Question	Strongly agree	Agree	Disagree	Strongly disagree
It is easy to find e-mail addresses for all colleagues located in the same office				
It is easy to find e-mail addresses for all colleagues located in other company offices				
It is easy to find e-mail addresses for all colleagues from other companies working on my projects				
It is easy to find telephone numbers for all colleagues located in the same office				
It is easy to find telephone numbers for all colleagues located in other company offices				
It is easy to find telephone numbers for all colleagues from other companies working on my projects				
Telephone equipment in meeting rooms provides good quality of communication during meetings				
Desktop telephone equipment provides good quality of communication during meetings				
It is easy to access company e-mails from other company locations				
It is easy to access company e-mails outside the company offices (for example, hotels, home)				
It is easy to connect to the company network and perform most project functions				

My suggestions to improve communications
over distance

Defining documentation and procedures

A good set of documentation and procedures must be in place to increase the adoption level of the new technologies by informing all project team members of the deployment steps of the new solutions and the new functions available. Table 16-2 provides one template for a basic assessment of key elements to increase collaboration on global projects, and can serve as a checklist to complete the implementation of the new technologies. The main items are described in more detail below.

REAL-LIFE TECHNOLOGIES

Some examples of other types of technologies being deployed to help teamwork over distance are:

- activity management systems – Accomplice (www.accomplice.com)
- sharable spreadsheets – Num Sum (www.numsum.com)
- people availability systems – WAY (www.gbpi.net)
- IP speakerphones – Avaya (www.avaya.co.uk), Polycom (www.polycom.com)

See more examples online at www.GlobalProjectManagement.org.

The *employees' basic information* must be readily available, so that anyone in the company can join colleagues by *telephone* or *e-mail* at any time. The information about the main *location* and the time zone of each employee is also very useful when planning for telephone contacts and local meetings. Details of the fluency level in different *languages* can be interesting to build rapport and to allow everyone to speak their preferred languages when possible. Consider implementing project virtual rooms (see Chapter 19) that can provide a user directory to all employees and allow you to add team members from other companies and locations.

It is also important for everyone to know how to use some special – although basic – telephone functions, like *conferencing*. For example, when someone rings with an urgent question, you may want a specialist to quickly join the call and have an immediate problem-solving session. When you are at your desk you may know how to make this happen. If you are in another country or location, the telephone system may have different codes to activate this function and you must be able to obtain this information without much effort. The same is applicable for other functions, such as *recording* facilities for legal and ethical reasons such as detailed minute taking and interviews, *muting* your telephone to allow better quality during audio conferences, and procedures to order accessories like *headsets*, which increase comfort during long periods on the telephone.

Instructions about some relatively trivial activities (like setting-up out-of-office messages to inform other people about your absence periods) can also be made available if the companies and locations participating in the project are using different software solutions or versions. The availability of information on *remote access* is fundamental for global projects, as people must know how to connect to the company network from any location in the world – starting with their own homes – to read e-mails, to use shared file servers and the corporate intranet, and to access other applications. Another essential facility for frequent travellers is the availability of *webmail* functions, for that quick look into your e-mail inbox while waiting for the delayed flight.

It is good practice to have all the information available in electronic format for all locations. For more information on this, please refer to Chapter 19.

Evaluating the implementation

Some time after implementing the technology, preparing the documentation and informing all project team members, it is appropriate to evaluate the improvements and detect if further corrections are required, by deploying the same assessment survey (Table 16.1) and comparing the new results with the initial findings.

Table 16.2   Checklist: documentation and procedures for basic technologies

	Information available	In electronic format	Published	Accessible by all locations
Employees' basic information				
Telephone and FAX numbers				
e-mail addresses				
Locations				
Picture				
Languages				
Telephone functions				
Basic conferencing facilities				
Recording facilities				
Mute facilities				
Headsets (how to order)				
SMS (Code of conduct)				
e-mail functions				
e-mail address (how to order)				
Accessing your e-mail from other locations				
Out-of-office automated messages				
Use of wireless handheld devices				
Remote access				
High-speed internet connection (how to order)				
Remote access to the company network				
Webmail				
Wireless handheld devices				

ACTIONS FOR IMPROVEMENT

Revisit the list or mindmap created at the beginning of this module. What additional weak points did you recognise? What recommendations can you make to improve you organisation's infrastructure?

Now share your thoughts with other people, and read about their own learning (www. GlobalProjectManagement.org).

17 *Interactive Audio and Video*

There are different ways to hold conversations over a distance. Audio conferencing is perhaps the medium used most often during global projects. Low cost, ease to set up and low risk of technical problems are the main advantages of holding an audio conference instead of a video conference, and few people in the business environment would consider using web conferencing without the audio support. This justifies special attention when implementing the audio conferencing service most adapted to your needs. The use of video conferencing can help to establish trust when the stakeholders do not have the opportunity of meeting face-to-face regularly, requiring some investment in equipment, documentation and training.

Evaluation of current audio conferencing solutions

Before changing the conferencing facilities or documentation, a survey can help you to evaluate the efficiency of the existing services and procedures. You could complete the survey shown in Table 17.1 with the help of the mindmap you created at the beginning of this chapter.

Evaluation of new audio conferencing solutions

When evaluating different audio conferencing service providers, you can take into consideration the items on the survey above and other criteria relevant to your organisation. The main element for comparison is the simplicity to set up. Usually, the organiser establishes the conference by dialling a telephone number and inputting the organiser's 'pin' code. The participants dial the same number and input the participant codes. The total time to connect

---

AUDIO AND VIDEO CONFERENCING IN YOUR ORGANISATION

Do you have any difficulties in setting-up an audio conferencing meeting with other project team members? Do you know how to use the main functions to control and help your audio conferencing participants? How often do you use the video conferencing facilities? With what frequency do you face technical issues with the equipment? How quickly are these issues resolved? What other issues do you face regularly, due to lack of equipment or the absence of documentations and procedures to use the devices and to investigate problems?

Write on a list or mindmap the main issues you experience with audio and video conferencing equipment. For each point, make a recommendation based on your current knowledge of the area. While you read this chapter, complete your mindmap with other ideas you may have to improve the quality of your audio and conferencing facilities.

Table 17.1   Survey to identify efficiency of audio conferencing

Question	Strongly agree	Agree	Disagree	Strongly disagree
It is always easy and quick to set up audio conferences				
It is always easy and quick to join audio conferences				
All meeting organisers consistently distribute correct information on the conference telephone numbers and pin codes				
I know how to instruct a new colleague to request a new audio conferencing number				
The audio quality always ensures good communication				
I know how to monitor who is joining the conference, and how to block people from joining if they are not allowed to participate				
General comments about audio conferencing				
Suggestions on how to improve audio conferencing technology				

should be less than 20 seconds. To simplify the task for people working in different time zones and joining the conference from home or mobile telephones, you may require the availability of 'toll-free' numbers in the different countries where your stakeholders are located, with instructions in the local languages.

Privacy and security are very important aspects for many projects and nobody will feel comfortable exchanging important information without knowing who else may be listening to the call. Most audio conferencing services provide a control panel over the web, enabling the meeting organiser to detect the telephone numbers of the participants, allowing into the conference only those who identify themselves when joining the call.

Different service providers calculate various cost elements, such as duration of the calls, number of participants and the use of toll-free numbers. Initially you should estimate average usage figures for your company and then ask for detailed bills to control the costs and adapt the conferencing usage – or change the service provider after an evaluation period by using the real usage statistics to perform a new cost comparison.

Another feature that can be important for specific types of meetings is the possibility of recording the calls, in order to write detailed meeting minutes afterwards. Ethical and privacy issues must be investigated beforehand and usually all participants must be informed that

REAL-LIFE TECHNOLOGIES

Some examples of audio conferencing services:

- PowWowNow (www.powwownow.co.uk)
- ConferenceNow (www.conferencenow.co.uk)
- Arkadin (www.arkadin.com)
- Verizon (www.verizon.com).

See more examples online at www.GlobalProjectManagement.org.

recording is taking place. Be aware that the meeting effectiveness may suffer, as some people can feel uncomfortable in expressing concerns, making decisions or voicing their opinions when recording is taking place.

Implementing changes

After an evaluation and trial period, you can select one global project team or a group of project managers in different locations to perform a pilot implementation. The goal of the pilot will be to compile the procedures and documentation adapted to the needs of your organisation, and to ensure that the connections work from different countries. Sometimes there are informal rules and procedures that people already operate and you can use them when writing the new documentation.

Once the pilot is completed, you need to publish the procedures and instructions and make them available to all team members in the scope of the implementation.

Defining procedures for audio conferencing set-up

All global project team members must know how to request their own audio conferencing number, how to set up their conferences and what features are available during meetings. You can prepare the documentation for these activities and make sure that this knowledge is available to all team members, including people from other companies and locations. In this documentation, you may also suggest that the meeting organisers distribute their conference numbers, country telephone and toll-free numbers, and participant pin codes to all attendees. You need to avoid a group of people sharing the same account (with a single conference number), or define clear procedures to avoid a 'double-booking' crisis. See the example of a checklist for the audio conferencing documentation in Table 17.2.

Evaluating the implementation

Some time after implementing the audio conferencing solutions, preparing the documentation and informing all project team members, evaluate the improvements and detect if corrections are required by deploying the same assessment survey (Table 17.1) and comparing the new results with the initial findings.

Table 17.2   Checklist: documentation and procedures for audio conferencing

	Information available	In electronic format	Published	Accessible by all locations
How to request an audio conference account				
How to set up an audio conferencing session				
Functions available to the audio conferencing moderator				
Functions available to the audio conferencing participants				
List of all access numbers in different countries				

Video conferences

During research interviews and informal discussions with global project managers, it was surprising to discover that many people do not consider visual contact essential for meetings over distance and seldom use video conferencing. They organise all meetings by audio conference, and when the sharing of application screens or presentations is required, they employ web conferencing. When trying to understand the main reasons for this, it was clear that technology was the main barrier as there is a general impression that video conferencing takes more time to set up and is more likely to present problems and have poor quality of audio and video, or bad synchronisation of sound and images. Others, however, consider the visual contact essential, employing video conferencing whenever local meetings are not possible. Generally, they agree with the likelihood of technical failures, mentioning the need to be in the meeting rooms in advance, asking a remote colleague to help them setting-up the video connection and allowing some time to fix problems when they appear. Both cases show the need for better quality video conferencing equipment, documentation of clear procedures in how to set up the conferences and solve common problems, and creating a support group that can solve complex technical issues.

The main objective of video conferencing is to improve trust on global projects by allowing a visual contact among the participants. Since good quality of video, audio and the synchronisation of sound and image is essential, the companies must engage network specialists to evaluate and monitor the connections among different sites in order to validate if they are correctly dimensioned (bandwidth and latency). Most systems offer the basic functions, like zooming, adjusting image and sound, providing an address book and taking snapshots. Therefore, the main item for comparison is user-friendliness. People from different technical backgrounds must be able to operate the video conferencing equipment and use the basic functions in an intuitive manner.

Other functions that can increase the benefit of video conferencing are the use of special devices to send images of documents and small objects. This can also allow the drawing of schemas to improve the quality of knowledge sharing, without the need to operate complex software tools in real-time to send the same information.

Another function, equivalent to the recording of audio conversations, is the possibility of saving the whole meeting, in visual and audio formats, for later reference. The ethical and privacy concerns must be carefully evaluated: is this allowed in all companies and countries where your team members are located? In a similar way to the recording of audio conversations (explained earlier in this chapter), you must also be aware that people can have different sensitivities to being filmed.

For small meetings, and when only one person is joining the conference in each location, web conferencing with webcams can provide an equivalent visual contact to video conferencing, with fewer constraints. You must involve specialists to validate the impact on the network usage, in order to have good quality communication without creating problems for other applications sharing the same resources. The evaluation of costs must consider the impact on corporate networks, as well as the purchasing of equipment.

Evaluating existing video conferencing solutions

You can measure the satisfaction of global project managers and team members with the existing facilities by requesting that they participate in a survey. You can measure their satisfaction with the simplicity and efficiency of the facilities, to understand if they know how to use them. One example for this survey is provided in Table 17.3.

REAL-LIFE TECHNOLOGIES

Some examples of video conferencing technologies:

- video conferencing hardware – Polycom (www.polycom)
- video conferencing software – FlashMeeting (www.webconference.com)
- high-quality video conferencing via satellite broadcasting communications – SCS (www.satellite-commsys.com), TKO (www.tkoworks.com)
- telepresence – solutions that provide 'a sense of being there without going', by using high-quality network and equipment, simulating eye-contact, directing voices to the speakers, employing large screens for real-size images and using the same types of furniture and decoration across all rooms – VirtualLife (www.teliris.com)

See more examples online at www.GlobalProjectManagement.org.

Implementation of new video conferencing solutions

The video conferencing equipment should be selected according to the criteria specified above and the survey results. You can organise pilot sessions to validate the functions and the facility to use them. Besides the usual two-point connections, these sessions must also be organised by setting up video conferences with at least three different rooms, using the same type of equipment. Three-point conferencing is the ideal condition to validate how the equipment behaves in identifying who is speaking and switching the image accordingly. Additional sessions

Table 17.3   Survey to identify efficiency of video conferencing

Question	Strongly agree	Agree	Disagree	Strongly disagree
It is always easy to set up video conferences, never taking more than 2 minutes to start the meeting				
I know how to use the main video conferencing functions, and can share the images on my computer screen with the other locations				
I know how to show images of books, documents or small objects in a video conference				
I have already shared images of books, documents or small objects in a video conference				
I know how to add and refer to entries in the video conferencing address book				
I know how to request help in case of problems				
The support team is always helpful and quick in solving problems				
General comments about the video conferencing equipment				
Suggestions on how to improve the video conferencing technology				

must also validate whether the equipment can connect to other types of video conferencing, by connecting to main clients and suppliers and validating all the functions.

The deployment of video conferencing in meeting rooms must be done with special attention to the visual aspects, by validating if the whole room can be covered in the camera angle, and taking out the chairs in the black spots. The sound conditions must also be considered, by distributing the microphones and speakers in order to capture and reproduce the voices with similar volumes.

Defining procedures for video conferencing set-up

It is important to have procedures that explain the steps required to establish the connection and use the different facilities, such as the TVs, projectors, microphones, speakers, cameras and computers connected to the conferencing device. The different functions available must be clearly explained so that meeting organisers and participants can make best use of them during meetings. Table 17.4 provides a template for a documentation checklist.

Request full documentation from the video conferencing suppliers as they may have audio and video tutorials, brochures, reference guides and other types of information. In this case you only need to instruct the video conference users on how to find the material and adapt it to the particularities of your organisation. They need to practice and be familiar with the technology before organising important meetings through video conferencing.

Evaluating the implementation

After implementing the technology, preparing the documentation and informing all project team members, it is time to evaluate the improvements and detect if corrections are required, by deploying the same assessment survey (Table 17.3) and comparing the new results with the initial findings.

Table 17.4   **Checklist: documentation and procedures for video conferencing**

	Information available	In electronic format	Published	Accessible by all locations
How to activate all devices				
How to establish the connection				
What functions are available during video conferencing				
How to have multi-point conferences				
How to finish the video conferencing session				
How to request support				

ACTIONS FOR IMPROVEMENT

Revisit the list or mindmap created at the beginning of this module. What additional weak points did you recognise? What recommendations can you make to improve you organisation's audio and video conferencing facilities? Revisit the mindmaps you produced in other chapters and identify if the implementation of new audio and video conferencing equipment can provide solutions to open problems.

Now share your thoughts with other people, and read about their own learning (www. GlobalProjectManagement.org).

CHAPTER

18 *Interactive Text and Images*

This chapter outlines the technologies that can allow two or more people to interact without the need for audio or visual contact. A new generation of team members, well accustomed to chats, BBS, newsgroups, SMS and other media that allow the exchange of ideas with simple and short text messages, will feel comfortable having discussions while performing other tasks or having knowledge exchange sessions that complement the tasks with questions, hints and tips. This can be accomplished very easily with desktop sharing tools that allow people working in different corners of the planet to share computer screens in order to understand complex processes and solve problems. The main difference between the two technologies is the number of people involved in the discussion. While instant messaging tools are suitable for a few people to exchange ideas in an informal manner, larger meetings require more preparation and a different technology set: web conferencing. Meeting organisers can mix these two technologies with audio conferencing to attain a high level of efficiency when clear procedures are in place.

Evaluating technologies for instant messaging

The name says everything: the main element for comparison between different solutions is the ease of establishing the connection … instantly. The conversation using these tools may start spontaneously; when team members have a question about a specific topic or have achieved a project milestone, they can simply look in the directory, click on the project manager's name, open a chat session and start an informal discussion. When the instant messaging tools are integrated with other technologies like e-mail, IP telephones and virtual rooms, the communication can start from many different virtual places, allowing a natural flow of conversation that can be quite similar to having the whole project team in the same building.

INSTANT MESSAGING AND WEB CONFERENCING IN YOUR ORGANISATION

Are you allowed to use instant messaging to communicate with colleagues in other locations? Do you know how to start the session and use the main features? How often do you make presentations via web conferencing to team members in other locations? Do you also use this media to share documents and collaborate over distance? Is it easy to organise a meeting through web conferencing and inform the other participants? How long does it take to have all participants connected to the web conferencing session?

Write on a list or mindmap the weak points in the technologies your organisation uses to share text and images during meetings. For each point, make a recommendation based on your current knowledge in the area. While you read the chapter, complete your mindmap with other recommendations you would make to improve this infrastructure in your organisation.

The second important feature of instant messaging software is desktop sharing. The effect on global teams is very similar to when two or more people are in the same room and they can all see the same computer screen. They can better understand how to use an application, work together on a design activity, review specific sections of a blueprint, follow a project plan or prepare a document together. The main elements to be evaluated when comparing different solutions are the quality of the images across the network, the elapsed time required to reflect the updates into the remote distances and the usage of network bandwidth.

As an additional feature, a whiteboard application allows the exchange of quick drawings. This feature becomes less useful when desktop sharing is available and allows the use of other graphic tools to attain the same objective in a better way. As a last element of comparison, some companies may be required to keep a log of the chat sessions for legal reasons, and not all software solutions provide this capacity (this requirement must be considered carefully for projects involving different countries and companies: investigate if all legislations and corporate policies allow this recording of informal and personal discussions).

Certain software solutions are now implementing third dimension virtual workspaces, where users select avatars to simulate a real world experience in meeting people, sharing screens, accessing 3D models and having conversations. This feature can be interesting in specific corporate or country cultures, or for selected age groups.

Evaluation of the existing instant messaging solutions

When an organisation already has an instant messaging solution available, a survey can confirm its simplicity and usefulness. One example is supplied in Table 18.1, which can be completed with the points in the mindmap created at the beginning of this chapter.

Implementation of a new instant messaging solution

The implementation of this tool may involve setting up a directory server, integrating it with other directories the company may have for e-mails and telephones and carefully selecting a group of people, located in different countries that participate in the same project, to perform a proof of concept. This group can confirm the efficiency of the new technology solution by using the same questionnaire (see Table 18.1). After an initial period, the tool can be deployed to other countries and global projects, with the use and efficiency increasing exponentially as the community includes more people. The questionnaire can be used again later when a new group of people discovers the technology, to identify cultural differences in using the tool and complement the existing documentation, fostering a more efficient adoption.

REAL-LIFE TECHNOLOGIES

Some examples of instant messaging technologies:
- Jabber (www.jabber.org)
- Miranda IM (www.miranda-im.org)
- Microsoft Office Communicator (office.microsoft.com/communicator)

See more examples online at www.GlobalProjectManagement.org.

Table 18.1   Survey to identify efficiency of instant messaging

Question	Strongly agree	Agree	Disagree	Strongly disagree
It is always easy to start an instant messaging session, never taking more than a couple of seconds to find my colleagues in the directory				
I know how to use the main instant messaging functions and how to share the images on my computer screen with other locations				
I prefer to use the chat feature instead of the telephone for simple discussions				
I use the chat feature sometimes but prefer using the telephone to hold discussions				
Instant messaging is an important tool for social discussions and to build a network of contacts				
On what professional occasions do you find instant messaging useful				
General comments about the instant messaging equipment				
Suggestions on how to improve the instant messaging technology				

Defining procedures for instant messaging set-up

When good and simple tools are deployed, the main procedures must explain how to start the instant messaging conversation, how to add people to the 'favourite' lists, give examples of desktop sharing and a troubleshooting session to allow the team members to quickly resolve their problems and continue using the tool. The documentation must include a reference guide to all functions available. The preparation of documentation and procedures can use a checklist to track the completeness of the different steps (see example in Table 18.2).

Evaluating the implementation

Some time after implementing the technology, preparing the documentation and informing all project team members, you ,may evaluate the improvements and detect if corrections are required, by deploying the same assessment survey (Table 18.1) and comparing the new results with the initial findings.

Table 18.2   Checklist: documentation and procedures for instant messaging

	Information available	In electronic format	Published	Accessible by all locations
How to start the software				
How to start a session				
How to create a list of people whom I need to contact frequently				
What functions are available				
How to share my computer screen with others				
How to finish the session				
How to request support				

Evaluating technologies for web conferencing

There are two types of platforms for web conferencing: proprietary client software (normally available only to computers inside the corporate network) and Internet-based conferencing (service hosted by a conferencing provider and available to anyone connected to the Internet, via a web browser). The first option usually requires the company to set up one directory server for easy meeting scheduling, and is only recommended when all participants in the project are connected to the corporate network. The second type is suggested when stakeholders are from different companies or attend meetings from locations outside the corporate network.

Web conferences often involve many participants and are scheduled in advance. They must be very easy to set up and join: usually the meeting requests include a web link or icon which directs the participants to the meeting workspace via the Internet. When all meeting attendees have joined the workspace, the main functions available to the organiser are chat, whiteboard and desktop sharing – already described in the instant messaging topic (see page 197). One additional feature available is voting, which can be used to gather opinions on specific topics in a well organised way. Instead of asking a general question ('does everyone agree with this decision?'), which is not efficient in meetings with many participants, the organiser asks the same question through a voting panel, requesting the participants to answer using the keyboard.

Similar to audio conferencing, the web conferencing price models can be based on the maximum number of participants and the connection time, thus requiring an up-front study on the potential needs of web meetings and periodic reviews of the real usage to decide on taking different price alternatives or changing the web conferencing supplier.

Evaluation of existing web conferencing solutions

A survey can allow an evaluation of the efficiency of the services and procedures, in order to improve their quality. One example is shown on Table 18.3.

Table 18.3   Survey to identify efficiency of web conferencing

Question	Strongly agree	Agree	Disagree	Strongly disagree
It is always easy and quick to set up web conferences				
It is always easy and quick to join web conferences				
All meeting organisers consistently distribute the correct link to join the conference				
I know how to instruct a colleague to create a new web conferencing account				
The quality and speed of the images always ensures good communication				
I know how to monitor who is joining the conference, and how to block people from joining if they are not allowed to participate				
General comments about the web conferencing suite				
Suggestions on how to improve the web conferencing technology				

Implementation of web conferencing

After selecting the ideal web conferencing service for your global projects, you can ask a limited group of users to evaluate the tool. After that, an international deployment must follow different phases, carefully measuring the impact on the network and avoiding impacts on the existing infrastructure. The different functions, the quality of support from the supplier and the time required to refresh the screens over distance are other examples of elements to be validated before a worldwide implementation.

Defining procedures for web conferencing set -up

Procedures must be available to all global project team members, explaining how to create a web conferencing account, how to schedule a meeting, how to start and manage the session and how to use the available features. It may also be useful to create a standard in how the meeting organisers distribute the conference instructions to all attendees in a quick manner. See an example of a checklist that contains the main documentation items in Table 18.4.

REAL-LIFE TECHNOLOGIES

Some examples of technologies being deployed to share text, images and applications across locations are:

- Web conferencing – Convenos (www.convenos.com), webconference (www.webconference.com), Microsoft Office Live Communications Server (office.microsoft.com/en-us/communicationsserver), WebEx (www.webex.com)

- Virtual worlds– Tixeo Meeting 3D (www.tixeo.com), www.activeworlds.com (www.activeworlds.com)

- Third-dimension design tools that allow collaborative work over distance – The CSIRO's Haptic Workbench (www.csiro.au)

See more examples online at www.GlobalProjectManagement.org.

Table 18.4   Checklist: documentation and procedures for web conferencing

	Information available	In electronic format	Published	Accessible by all locations
How to request a web conferencing account				
How to include the web conferencing information in the meeting invitation				
How to start a session				
How to share a computer screen				
What functions are available to the meeting moderator				
What functions are available to the meeting participants				
How to avoid unwanted people joining the conference and accessing the information				
How to finish the session				
How to request support				

Evaluating the implementation

After implementing the technology, preparing the documentation and informing all project team members, it is time to evaluate the improvements and detect if corrections are required, by deploying the same assessment survey (Table 18.3) and comparing the new results with the initial findings.

ACTIONS FOR IMPROVEMENT

Revisit the list or mindmap created at the beginning of this module. What additional weak points did you recognise? What recommendations are you going to make to improve you organisation's infrastructure? Revisit the mindmaps you produced in other chapters and identify if instant messaging and web conferencing can provide solutions to your challenges. Share your thoughts with other people, and read about their own learning (www.GlobalProjectManagement.org).

19 *Knowledge Sharing*

Collaborative environments need to be available on global projects to facilitate the sharing of information about the project and the products. The project manager can create the project management plan with the participation of team members in all locations, and keep all its documents in a shared workspace. The team members can organise review cycles for design documents, keeping different versions and a history of the changes. Project-related information, like the global project binder, can be maintained in shared tables or spreadsheets, allowing the owners of tasks, issues and risks to keep their information accurate in real time and accessible to all stakeholders.

Another form of collaboration goes beyond formal documentation, by collecting knowledge in an informal manner, through discussion groups, web links and project announcements. Originated from the BBS (Bulletin Board Systems) and newsgroups, and using a similar language and structure to chat rooms, discussion boards have the advantage of keeping discussions stored in a shared place and allowing the stakeholders to search for information at any time during the project. Global project offices can establish procedures to archive the knowledge base so that it can serve as a basis for future projects.

Evaluating technologies for knowledge sharing

International companies need to consider different software solutions to satisfy all their knowledge-sharing requirements and the main objective of the evaluation phase is to guarantee a good integration level among the different collaborative tools, which might also be combined with e-mail, web conferencing and calendar systems. Proprietary software can force companies to use a complete suite of tools from the same supplier and sometimes these are not the best options available. Global organisations might consider the use of open solutions for better integration and a wider choice of complementary packages.

KNOWLEDGE SHARING INFRASTRUCTURE IN YOUR ORGANISATION

Is there a standard knowledge-sharing tool in your company? Is it easy to use? How long does it take to publish a project document? How long does it take to find a document within the sub-directories and folders? How many team members use the knowledge-sharing infrastructure, instead of distributing files by e-mail? Are you sharing other type of information, besides documents and project status?

Write on a list or mindmap the weak points in your organisation's infrastructure. For each point, make a recommendation based on your current knowledge of the area. While you read the chapter, complete your mindmap with other ideas for improvement.

The first requirement for knowledge-sharing suites is a good system for document collaboration, which allows different team members to checkout, update documents, submit them for review, and publish a final version. The software must recognise all document types: text editors, spreadsheets, presentations, design schemas, program sources, blueprints and other files applicable to the different projects in your company. The usual knowledge management activities must be performed as easily in the knowledge-sharing software as in older file sharing systems: that is, to look for a specific document, to edit it and to save a new version. The creation of historic versions, back-ups, archiving and indexing must be performed smoothly by the software with little or no human intervention. Complex or time-consuming activities may inhibit the use of the collaborative environment.

A second requirement for knowledge-sharing software is the management of discussion groups. The project office or project manager can create various groups, according to the categories of information and the types of stakeholders exchanging information (for example, environmental aspects, engineering standards, technical discussions, marketing strategies, sales forecasts, and so on). The project team members can create discussion threads, one for every topic of interest: technical or environmental discussions, suggestions to improve the quality or reduce the cost of the project deliverables, informal conversations that may reveal potential risks, opportunities or issues. When analysing the efficiency of the tool to manage the discussions, think about how intuitive it would be for any project stakeholders to write new discussion threads, to be informed about threads created by other people, to detect which replies were given to specific threads and to search for information in all threads.

Project announcements are an additional and important feature, since global project teams cannot have wallboards to share personal events (like birthdays and marriages), project matters (new project members, important milestones, decisions, changes), external events that may affect the project (press releases, environmental reports, changes in the organisational structure) and project metrics (for example, important deviations on cost, schedule, quality and customer satisfaction). The announcement board must allow the posting of text, pictures and hyperlinks to project documents with detailed information on the topics being published.

REAL-LIFE TECHNOLOGIES

Some examples of technologies being deployed to share information over distance and to publish project information are:

- Content Management Systems (CMS) – Microsoft Office SharePoint Server (sharepoint.microsoft.com)

- Open Source Content Management Systems (CMS) – Joomla (www.joomla.org), Mambo (source.mambo-foundation.org), PostNuke (www.postnuke.com), Typo3 CMS (www.typo3.com), see site OpensourceCMS (www.opensourcecms.com) for a comprehensive list

- Collaborative authoring software ('wiki') – MediaWiki (www.mediawiki.org), Tikiwiki (www.tikiwiki.org)

- Web logs (blogs) – WordPress (www.wordpress.org)

- SPIP (www.spip.net)

- Information sharing – Microsoft Office Groove (office.microsoft.com/groove)

- Discussion groups – phpBB (www.phpbb.com)

See more examples online at www.GlobalProjectManagement.org.

Evaluating the existing knowledge-sharing solutions

When the organisation or project already deploys knowledge-sharing solutions for collaboration among distant team members, a survey (see example in Table 19.1) can identify the simplicity of use and compliance with the requirements identified in the section above. In this survey, you can confirm if other team members share your impression, by comparing the results with the mindmap you created at the beginning of the chapter.

Implementing a new knowledge-sharing solution

After all the different components are selected, validated and integrated, a pilot implementation is recommended to identify how the stakeholders are using the different functions and to

Table 19.1   Survey to identify efficiency of existing knowledge sharing suites

Question	Strongly agree	Agree	Disagree	Strongly disagree
It is always easy and quick to publish information about the project				
It is always easy and quick to create and update the project documents				
It is always easy and quick to find the project documents and information				
All team members consistently publish up-to-date information and documents about the project tasks under their responsibility				
I know how to instruct a new colleague to obtain access to the knowledge-sharing system				
I consider it important to share personal events, external information and the evolution of the project metrics with the project team members and other stakeholders				
I find it easy to share personal events, external information and the evolution of the project metrics with the project team members and other stakeholders, using the knowledge-sharing suite				
General comments about the knowledge-sharing suite				
Suggestions on how to improve the knowledge-sharing technology				

Table 19.2   Checklist: documentation and procedures for knowledge sharing

	Information available	In electronic format	Published	Accessible by all locations
How to request access to the knowledge-sharing solution				
How to request installation of desktop software required by the knowledge-sharing solution				
How to access the knowledge-sharing software				
How to find and publish project information				
How to find and publish project documents				
How to create a new discussion group				
How to post new threads or topics on the discussion groups				
How to search for information on the discussion groups				
How to use pictures or hyperlinks in the project announcements				
How to lock files, to avoid other people changing them at the same time as you				
How to create online lists and tables that allow the update of information items by various team members at the same time				
How to finish the session				
How to request support				

determine the best approach to deploy the knowledge-sharing suite into all global projects. This approach is also recommended when some components are being added or updated in the existing knowledge-sharing suite.

At the end of the pilot phase, the evaluation survey can be announced to all the participants, identifying if the implementation can proceed to other projects or locations in the same organisation, or even extended to partner companies. Depending on the survey results, a second pilot phase can be organised to correct important gaps between the requirements and the solution in place.

Defining procedures for knowledge-sharing set-up

All global project stakeholders must know how to prepare their computers to access the knowledge-sharing systems (for example, by installing client software or plug-ins), how to obtain access to the applications (for example, by requesting user identifications, passwords or access rights) and how to use all the basic knowledge-sharing functions. The structure of the documentation must show how the various applications are integrated, how to publish the information and how to search for it. You can use the checklist in Table 19.2 opposite to produce and publish the documentation to help all project stakeholders accessing and using the knowledge-sharing suite.

Evaluating the implementation

Some time after implementing the new technology components, preparing and publishing the documentation and announcing the new solution to all project team members, you may evaluate the improvements and detect if corrections are required by deploying the same assessment survey (Table 19.2) and comparing the new results with the initial findings.

A new implementation cycle can start to correct problems or to improve the quality of the knowledge-sharing tools and the documentation.

ACTIONS FOR IMPROVEMENT

Revisit the list or mindmap created at the beginning of this module. What additional weak points did you recognise? What recommendations can you make to improve your organisation's knowledge-sharing infrastructure? Revisit the mindmaps you produced in other chapters and identify if the knowledge-sharing infrastructure can provide solutions to open problems.

Now share your thoughts with other people, and read about their own learning (www. GlobalProjectManagement.org).

20 *Collaborative Project Management Software*

Collaborative project management software is the technology platform that provides global project managers and project office administrators with the automated tools to create the project management plan, to monitor the execution of the deliverables, to control the issues, risks, quality, cost and time and to obtain approval for the project closure. Project management software is an important tool for traditional projects during processes that include calculations and diagramming techniques, such as 'activity sequencing', 'activity resource estimating', 'schedule development', 'schedule control', 'cost estimating' and 'cost control' (PMI, 2004). For global projects, the implementation of collaborative project management software is also essential for all processes that require effective collaboration between the project manager and the team members in different locations when defining activities, identifying and analysing risks, directing and managing project execution, monitoring progress and controlling project work. This chapter considers the collaborative project management software as the subset of the Project Management Information System (PMIS), which is composed of the essential tools, methods and processes that ensure successful management of global projects.

Collaborative project management software can also help to satisfy the organisational governance requirements, by providing program managers, portfolio managers, project managers and executive stakeholders with summarised project performance measurements and consolidated metrics, simplifying the reporting preparation and information distribution activities

Evaluating collaborative project management software tools

The main objectives of collaborative project management software tools are to centralise the project information (including project plan, schedule, risks, issues and cost) and create

---

COLLABORATIVE PROJECT MANAGEMENT SOFTWARE IN YOUR ORGANISATION

What type of project management software do you use in your organisation? What types of project information are maintained using this tool? How long does it take to add new information items with the tool? How long does it take to extract and summarise the information? How many stakeholders consult the tool to update the project items and check on the status of your project? Is this tool integrated with other tools, or do you need to enter the same information twice in different applications?

Write on a list or mindmap the weak points in your organisation's project management software. For each point, make a recommendation based on your current knowledge of the area. While you read the chapter, complete your mindmap with other recommendations to improve the project management software in your organisation.

automated rules for project administration. These rules will trigger the distribution of project reports, remind project team members of due actions and issues, alert the project manager of imminent risks and raise the project management awareness of deviations in schedule, cost or quality. International companies can follow the steps below to evaluate the various software alternatives, and compare with the existing system:

1. Define the main objectives of the project management software, together with the company senior management and a representative number of project managers and stakeholders from different countries. Agree on measurable success criteria for the implementation.
2. Analyse past and ongoing global projects in a representative number of company locations, to create an inventory of the different project documents, reports and tools. This will result in a comprehensive view of the various types of project information.
3. For each type of document, report and tool, classify the information items into *mandatory*, *beneficial* or *optional*.
4. Identify the main information items that can trigger *alerts* and require *actions* from the project manager or stakeholders.
5. For each software solution being evaluated, identify the items completely or partially available.
6. Evaluate the integration of each solution with other knowledge-sharing and project management tools, such as timesheet allocation, scheduling diagrams, cost tracking mechanisms and quality assessment.
7. Compare the percentages of information available for each PMIS solution and determine which alternative best fits the company requirements.
8. Complete this information with the items in the mindmap you created at the beginning of this chapter.

Table 20.1 provides an example of an evaluation sheet for three collaborative project management software solutions, illustrating a possible output of the steps above.

To increase the adoption of the new tool by the project team members across the globe, a survey can be prepared to gather various opinions on the software solutions being analysed. This survey can be used to collect information on the existing software tools, providing additional criteria for the evaluation of the new solution. Table 20.2 shows an example of this survey.

REAL-LIFE TECHNOLOGIES

Some examples of collaborative project management systems are:

- Microsoft Office Project server – www.microsoft.com/project
- Microsoft Office Project Portfolio server – office.microsoft.com/en-us/portfolioserver
- Primavera – www.oracle.com
- Clarity – www.ca.com
- Compuware changepoint – www.compuware.com

See more examples online at www.GlobalProjectManagement.org.

Table 20.1   Collaborative project management software – comparison matrix

Documents, reports and tools	Existing software	Software A	Software B
Network diagramming tool (mandatory)	Yes	Yes	No
Schedule network analysis (beneficial)	Yes	Yes	No
Project detailed schedule (mandatory, with automated 'red' warning to the activity owners on due actions, and 'green' when all predecessors are completed and the activity can initiate)	Yes	Partial (no warnings)	Yes
Automated milestone schedule (mandatory)	Yes	Yes	No
Online risk log (mandatory, with automated warnings to the risk owners)	No	Partial (no warnings)	Yes
Risk bubble chart (beneficial)	No	No	Yes
Online issues log (mandatory, with automated warnings to the issue owners)	No	Partial (no warnings)	Yes
Change control system (mandatory, with online approval)	Yes	Partial (no warnings)	Yes
Progress report (mandatory, with distribution to executive stakeholders)	Partial (distribution manual)	Partial (distribution manual)	Yes
Integration with project request system	No	Yes, by scripts	Yes, by scripts
Integration with timesheet (time allocation) systems	No	No	Yes, by scripts
Integration with financial systems	Yes	Yes, by file transfer	Yes, by scripts

Software B is recommended, as most automated functions are available and the integration with existing systems is possible. A separate tool is required to provide network diagramming and schedule network analysis.

Defining procedures for the collaborative project management software

All global project stakeholders must know how to prepare their computers to access the collaborative project management systems (for example, by installing client software or plug-ins), how to obtain access to the applications (for example, by requesting user identifications, passwords or access rights) and how to use all the basic functions of the different software components. The structure of the documentation might show how the various components are integrated, how the software is integrated with other company tools, how to update the information and how to extract reports and perform consolidations. You can use the checklist on Table 20.3 to produce and publish the documentation required by all project stakeholders who need to access and use the collaborative project management software.

Table 20.2   **Survey to identify efficiency of the collaborative project management software**

Question	Strongly agree	Agree	Disagree	Strongly disagree
It is always easy and quick to enter the project information in the project management software				
It is always easy and quick to obtain information from the software tool				
All global project managers consistently use the tool to ensure the project information is up-to-date				
The method used to inform me of my due items is very efficient				
It is always easy and quick to update the action and risk items assigned to me				
I know how to find and update the items assigned to my colleagues when they are absent				

General comments about the collaborative project management software
Suggestions on how to improve the collaborative project management software

Implementing the new collaborative project management software

Perform a trial installation to validate whether the required functions perform as expected and allow a number of project managers and stakeholders from different countries to use the selected tool. Discuss their impressions on the ease-of-use, intuitiveness and completeness of the different alternatives. You can use the survey (Table 20.2) to evaluate the new software and compare with the existing solution, and detect what the real improvements are, from the perspective of the project team members.

Evaluating the implementation

Some time after implementing the new collaborative project management software, preparing and publishing the documentation, announcing the new solution to all project team members and providing training, you may evaluate the improvements and detect if corrections are required by deploying the same assessment survey (Table 20.2) and comparing the new results with the initial findings. The results will serve as a basis for the preparation of a strategy to correct the problems, improve the usability and increase adoption.

Table 20.3   Checklist: documentation and procedures for the collaborative project management software

	Information available	In electronic format	Published	Accessible by all locations
How to request access to the project management software				
How to request installation of desktop software, add-ons and plug-ins required by the project management software				
How to access the project management software				
How to update project information				
What information is synchronised with other company systems				
How to produce consolidated reports				
How to find and update the items assigned to my colleagues when they are absent				
How to request support				

ACTIONS FOR IMPROVEMENT

Revisit the list or mindmap created at the beginning of this module. What additional weak points did you recognise? What recommendations will you make to improve your organisation's project management software? Revisit the mindmaps you produced in other chapters and identify if collaborative project management software can provide solutions to open problems.

Now share your thoughts with other people and read about their own learning (www. GlobalProjectManagement.org).

Part IV: Key concepts

There are different types of technologies that can improve collaboration during global projects: basic infrastructure (telephones, e-mails, directories and remote access tools), solutions for interactive audio and video conferencing, solutions for interactive exchange of text and images (chat and web conferencing), knowledge-sharing packages and collaborative project management software.

- The main steps to select and deploy collaborative tools for global projects are the understanding of the technological alternatives, the evaluation of existing technologies, the implementation of changes, the preparation of documentation and procedures and the post-implementation evaluation.

- Surveys can help to identify problems with the existing technologies and the lack of documentation.
- Well-prepared trial periods and pilot groups are extremely helpful for the evaluation of new technologies.

Part IV: Further reading

Edwards, A. and Wilson, J.R. (2004) *Implementing Virtual Teams: A Guide to Organizational and Human Factors*

The authors provide a good analysis of current and future technologies for communications in virtual teams.

Khazanchi, D. and Zigurs, I. (2006) *Patterns of Effective Management of Virtual Projects: An Exploratory Study*

The authors present a comparison of tools for virtual collaboration and project management.

Part IV: Interactive section

Share your experience of collaborative tools during global projects (www. GlobalProjectManagement.org):

- How did you adapt the checklists to your situation?
- How did you adapt the surveys to your organisation?
- What is your opinion on the tools available on the market, do you have positive or negative experiences to share with other people?
- Are you using a different category of tool not covered in this book? What feedback can you provide on these tools?

V Adoption of Collaborative Tools

Staples, Wong and Cameron (2004) identified that companies must establish conditions for the collaboration and communication systems to be employed and that these must, 'fit with the strategy, structure, culture, processes, and IS infrastructure (for example, training and support).' Project team members will exchange more information using the collaborative tools, write more project documents in the project management system and capture more ideas during meetings, once they know how to use the technology in an effective manner and see the benefits of doing so.

The first objective of this chapter is to present a strategy to improve the efficiency of global projects, by fostering the use of the collaborative tools implemented in your company, improving the communication channels among global team members.

The second objective of the recommendations in this chapter is to identify the way people communicate in their day-to-day tasks, in order to prepare the collaborative tools to simulate their local activities. When the communication technology in place does not allow the ideas to flow naturally, there is a tendency to favour local contacts rather than distant colleagues. The number of informal contacts among global team members – and therefore the global communication channels – can increase if technology is available to allow social discussions to complement work-related conversations.

When global team members can complement verbal discussions by drawing schemas, sharing applications and taking online meeting minutes, they increase the quality of information exchanged. This reduces the time lost during meetings and discussions, minimises the number of misunderstandings and raises the quality level of the project information. The third objective of this chapter is to allow the use of rich media to improve the quality level of information exchanges during the whole project life cycle.

At the end of this chapter, you will know how to increase collaboration during global projects, through the correct and effective use of all collaborative tools implemented in your organisation.

21 *Getting Connected*

Most companies have a set of basic tools in place, without formal recommendations and procedures to help new employees to get connected to global collaboration. Some people do not adapt their communication style to the different types of technologies available, generating misunderstandings and conflicts. This chapter describes how the implementation of basic rules and practices can improve the efficiency of communications by e-mail and telephones.

Understanding what can be improved

The first step is to understand how the global team members see the use of e-mails, telephones and other basic technologies, identifying areas for improvement. You can develop a structured interview (illustrated by Table 21.1) to identify positive and negative aspects and start collecting recommendations. The first step is to adapt the questions to your organisation and technologies, including discussion topics for webmail, remote connections and other components of the basic infrastructure discussed in Chapter 16. When this is completed, perform a pilot interview with some colleagues in the same location as you, to validate and improve the questions. With the help of colleagues from other countries, you can then translate the questions to the various local languages, asking them to conduct local interviews. The next step is to combine all the suggestions received with the basic recommendations in this chapter, and write the first set of good practices. You can use the same interview at a later stage in order to detect the effectiveness of the practices and to identify areas for improvement.

The following list of recommendations is especially applicable to global project team members, based on the Netiquette and other sources of good practices for virtual teams and virtual projects:

- Keep in mind that global project stakeholders travel across time zones and sometimes will not answer to e-mail messages quickly simply because of the time differences. You should

---

YOUR EXPERIENCE OF E-MAIL AND TELEPHONE COMMUNICATIONS

Write on a list or mindmap the situations when e-mails or telephones are not used correctly, in your opinion. On a separate list, write your observations on good practices in the use of these communication media. Using all the e-mails you received in the last working day, take some time to mark the good and bad examples of communication.

While you read this chapter, and during the next week, complete your mindmap with the main characteristics of remarkable e-mail messages you receive (the ones that strike you with their simplicity and effectiveness on conveying a message). For every message that annoys you, or creates misunderstanding, note down the main reasons why it is bad communication and what recommendations you would give to avoid this type of e-mail in the future.

Table 21.1   Interview to understand the use of e-mails and telephones

Question	Note all answers below
Do you think you receive too many e-mails? If yes – give some examples of the types of e-mails you should stop receiving.	
Do you think people should use other communication media rather than e-mails – such as telephones and chat? Please give examples of when this would be the case.	
What suggestions would you give to other people in order to improve the overall understanding of e-mail messages?	
What suggestions would you give to other people in order to improve the understanding of telephone discussions?	
Do you think your colleagues use mobile phones appropriately? If not, do you have any examples of situations when they could have used another type of communication?	
What do you think about the use of mobile phones and e-mails outside office hours – is it appropriate or disturbing? What are your recommendations?	

also consider local holidays and vacations to understand possible reasons for delays in receiving a reply.

- Inverse your position on the previous point: develop a practice of always replying to important messages on the same day, and when your answer requires more investigation, inform the sender of this and give an estimate of when you can write the full reply. This way your usual correspondents (which are your global project team members and colleagues) will know that 'no reply' means 'not available at the moment', and they may try another person or wait longer.
- Remember to write 'out of office' automated messages, which will inform your correspondents when you plan to be out of the office or in full-day meetings, without access to your e-mails.
- Be aware of cultural differences when reading or writing sentences with humour, slang and local acronyms, always avoiding sarcasm.
- Remember that time zones, date formats and measurements can vary from your own. As an example, prefer to specify, 'at 17:00 CET on 5 April 2006', instead of '5/4/2006 - 5:00'.
- Rules of conduct differ according to the context (private discussions with old friends versus business discussions with colleagues you never met face-to-face), countries and company cultures. Always remember that your message can be forwarded to other people in different contexts.

REAL-LIFE EXPERIENCE

Before trying to define a complete set of recommendations for electronic media, international companies must ensure that all employees know and comply with a basic set of guidelines. The 'Network Etiquette' (Netiquette) from the Internet Engineering Task Force provides some interesting recommendations (adapted from Hambridge, 1995):

- Use only mixed case (NEVER SENTENCES IN UPPER CASE) and think twice before writing a smiley ;-).
- Always write a subject heading and make it representative of the e-mail contents. e-mail applications can group items with the same heading and use it to find similar messages, thus the headings should be changed only when the conversation topic changed from the original message. To avoid confusion, always write a new message when you want to talk about a different topic to the initial discussion.
- Wait overnight to send emotional responses to messages.
- Be careful when replying to messages sent to a large group of people. Prefer to have direct conversations with a few of them until a conclusion is reached, and then inform everyone who received the original message.
- Always include a short signature, with your e-mail address for replies, and with your telephone numbers when you prefer the conversation to continue via that medium.
- Before replying, always carefully check your e-mail for more recent messages on the same topic, as they can change the requirements – or simply remove the need for your answer.
- Most e-mails exchanged over the Internet are not secure (except if special measures are in place). Never write sensitive or confidential topics in unsecured messages.
- Understand and comply with the copyright laws of all the countries involved in the project, before distributing material from other authors in e-mails.
- Always keep the original text intact when forwarding one message to other recipients. Consider asking for authorisation (beforehand) and including the original sender as a recipient in the forwarded e-mails, mainly for sensitive topics.

- Try to avoid sending messages with large attachments (a good rule of thumb is to avoid sending files with more than 2GB, as they may be blocked by some networks or fill the available space in your correspondent's e-mail account). A good option is to always store documents in the knowledge-sharing systems (see Chapter 19) and send links in the e-mail message. When you have a valid reason to send the attachment (for example, to people without access to the knowledge-sharing system), also include the link in the e-mail message. This will allow other people receiving the e-mail to decide if they want to suppress the attachment, while keeping only the link to the original document.
- A good rule of thumb, mainly in multicultural environments, 'Be conservative in what you send, and liberal in what you receive' (Hambridge, 1995).

What to avoid in e-mail discussions

Generally, avoid writing or saying anything you would not state in a face-to-face discussion. Moreover, avoid discussing any sensitive or personal topics that can give scope for misunderstandings and generate conflicts. Face-to-face and telephone contact should be kept as your preferred communication method for these types of dialogue.

Other rules of thumb that are especially applicable to global projects are:

- Avoid using e-mails for urgent information or requests when you cannot be sure of other people's locations, time zones or availability. If you do so, use 'read receipts' to confirm if all the target audience received the messages on time.
- Avoid adopting e-mail as your main communication tool when managing a global project. Checkpoint meetings, steering committee meetings, knowledge-sharing tools, collaborative project management systems and informal discussions must continue to exist, being your main instruments for project monitoring and control.
- The e-mails should not be used as a 'file transfer' tool. Companies deploy antivirus solutions that scan e-mails and suppress attachments that may contain malicious code. Projects need to provide file transfer platforms for the exchange of computer programs, scripts and all other file types, giving access to all project team members. The project virtual room can also serve this purpose, but sometimes it has limitations on the file sizes, blocking the information exchange at critical moments of the project and impacting the schedule of important activities.

Using telephones

Telephones should replace e-mails on quick and timely communications, to understand concerns, feelings and motivations of global project team members, to discuss sensitive matters, to solve conflicts and to build trust.

As telephone calls can be disruptive, check the calendars and availability plans before making the call. This rule is especially important for mobile phones in order to avoid disturbing meetings. With the added complexity of people travelling across time zones, knowing the location of your correspondents can ensure you will only call other team members outside business hours for urgent subjects. When calling people from other countries, you should understand what their working days and hours are, and their country cultures and company policies applicable to telephone use outside office time.

If the communication is not urgent enough to justify calling your colleagues outside business hours, you can always leave a voice mail message, asking them to return your call – specifying your location and a preferred time to call you. If they do not return your call in an acceptable time, do not assume there is a problem: you should check their availability in their electronic calendars, with other colleagues or their managers.

What to avoid in telephone discussions

You should always try to have face-to-face discussions for sensitive matters and conflicts. When the telephone must be used, ensure that you and the other person are isolated from other colleagues, reserving time in advance for the discussion.

YOUR LEARNING ON E-MAIL AND TELEPHONE COMMUNICATIONS

Revisit the list or mindmap created at the beginning of this module. What additional recommendations would you give to global project managers and team members? Which recommendations in this chapter would not work in your company or country?

Now share your thoughts with other people, and read about their own experiences (www. GlobalProjectManagement.org).

22 *Effective Audio and Video Conferences*

Many global project managers and team members have had poor experiences of meetings held via audio and video conferencing. Misunderstandings, conflicts, background noises and excessive idle time until all participants are connected are all examples of situations that create frustration for the meeting participants.

This chapter describes how the meeting organisers and participants can follow some basic rules and practices to improve the efficiency of communication by audio and video conferencing, when planning, moderating, participating and closing the meeting.

Understanding what can be improved

The first step is to understand how effective meetings via audio and video conferencing are currently, and identify the areas for improvement. You can develop a structured interview (illustrated by Table 22.1) to understand the current caveats and start collecting recommendations. After conducting interviews, combine the answers with the other recommendations in this chapter, and write the first set of good practices for audio and video conferences.

You could use the same interview later, in order to detect the effectiveness of the good practices, and to identify areas for improvement.

Using audio conferences

Audio conferencing connects two or more sites with audio links so that participants can converse, interact and share views. It is used frequently during the project execution, monitoring and controlling activities, when the team is already established, and after the project plan has been prepared.

YOUR EXPERIENCE OF AUDIO AND VIDEO CONFERENCING

Write on a list or mindmap the situations when, in your opinion, audio and video conferencing facilities are not used correctly. Make another list of what you consider to be good practices for the use of these communication media.

When you read this chapter, and during the coming weeks, complete your mindmap with the good practices employed by other people to organise and host audio and video conferencing. Note the constructive behaviours other people adopt during these meetings and how they help to increase understanding and collaboration. Observe the situations when certain attitudes generated tension or conflicts, and what recommendations you would give to avoid this behaviour in the future.

Table 22.1   Interview to understand the use of audio and video conferences

Question	Note all answers below
In your opinion, what types of meetings are most suitable for audio conferencing?	
What meetings are not suitable for audio conferencing, and what type of media would you use instead?	
What are the main reasons for misunderstandings during audio conferencing, and how to avoid them?	
When scheduling and preparing a meeting by audio conferencing, what are the mandatory steps?	
In your opinion, what types of meetings are most suitable for video conferencing?	
What meetings are not suitable for video conferencing, and what media would you use?	
What are the main reasons for misunderstandings during video conferencing, and how to avoid them?	
When *scheduling and preparing* a meeting by video conferencing, what are the mandatory steps?	
Do you have any other suggestions for people *organising* audio and video conferencing?	
Do you have any other suggestions for people *attending* audio and video conferences?	

This chapter discusses how to achieve a good level of efficiency during audio conferences, by suggesting good practices for meeting preparation, hosting and participation. The next chapter will show how to combine audio and web conferencing to improve the efficiency further.

Any good meeting starts with excellent *preparation*. For audio conferences, some good practices are:

• Always issue the meeting request a few days in advance along with the conference telephone number details and the access numbers for all countries attending the meeting.
• Never organise an audio conference with a duration of more than 2 hours. When the number of topics requires more time, separate the meeting into two distinct parts, leaving at least 10 minutes interval between them. A preferred approach is to divide the meeting into logical sections, and to schedule them on different days.

- As a meeting organiser, commence the conferencing facilities at least 5 minutes prior to the meeting.

When *hosting* an audio conference, you could use the following rules to improve the efficiency of the meeting:

- Open the meeting by confirming that every invitee has joined the audio conference. Start the meeting on time. If mandatory attendees are not present, agree with the other participants whether the meeting should proceed or be adjourned.
- Make sure that new project team members introduce themselves, their roles and main responsibilities to the other participants. Hold a separate session to explain the project organisation and the project background exclusively to the new members, to avoid disrupting the meeting flow.
- Always speak slowly and clearly. If other participants are not following this rule, you should politely request that they do so.
- Press mute when not talking, this will avoid background noises disturbing the meeting flow. Always ensure that other people in the same room know that the phone is muted, and reactivate the microphone when anyone wants to speak.
- Proactively engage participants throughout the conference. Keep a list of all attendees and identify which ones are not participating in the discussion. You should invite them, by name, to confirm their agreements, give suggestions or voice their opinions.
- After taking important decisions or concluding an important discussion, have a round table inviting all participants to voice their opinion.
- Capture all action points during the meeting, and confirm their ownership and expected completion date and time before concluding the meeting.
- Conclude on time, allowing a few minutes for wrap-up.
- When the time allocated is not enough to discuss all points and reach agreement, you can request to extend the meeting and ask if all participants are able to continue with the call. If key participants have other commitments, the meeting should be adjourned and a new date and time set to continue the discussion. Before closing the meeting you should identify preparatory actions and one-to-one discussions to be completed before the next meeting, aiming to reduce the duration of the next conference.

To increase the success of the meeting, all *participants* should follow a basic set of principles, such as:

- Always introduce yourself when joining the call, by stating your name, location and company – if applicable.
- Identify any constraints in advance (for example, need to leave the meeting early, attending from the car or airport, and so on).
- When other participants do not know you very well, identify yourself before speaking.
- Always speak slowly and clearly. If other participants are not following this rule, you must politely ask them to do so.
- If you can't understand any sentence or subject, don't be afraid to ask for clarification.
- Always focus on the meeting content and avoid distractions like e-mails and mobile phones.

- Avoid attending conferences from open spaces; try to attend from a small meeting room or separate office when possible to avoid discussions and noises in the background damaging the communication in the conference.
- Be aware that your participation in the audio conference can disturb other colleagues sitting next to you.

General points *to be avoided* during meetings held via audio conference:

- Avoid speaking quickly, using slang or exaggerated accents.
- Avoid speaking far from the sound station or microphone.
- Avoid unnecessary background noises when participating.
- Avoid unnecessary or unplanned discussions outside the meeting agenda.
- Avoid going over the allotted meeting time.
- Avoid joining the conference from a mobile phone in noisy locations.
- Avoid doing parallel activities during the meeting.
- Avoid drawing on paper and flipcharts. This excludes or marginalises people not in the same physical room. Use web conferencing tools instead.

Using video conferences

Video conferencing equipment connects two or more sites with audio and video links so that participants can converse, interact with oral and verbal communication and share documents. You can use video conferencing to establish an initial contact among project team members located in different company offices and countries when travel is not possible.

As visual contact can improve empathy, you can use video conferencing to re-establish team dynamics in difficult project phases, to improve the level of trust among global team members and to keep a regular contact with a team that has few occasions for face-to-face meetings and social gatherings. In these situations, team-building activities and informal discussions about social events can help to start a good meeting.

Good practices for meeting organisers when *planning* the video conferencing session:

- Determine the time and length of the conference. Never organise a video conference for a duration of more than 3 hours. When the number of topics requires more time, separate the meeting into two distinct parts, leaving at least 10 minutes interval between them.
- Appoint a leader for each site.
- When connecting to new sites, plan for a separate test or practice call, requesting local coordinators to be present.
- With the help of the coordinators, connect with the remote sites around 15 minutes prior to the meeting. Remember to book this extra time in their agendas.
- Note in the meeting request all the conferencing telephone numbers and the conference rooms' telephone numbers. Be sure that the leaders have your mobile phone number, and use it to solve problems with the video conferencing connection.
- As the meeting organiser, you should always initiate the conference call, by dialling the conferencing numbers in other locations. Ensure the audio and video are working perfectly – including the visualisation of computer screens if applicable – before including other locations in the call.

When *hosting* the video conference, you and the local coordinators can use the following practices to improve the efficiency of the meeting:

- Open the meeting by introducing all participants and confirm if any attendees are not visible. If this is the case, ask the local leader to rearrange the people in the room, so that all attendees appear on screen.
- Always speak slowly and clearly. If other participants are not following this rule, politely request that they do so.
- If the background noise in your location is breaking the audio signal, press mute when not talking. Always ensure that other people in the same room know that the phone is muted and reactivate the microphone when anyone wants to speak.
- Proactively engage participants throughout the conference.

When *participating* in a video conference, you can also use some simple practices to ensure a successful meeting:

- Always be on time.
- Try and pretend you are having a face-to-face meeting: be yourself and imagine the participants are sitting opposite you.
- The camera position and angle should be set at the beginning of the meeting and not changed as this can distract participants.
- Speak naturally and direct your voice to the closest microphone.
- End your statements with 'thank you' or ask for confirmation of understanding to let the other attendees know you are finished,
- Pause occasionally so others may speak.

REAL-LIFE EXPERIENCE

The use of video conferencing only has a clear advantage over audio conferencing in meetings where the interaction among participants is stimulated. In a kick-off meeting, where people only stare at each others faces while they speak, the use of video can add little value. However, participants can benefit from the use of video conferencing by sharing presentations, objects and documents, and drawing together the project strategies and overall planning. Some people are not technically savvy enough to create drawings using software tools during the meetings. In some situations, these team members will not make full use of the web conferencing tools described in Chapters 18 and 23 to express their opinions. Instead, they can use their creativity during video conferencing.

In a technical design meeting, the Swiss engineers made a quick paper drawing of their proposal for the new product and shared it with the American engineers by using a document camera. The American team wanted to suggest a change in the design, but did not have a document camera in their video conferencing room. Instead, they focused the video conferencing camera on a white board, and drew their recommendations on it. The Swiss team agreed and reflected the change into their drawing, obtaining an agreement on the first draft of the product design. When the teams reconvened the day after, a computer-generated 3D drawing was shared on the screen and used as the basis for a storm of new ideas and risk identifications.

On other occasions, people share documents by using fax or scanners during audio and video conferencing meetings, making use of basic technologies to achieve a high level of efficiency.

General points *to be avoided* during meetings held via video conferencing:

- Avoid speaking quickly, using slang or exaggerated accents.
- Remember the interference caused by background noises: avoid coughing and tapping pencils or fingers near the microphone. Avoid holding side conversations.
- Avoid unnecessary or unplanned discussions outside the meeting agenda.
- Avoid exceeding the allotted meeting time.
- Avoid doing parallel activities during the meeting.

YOUR LEARNING ON AUDIO AND VIDEO CONFERENCING

Revisit the list or mindmap created at the beginning of this module. What additional recommendations would you give to global project managers and team members? Which recommendations in this chapter would not work in your company or country?

Now share your thoughts with other people, and read about their own experiences (www. GlobalProjectManagement.org).

---

23 *Coordinating and Attending Online Meetings*

Not all meeting moderators use video and web conferencing to share documents and electronic whiteboards during meetings over distance. Instead, they usually distribute documents before the meeting, read the material during the session and take paper notes. After the meeting, they must transcribe the notes into meeting minutes or other types of documents, distribute to the audience, gather feedback on possible misunderstandings and obtain the approval of the meeting records. On many occasions, the meeting attendees who are away on business trips do not receive the material on time, losing their focus on the discussions. In the worst case, the meeting records are not distributed until a week after the meeting, when the participants do not recall the discussion and decisions. This may be one of the main sources of misunderstandings on global projects.

This chapter introduces the concept of online meetings, where collaboration and interaction are at their best, and the meeting organisers can reduce misunderstandings and formalise acceptance on the decisions and action points during the sessions.

Understanding what can be improved

You can develop a structured interview (illustrated by Table 23.1) to understand the current caveats and start collecting recommendations. After conducting the interviews, combine the answers with the other recommendations in this chapter, and write the first set of good practices for online meetings.

You can use the same interview later, in order to detect the effectiveness of the good practices, and to identify areas for improvement.

YOUR EXPERIENCE OF ONLINE MEETINGS

How many meetings have you attended without having received the material being discussed? How long does it take you to write down and distribute the meeting records to the audience? How many people provide you with feedback on this material?

Write on a list or mindmap the situations that reduce the efficiency of meetings over a distance. Note your suggestions to increase this efficiency, by sharing the meeting material through web conferencing and updating the project records during the session, showing them to the audience as you type.

While you read this chapter, and during the coming weeks, investigate if anyone else in your company organises this type of meeting, and ask to be invited to some of these meetings. Complete your mindmap with the good practices employed by other people to organise and host online meetings, noting down how they help to increase understanding and collaboration. Observe the situations that did not work well, and identify possible reasons for this, trying to make suggestions for improvement.

Table 23.1   Interview to understand the use of online meetings

Question	Note all answers below
In your opinion, what types of meetings justify the information sharing using computer screens?	
What occasions are not suitable for online meetings, and what media would you use instead?	
What are the main mistakes people make during online meetings, and how to avoid them?	
What are the mandatory steps when scheduling and preparing online meetings?	

Communication style during online meetings

The recommendations in this chapter are divided into two different types of situations. The first one is the use of instant messaging tools and visual media – computer applications, whiteboards and chat-rooms – allowing a few people to share knowledge in a direct, unplanned manner. The second is the use of audio and web conferencing suites with the same visual media, in scheduled meetings with many attendees.

The main recommendation to the team members sharing their applications with colleagues in distant locations is to be proficient in what they are doing, and to know the tools. When the whole team is in the same room, flip-chart meetings let the ideas flow as rapidly as one can write on the board. People familiar with this traditional style can become impatient when technology causes interruptions to the meeting flow. Global team members can start by practicing the use of computer tools during face-to-face meetings, acquiring more confidence to do the same over a distance.

A three-step method (learn-practice-share) can help in achieving this self-confidence: meeting organisers must *learn* to use the software tools on their own, and *practice* their skills in face-to-face meetings until they are comfortable with *sharing* the software screens over a distance. Depending on the complexity of the software tool, each of these steps can take days or weeks to be completed.

The practice level must be achieved in meetings with familiar stakeholders, who will understand if you get things wrong during the initial use, and who will motivate you to go ahead and continue learning. You can ask a software specialist to be present in the first meetings to provide you coaching on the tools (see also Chapter 5 when the coach is not at the same location as you).

Special considerations for instant messaging discussions

The recommendations on telephones and e-mail in Chapter 21 are a good starting point for the good practices for instant messaging, which can be seen as a combination of e-mail (written

---

REAL-LIFE EXPERIENCE

The Netiquette guidelines from the IETF also provide a set of rules for chat (or 'talk', using the IETF terminology), some of them can serve as a basis for the recommendations for the use of instant messaging on global projects (adapted from Hambridge, 1995):

- Instant messaging is an interruption to the other person. Your first question must be if the time is appropriate for a conversation.

- If you cannot get a reply when inviting someone to a session, think about the different reasons for it – technical problems, absence – before making assumptions.

- Always make clear to the other parties that you have finished writing, and are waiting for their comments or answers.

- Never start replying or making comments before the other participants have completed their flow of thoughts. This can be a bit tricky when more than two people are in the same conversation, requiring some *savoir-faire* to avoid a messy conversation.

- Always be careful when you have more than one chat session open at the same time, to avoid mixing different topics and writing to the wrong person.

- Always inform the other participants when you must close the chat session, waiting for their farewells before closing it.

---

media) with telephones (synchronous communication). As many companies keep a history of all conversations on instant messaging, there is no reason for you to write anything during a chat that you would not say in a telephone discussion or e-mail.

Special considerations for online meetings via web conferencing

The main advantage of having online meetings in addition to audio conferencing is the use of visual media to increase the richness of knowledge and validate understanding. Thus, the recommendations in Chapters 7, 9 and 22 are valid for these meetings. Moreover, some specific topics that can help you to *prepare* productive audio and web conferencing meetings are:

- Always write clear instructions to people joining your web conference, using hyperlinks to the conference website, to the set-up documentation (Chapter 18) and to the set of good practices you might publish after reading this chapter.
- Some conferencing tools are integrated to e-mail and calendar systems. If this is the case, always state the conference server and your conference identification in the meeting request, making it easier for attendees to join the call.
- Always practice before your first web conference. Use a second computer or ask a local colleague to connect to a trial meeting, and understand how your computer images appear to the attendees. Practice all the functions you are planning to use during your calls.
- When you are setting up a new project team, or if you have new team members, always schedule a trial meeting to allow them to learn how to join the conference, how to use the functions and how to share their applications. This will improve their confidence when attending your meeting and can allow more ideas to flow, with different people

having various meeting roles and sharing their computer applications when needed. See the recommendations in Chapter 5 for coaching over distance.

Consider the following suggestions when *moderating* a web conferencing meeting:

- Always start the web conferencing session before the meeting time, together with the audio conferencing.
- Never spend too much time writing and drawing. Keep to the essentials, take only the major points online and complete the details when the meeting ends.
- Ask participants to prepare presentations on their topics before the meeting, to reduce the amount of drawing during the conference.
- Be familiar with the document content, formats and automated functions beforehand.
- Avoid switching screens too quickly and using shortcuts when the participants need to understand the way actions are being performed (for example, showing the steps required to access applications). However, this rule is not relevant if the action itself is not important (for example, updating project records). In this case, quick actions are very useful.
- Ask the other participants to store all material on a shared space, preferably the project virtual room. This way you can use them during the meeting, in case other participants cannot share their computer screens. People that cannot access the web conference for technical reasons might download the documents from the virtual room and use them during the meeting.
- When opening new documents, always check that everyone can see them. Also confirm that other people can read the document contents (sometimes you will need to increase the font size or perform zooming to allow everyone to read text in small fonts).
- Be careful when using colours if these are important to the understanding of the points being discussed (compression algorithms reduce the quality of colours, sometimes changing tones significantly).
- If possible, close other software running on your computer (avoid pop-ups and reminders distracting the participants).
- When sharing your whole computer screen (desktop), close applications with sensitive or private information (for example, e-mails, calendars).
- Always consider using graphic tools and drawings to improve understanding of complex topics across locations.
- Prefer to use graphic drawing applications, instead of the whiteboard facility provided by the conferencing suite, to keep the discussions documented and in a convenient format for future meetings.
- When inviting a group of people located in the same office, investigate if they wish to attend the meeting in the same room, assigning one coordinator to reserve and prepare the space, and to establish the audio conference on time.

People *participating* in web conferencing meetings can benefit from the following good practices:

- Know the tool in advance. If you are not comfortable with using it, ask a colleague to explain it to you, organising a trial meeting for you to practice beforehand.
- Always join the meeting on time to ensure you can connect to the web conference. This way you can ask the meeting organiser to help you, without disturbing the meeting flow.
- Pretend you are in a face-to-face meeting and keep the focus on the discussion, avoiding distractions from your office space or other computer applications (for example, e-mail).

- When the moderator refers to a document, and you cannot see it, check if the meeting screen is minimised or hidden behind another application. If you are sure the document is not available, politely ask the meeting organiser to verify if the application is being shared correctly. Confirm if other participants can see it.
- When the moderator shares a document with small fonts or images, and you cannot read the information on them, politely ask the meeting organiser to increase the font or image size.
- Prepare documents in advance to explain topics under your responsibility. Share them with the meeting organiser in advance and with the other attendees during the meeting.
- Be aware of sensitive material being shown on your computer screen, when other people are in the same working space as you.

YOUR LEARNING ON ONLINE MEETINGS

Revisit the list or mindmap created at the beginning of this module. What additional recommendations would you give to global project managers and team members? Which recommendations in this chapter are the most difficult for you to implement?

Now share your thoughts with other people, and read about their own experiences (www. GlobalProjectManagement.org).

24 *Fostering Knowledge Exchange*

The open exchange of information during all the phases of a project improves the quality of the project management processes and deliverables (Gardiner, 2005). Traditional projects may lose important knowledge if the information exchanged during informal discussions or formal meetings is not captured in the project documentation. Global projects face the same threat, with the additional challenge of having e-mail threads as an important source of project discussions, decisions, risks, issues, changes and meeting minutes. Some project managers are comfortable with using e-mail as the project knowledge repository, but what happens when key people are absent, or leave the project? A good part of the knowledge is often lost, or transferred to other people, using an unstructured format that makes it difficult to find information when needed.

This chapter discusses some formal and informal communication guidelines that can stimulate the global team members to exchange, capture and combine tacit knowledge, by using the knowledge-sharing infrastructure to foster collaboration with team members in other locations.

Understanding what can be improved

You can develop a structured interview (illustrated by Table 24.1) to understand the current caveats in the existing knowledge-sharing suite, and start collecting recommendations. After conducting the interviews, combine the answers with the other recommendations in this chapter, and write the first set of good practices for knowledge sharing. You could use the same interview at a later date, in order to detect the effectiveness of these practices, and to identify areas for improvement.

YOUR EXPERIENCE OF SHARING KNOWLEDGE

How many e-mails with attachments do you receive on a daily basis? How often do you need to request that people send you the most recent version of project documents that are not stored in shared areas? How do you ensure that people in other locations review and complete your project documents?

Write on a list or mindmap the situations that increase collaboration through the sharing of knowledge. Note down the practices that are detrimental to teamwork across borders.

When you read this chapter, and during the coming weeks, look at some of your company's project virtual rooms, and try to obtain the project status and find the main project records. Complete your mindmap with the good practices employed by other people to organise their project virtual rooms. In the instances when you could not find the right information, write down your suggestions for ways the organisation of virtual rooms can be improved.

Table 24.1   Interview to understand the use of knowledge sharing

Question	Note all answers below
Do you think that all project managers in your company use the same knowledge-sharing suite?	
Do you think that all team members on your project use the same knowledge-sharing suite to store their documentation items?	
Do you think that all global project managers consistently update the project information in the project virtual room?	
Do you think that all global team members consistently update the project information in the project virtual room?	
Do you have any suggestions to improve the structure of the project documentation?	
Do you have any suggestions to improve the contents of the project documentation?	
Do you have any suggestions to improve the use of the knowledge-sharing suite?	

Defining the rules for knowledge sharing

A knowledge-sharing suite should be deployed by using the recommendations in Chapter 19, and then a 'project virtual room' must be defined for each project, with a structure that represents the usual project documentation in your company, like 'project plan', 'project standards', 'project monitoring and control' and 'project deliverables'. If possible, all projects should use the same structure, so that team members can follow the same criteria to store and retrieve the documentation. Otherwise, you can define a standard that will fit the requirements of most projects in your company, and explain how other project managers might create a classification system for documentation specific to their projects, or to different countries.

Global organisations can define standards for knowledge sharing, following these recommendations:

- All program and project managers, or at least representatives from key departments, should participate in the definition of the rules for knowledge sharing.
- All project team members should know and reinforce the rules of knowledge sharing.
- All project team members must have the right to voice their opinion on the existing rules, and provide recommendations for improvement.
- Project QA reviews must verify the application of the knowledge-sharing principles.
- The organisation must review the knowledge-sharing structure periodically, but leave a certain time of stability before changing the formats or rules (usually the rules must remain the same during cycles of 1–3 years).

Leading people to share information

The project virtual room must contain the information produced during all process groups: initiating, planning, executing, monitoring and controlling and closing. During *initiation*, the project manager is responsible for:

- establishing the project virtual room with a basic file structure;
- storing the initial information in the project virtual room (usually the project charter and the preliminary project scope statement);

REAL-LIFE EXPERIENCE

Bad practice: using e-mails	Good practice: using the project virtual room
'Please find attached the revised components of the project management plan, which you should update and return to me today (…).'	'Please find the revised components of the project management plan in the project virtual room (link), which you should update today.' *Use the project communications plan to specify the rules for document updating, such as 'creating a new version in the same directory' and, 'No need to inform other people as they receive an automated notification when any file is created or changed.*
'I request a change in the project scope, to include the development of a new interface to solve the problem found yesterday. Please let me know if you agree or if you have any other suggestions in mind (…).'	'I registered the scope change request #20 (link) to resolve the issue # 32 (link) reported yesterday. Please approve it if you agree, or call me to discuss other alternatives (…).'
'Dear all: please find below the outcome of the meeting we had last week (…) please let me hear your comments.'	'Dear all: the minutes of today's meeting are now stored in the knowledge base (link), please let me have your comments.'
'After the discussion on the special feature that the customer requested during today's meeting, I would like to inform everyone of a risk of exceeding the project budget and missing the delivery date (…).'	'I've registered the risk # 21 (link) to raise your attention to the potential impacts of the special feature requested by the customer today (…).'
'Find the latest work performance reports attached to this e-mail.'	*No need to send an e-mail as the interested parties will receive an automated notification when you save the files on the 'work performance reports' directory.*
'I am sending the signed version of the contract to you by express mail, keep it confidential.'	*No need to send an e-mail as the procurement and project office teams will receive an automated notification when you publish a scanned copy of the contract on the 'signed contracts' folder. There is no confidentiality risk as this folder can only be accessed by the procurement and project office teams.*

- organising a kick-off meeting with all key team members to explain the objectives and structure of the project virtual room and the project intelligence;
- discussing the good practices in knowledge sharing and obtaining a common agreement on the rules to be adopted for the project;
- always following the practices;
- always reinforcing the practices when team members do not follow them correctly.

Once you establish the project virtual room and define it as the basis for the project intelligence, you must use it to store all documentation and information related to the project. All e-mails must point to the project virtual room or to the project management system (see Chapter 20), instead of having document attachments. During planning, executing, monitoring and controlling activities, all project documents, reports and records should be stored in the project virtual room.

When *closing* the project, the project manager is responsible for coordinating the following activities with the Project Management Office:

- completing all formal acceptance documents and project closure documents, storing them in the project virtual room;
- requesting a safe copy of the contents on the project virtual room, keeping one copy and distributing other copies as requested by the organisational policies;
- identifying historical information documents and copying them to the knowledge repository as specified by the organisational policies;
- documenting lessons learned, creating a copy in the respective knowledge repository as specified by the organisational project management methodology.

YOUR LEARNING ON KNOWLEDGE SHARING

Revisit the list or mindmap created at the beginning of this module. What additional recommendations would you give to global project managers and team members? Which recommendations in this chapter are the most difficult for you to implement? What types of resistance would you face from other project managers and team members? What role can the project office play in improving the knowledge-sharing standards of your organisation?

Now share your thoughts with other people, and read about their own experiences (www. GlobalProjectManagement.org).

25 *Collaborative Project Management*

Most companies use scheduling software tools and have templates for project records, such as issue logs, risk logs and meeting minutes. Other companies have consolidated the project records into a global project binder (see Chapter 7), to improve the effectiveness of online meetings. All these companies can improve their maturity on global project management by implementing collaborative project management software tools, as discussed in Chapter 20.

This chapter makes suggestions on how to improve the adoption of collaborative project management software, by having all project managers and team members across the globe using the same rules and practices, with the help of senior stakeholders. All e-mails discussing important project elements – such as actions, issues, risks and changes – should always refer to the project management system, which must in turn be updated with the results of the discussion. The information in the project virtual room and the project management system will then form the basis for all regular meetings.

Understanding what can be improved

You can develop a structured interview (illustrated by Table 25.1) to identify the opinion and recommendations of program managers, project managers, project office teams and the team members on the current project management software (if any). After conducting the

---

YOUR EXPERIENCE OF COLLABORATIVE PROJECT MANAGEMENT SOFTWARE

How many different standards does your organisation have for project records? Does everyone know where to find these standards, and how to update them? Do you know how to obtain the status of issues and risks, for all projects in your company? Is there a standard change control procedure? Is it used consistently by all project managers?

Write on a list or mindmap the situations that reveal good usage of the collaborative project management software. Note down the occasions when these practices are not followed consistently across the various company offices and departments.

While you read this chapter, and during the coming weeks, consult the information on different projects, and try to obtain the status of the main risks, issues and changes. Complete your mindmap with the good practices employed by global project managers to effectively use the collaborative project management software, and keep the project records up-to-date. Investigate good practices from team members on how to use the software to improve their participation in the project. Make suggestions to foster the use of these practices by other project managers and team members in your organisation.

Table 25.1   **Interview to understand the use of the collaborative project management software**

Question	Note all answers below
Do you usually draw a WBS diagram using the software before identifying the project activities?	
Do you write the WBS diagram online with participation from the main project team members?	
Do you use the software to define the detailed schedule online with the project team?	
Do you create the project risks in the software as soon as they are identified?	
Do you maintain the list of project risks in the software during the status meetings?	
Do you create the project issues in the software as soon as they are identified?	
Do you maintain the list of project issues in the software during the status meetings?	
Do the project team members update their tasks, risks and issues directly on the project management software?	
Do the project stakeholders use the software to extract consolidated information?	
Do you use the software functions to extract consolidated information?	
What are the main mistakes people make on the project management software, and how to avoid them?	

interviews, combine the answers with the other recommendations in this chapter, and write the first set of good practices.

You could use the same interview at a later stage, in order to detect the effectiveness of the practices you have implemented, and to identify areas for improvement.

Updating information on the project management software

Global projects involving people in different time zones will have fewer opportunities for synchronous communication. In this case, a planning workshop with the whole team in the same location becomes almost mandatory for project success. However, the project execution, monitoring and controlling processes will rely almost exclusively on asynchronous information

REAL-LIFE EXPERIENCE

The collaborative project management software can be combined with video or web conferencing tools, to allow team members from different locations to work together when producing the project information. The synchronous collaboration replaces the traditional 'flip-chart and stickers' methods, when the project team members cannot be in the same location during the project planning and follow-up meetings. Some examples of this online collaboration are:

- During project planning, the creation of a WBS (Work Breakdown Structure) organises the total project scope, decomposing the project deliverables into work packages (PMI, 2004). The WBS is a hierarchical diagram that can be drawn by many graphic tools. However, a good alternative is to use a software program that can convert the WBS into the activity list, the network diagram and the project schedule, allowing the other planning tasks to start immediately. The best alternative is to have software that synchronises the changes in all these components (WBS – Activity list – Network diagram – Project schedule), to allow them to be created and maintained concurrently.

- The definition of the project activities based on the WBS is another task that can be performed online, allowing the main project team members to validate the completeness of the project scope, to check the correctness of the WBS decomposition, to define the attributes of each activity and to identify the milestones. Other planning processes might update the activity attributes during online meetings, by estimating the resources, duration and costs.

- The activity sequencing process, which uses network diagrams (usually based on the precedence diagramming method or the arrow diagram method) can also benefit from a project management software tool with graphic capabilities integrated into the other project information lists and diagrams.

- The project schedule development will use the activity list, the activity attributes and the network diagram to produce milestone and bar charts for the project execution, monitoring and control. The creation of a project schedule during online workshops can obtain buy-in from the project team members, who will validate the project activities and sequence, and work together on the schedule compression. The use of a software tool in the preparation of the project schedule is also recommended when all the project team members are working in the same location during the planning workshop. This will ensure that everyone becomes familiar with the tool, and that the project manager, planner or PMO administrator responsible for the project schedule uses the software from the beginning. A good software know-how will increase the success rates of the follow-up meetings that will be performed over video or web conferencing.

- Project status meetings can use the collaborative project management software to review the project schedule, the risks and open issues. When the meeting moderator updates the information directly on the software tool, the time required for maintaining the project information is reduced (suppressing the need for updates after the meeting), the probability of misunderstanding is minimised (everyone can validate the information being updated and react immediately if there is any mistake), and the need for validation of the information after the meeting by the participants is suppressed.

exchange to complete the project scope within acceptable levels of cost, time and quality. The project team members must update the information on the project management software as soon as possible, allowing other team members to be informed of the changes, and making the project metrics reflect the reality. Some examples of updates that must be performed by every project team member are:

- Activities must be marked as complete, as soon as they are performed.

- The project manager must be informed as soon as variances are detected in the target duration, resources required, or estimated costs. The team members can proceed with updating the activity attributes with the variances, and the software tool sends an e-mail to the project manager automatically. When the tool does not provide this option, the team members can send an e-mail, instant message or make a telephone call to the project manager who will update the information directly, and perform an impact analysis of the change. Depending on the methodology in place, and the degree of variance, a change request may be required.
- When the project stakeholders need to update the project scope, time, cost or quality elements, they can raise a change request automatically on the project management software. The software will need to activate a process workflow to inform other stakeholders, and request approval for the change. In these instances, the project manager will need to perform a detailed impact analysis before requesting the approval and making the updates.
- The project stakeholders can update the risks under their ownership directly on the project management software, or insert new risks when they are identified. The software tool must then inform the project manager, who will coordinate the risk analysis and response planning processes.
- When the ownership of any activity, risk or issue is transferred to another team member, this must be reflected in the software tool, which will inform the project manager, the former and the new owner. This will avoid duplication of activities (as the former owner will be informed and stop handling it), the lack of follow-up (the new owner will receive the information and start handling it) and the lack of monitoring (the project manager knows who can provide more information on the status of the item).

Information pushed by the project management software

The software tool can help project managers to monitor the activities, risks and issues under the responsibilities of team members in different time zones, by sending automated messages. Some examples being:

- **Actions** that are due shortly. The team members must update the actions if they are completed, or follow the established process if the activity will be delayed.
- **Issues** that are due shortly. The team members must use problem-solving techniques (see Chapter 10) and update the project management system with the issue resolution strategy.
- **Risks** that are about to be triggered. The risk owners must review and complete the risk register with the recommended corrective and preventive actions, as well as revisiting the risk response.
- **Risks** that just happened. The owners must activate the risk response plan and conduct an impact assessment, involving and informing the project manager.

Pulling information from the project management software

The project manager can identify the stakeholder requirements when performing the communications planning, and produce an index of the information available directly in the project management software tool, with instructions on how to obtain it. The project manager can also work with the PMO administrators to define shortcuts in the software interfaces for the different types of information requested. The stakeholders must use the software to obtain more information on the project, and only request it from the project manager when specific requirements cannot be satisfied by the existing reports and interfaces. Senior executives and members of the project office may also follow this rule and inform the project managers when the information cannot be found. By doing this, they can reinforce the use and adoption of the software tools. Some examples of information that can be produced automatically by the software tools are:

- up-to-date milestone chart;
- list of the ten risks with higher probability and impact;
- list of the ten open issues with higher impact;
- earned value metrics, indicating the project performance;
- project budget and variances;
- consolidated views of the project portfolio metrics;
- consolidated views of the program metrics.

Interfaces between the project management software and other tools

The project management system may not contain all tools for specialised tasks, but should provide easy interfaces with them. Some examples being:

- **Quality tools** – statistical and flow-charting tools used during quality planning and control activities will often be related to the project domain (for example, chemical, construction and manufacturing). Ideally, these tools will send a summary of the control measurements to the project management system, which will help the project manager to trigger corrective or preventive actions.
- **Procurement tools** – organisations usually have strict standards for the financial analysis tools and spreadsheets, supply relationship management suites, screening systems and payment systems, some of them interfacing with the project management software. Project managers can benefit from direct information exchanges related to the project budget and to the completeness of contractual and payment activities that have an impact on the project schedule.
- **Risk tools** – the outcomes of brainstorming sessions, cause-and-effect diagrams, process flow charts, statistic tools and modelling techniques will produce a list of risks that can be imported into the project management software.
- **Financial systems** – information on project costs and budget can be exchanged with the organisational financial systems, which will reflect the actual project expenditure, trigger invoices and monitor the payments.
- **Timesheet entry systems** – when the project management software does not provide a consolidated timesheet system that allows project team members to report the time spent on different projects together with non-project activities, an external system may be required. This system must be synchronised with the project management software, to allow the tracking of project costs and earned value management

YOUR LEARNING ON COLLABORATIVE PROJECT MANAGEMENT

Revisit the list or mindmap created at the beginning of this module. What additional recommendations would you give to global project managers and team members? Which recommendations in this chapter are the most difficult for you to implement? What types of resistance would you face from other project managers and team members? What could be the role of a project office to improve the use of project management software tools in your organisation?

Now share your thoughts with other people, and read about their own experiences (www. GlobalProjectManagement.org).

Part V: Key concepts

- The implementation of software tools is not sufficient for effective collaboration between team members located in different countries. The development of a collection of organisational good practices and appropriate training will ensure that all stakeholders know how to use the tools during all the project activities.
- The use of basic collaborative tools – such as telephone and e-mail – can benefit from the 'netiquette' and other good practices that establish protocols for rapid answers, time and date formats, cultural differences and copyright laws.
- Audio and video conferences can be more effective with good preparation, pro-active participation from remote participants and a common ground for visual and audio communication.
- The correct use of software tools and the online updating of project documents and information can improve collaboration during meetings.
- Pro-active participation from the team members and the PMO administrators when setting-up the project structure will foster the knowledge sharing during the project execution tasks.
- The project manager must implement rules and procedures for the use of the project management software tool and coach all stakeholders on the synchronous and asynchronous collaboration modes, so that the project activities, risks and issues will always be up-to-date and automatically trigger the information to the team members participating in them.

Part V: Further reading

Hambridge, S. (1995) *Netiquette Guidelines*

The netiquette provides some basic recommendations on the use of e-mail, chat and newsgroups that remain applicable after more than 10 years. It is surprising to see how often they are not applied during business communications.

Rowley, J.E. and Farrow, J. (2000) *Organizing Knowledge*

This book is fully dedicated to knowledge management and provides interesting recommendations to structure and classify information, with one chapter dedicated to internet publishing.

Jolliet, Y. (2006) *Des difficultés a gérer la connaissance à l'échelle d'une multinationale*

This article (in French) presents a real-life experience that consolidates the learning from the implementation of a global knowledge-sharing method in an international enterprise.

Wikipedia (http://en.wikipedia.org/wiki/Collaborative_software)

This entry on wikipedia provides a good summary of the different types of collaborative software available, with links to more detailed information on specific technology solutions, and some recommendations on the use of the tools.

Part V: Interactive section

Share your experience of the use of collaborative tools during global projects (www. GlobalProjectManagement.org):

- How did you adapt the interviews and recommendations to your organisation?
- Do you think that most people are using collaborative tools effectively?
- Do you think that a new generation of workers, who use the Internet and collaborative tools regularly at home, will change the collaboration in global projects?
- Do you have interesting stories about good and bad use of collaborative tools in your academic or professional experience?

VI *Implementing the Global Project Management Framework©*

The implementation of the Global Project Management Framework© can follow various methods, but is more likely to succeed when performed in a phased manner. You may start with the chapters that resolve existing problems in your company or projects, and then apply some recommendations that can realise immediate benefits. The implementation might also be performed on a single program or project, before deploying the new model of good practices across divisions and company borders.

Independently of the strategy you select, obtaining acceptance from all stakeholders will be the key for a successful implementation. You must engage them from the beginning of the project, making a summarised list of the potential benefits for your company, and establish clear objectives for each implementation phase. The chapters in this part provide an example of such analysis, and present different alternatives for the project implementation strategy. You can choose the method according to your company culture, by comparing the alternatives below with the methods employed during successful organisational change projects.

26 *A Charter for the Framework*

Your company can initiate a study to evaluate the efficiency of existing practices and procedures used by global project managers. With the help of the various mindmaps you have created while reading this book, you can prepare questionnaires and interviews to assess the opinions of program managers, team members, customers, project managers and senior executives.

The conclusions of this study may form a project proposal, which presents the requirements of the people who participated in the survey and the chapters on the Global Project Management Framework that can satisfy them. If the proposal is accepted, the results of the study might form the project charter, describing how you will implement the framework and measure the stakeholder satisfaction.

Stakeholder needs and expectations

Refer to the mindmaps you prepared for each chapter of the framework and identify the questions you could ask to understand how program managers, team members, customers, project managers and senior executives view the efficiency of global project management at your company. Some examples of these questions are:

- **Cross-cultural competence** – do you believe that most project managers understand and respect the cultural beliefs of team members and other stakeholders? Have you experienced a situation where team members generalise their impressions of colleagues in other locations, creating conflicts and reducing productivity and collaboration? What recommendations would you give to global project managers and team members on cross-cultural communication and collaboration?
- **International leadership** – do you believe that most project managers employ leadership styles adapted to international teams? What leadership skills are especially important across country borders?
- **Trust across borders** – do you think that your local colleagues usually trust the competency and effectiveness of team members in other locations? Do you think that your remote colleagues trust you and your local colleagues? What can be done to increase the trust level?
- **International conflicts** – have you seen the same type of conflicts on both traditional and global projects? How did the project managers manage conflicts over a distance? What suggestions would you give to improve the conflict management on global projects?
- **Global coaching** – is there a formal coaching process at your company? Does this process work equally well for coaching sessions over distance? What are the challenges of providing coaching over the telephone or via video conferencing? What recommendations would you give to cope with these challenges?

- **Global stakeholders** – do you believe that global stakeholders tend to react in a different way to local stakeholders? How did the project managers involve and manage local and global stakeholders? Were the stakeholder needs equally satisfied? What recommendations could you give to improve the management of global stakeholders at your company?
- **Meeting rules and templates** – how productive are meetings you attend with people from different locations? Are they managed correctly? What is the participation level from people in other locations? Are your project documents adapted to online meetings (where the moderator shares and updates the project records during the meeting)? What could be improved in meetings involving people from different countries?
- **Global communication strategy** – how formalised are the stakeholder communication requirements? How well are they satisfied? Does everyone know the different communication channels, frequency and media? Do all team members know their roles in the preparation and distribution of information?
- **Global communication techniques** – how do the project managers and PMO collect information on their projects? What is the quality level of the information collected? How effectively do they distribute the project information to the stakeholders, compared to their requirements? How would you rate the quality of information exchange during project status meetings? What suggestions would you give to improve the techniques used to collect, distribute and share information?
- **Global creativity** – how often are people from different locations involved in brainstorming sessions? Is there a feeling that everyone is equally involved to generate ideas? How effective are the creative sessions over distance? How could project managers increase the number and quality of ideas generated?
- **Global project structures** – are there local coordinators appointed to global projects, or is the project manager responsible for communicating directly with all team members? Are there functional coordinators responsible for complex work packages? Do you have projects running 24x7, with local project managers working in shifts? Do you believe that the project structures are usually well adapted to the location of team members and the complexity of the project?
- **Selection of international resources** – is your company hiring the best candidates in the right location? Does the evaluation process take into account the global communication and collaboration skills when hiring global project managers and team members? How effective are interviews when held over a distance? How can the selection process of international candidates be improved?
- **Global program and project offices** – is there a department performing the functions of a PMO at your company? Are there PSO roles assigned to major programs and projects? How effective are these project offices in communicating and increasing collaboration over a distance? What improvements can they make to increase the effectiveness of global projects?
- **Organisational support** – do the senior managers at your company understand the challenges and benefits of global teams? Are they effective in providing support to global programs and projects in order to address these challenges? Are the benefits well exploited and measured? How can your company provide additional support to global initiatives?
- **Global collaborative networks** – have you been involved on a strategic alliance or partnership with companies located in other countries? How effective was the collaboration across company and country borders? What lessons have you learned to improve the effectiveness of similar programs and projects?

The questionnaire can be completed with questions from the assessments provided in Chapters 16–25 to evaluate the status and effectiveness of the communication tools and techniques. Another alternative is to keep these assessments for a later stage during the project implementation.

The benefits of the framework implementation

Beyond stakeholder needs identified by qualitative instruments, such as the questions defined above, the framework can also address more specific organisational requirements, some examples being:

- **Increase customer satisfaction** – your company organises a survey to obtain feedback from various customers, discovering that global projects receive poor appreciation. One of the reasons may be the lack of communication skills and cultural awareness from the global project managers.
- **Increase quality levels** – the quality department may detect that the deliverables being produced by global project teams are not compliant with your customer quality standards, and hint that this is the reason for poor customer satisfaction. It is possible that team members across geographical regions do not have the same standards for quality and base their services on different service level agreements. Misunderstandings during the communication of the quality requirements and measurement techniques can also be behind the lack of compliancy.
- **Reduce budget overruns** – the finance department may conclude that global projects tend to deviate more from their original budget than the traditional projects. Your project office detects that the travel budgets are underestimated at the beginning of the project, and an important amount of face-to-face meetings are required to resolve conflicts and correct misunderstandings. The amount of travel and rework can be one of the main causes for the budget overruns.
- **Avoid project delays** – the corporate project office may reveal that a high number of global projects are completed behind schedule without valid justifications, when compared to traditional projects. Investigations by the PMO director may conclude that the project delays are due to misunderstandings between team members across borders, the excessive amount of rework and the time people spend waiting for distant colleagues to inform them of completion of pre-requisites.
- **Avoid scope creep** – the corporate audit department may detect that global projects are failing to track scope change requests and approvals, and suggest this as the main reason for most of the other problems. The lack of formalised and agreed procedures and documents across the companies and locations can be the main reason for this problem.
- **Increase morale** – the human resources department may detect a high incidence of absences and low motivation among global project managers and team members. The senior directors received many complaints from their subordinates about the excessive amount of work outside office hours and noticed a general frustration with the lack of response and collaboration from remote colleagues. The implementation of collaborative tools and techniques may reduce these problems.
- **Improve the communication across borders** – the corporate project office is facing problems in obtaining the project documentation and status from global project managers, and the main reason for the delays is the excessive amount of time they spend

travelling, conducting meetings and preparing meeting minutes. The implementation of a clear communications management plan and effective rules and templates might resolve this issue.

- **Improve the risk assessment and management** – your project office detects that the issue logs contain too many entries in global projects, when compared to the risk logs. After careful analysis, they conclude that risk identification sessions over a distance are not effective to detect potential problems, and do not include the threats from the different cultures, locations, laws and regulations.

If your organisation detects that traditional projects (executed by the whole team in the same location) have the same needs, this may be a good opportunity to implement a corporate standard for project management together with the Global Project Management Framework©, using as a basis one of the existing bodies of knowledge (PMBOK® Guide, PRINCE2® or a model based on the IPMA ICB, such as the APM Body of Knowledge).

Defining a scope for the implementation

The framework can be implemented in a reduced number of projects, in order to measure the costs and benefits before a global deployment. You can evaluate your company's projects with the help of an existing classification system (adapted from Gardiner, 2005):

- Participant mix – projects can be self-contained within an organisation (internal projects), entirely contracted out to an outside organisation (external projects) or have subcontractors and consultants take responsibility for parts of a project (mixed internal-external projects).
- Degree of standardisation – project deliverables, roles, systems, procedures and communication infrastructure can be clear and well defined (concrete projects), drawn-up for the first time (occasional projects) or informal and difficult to describe in detail (open projects).
- Project visibility – high (critical to market position or organisational survival, with a high risk level) or low (little attention from senior management and lower risk level).
- Size and complexity – projects can be compared according to their relative budget, scope and schedule.
- Industry – software, building, construction, and so on.

Your organisation can take the categories above into account and determine if it is worth deploying the Global Project Management Framework© to all projects, or only to large, complex or critical projects. As another example, organisations can declare the good practices *mandatory* for internal projects and *recommended* for mixed projects, while evaluating the sellers' capacities on global project management when planning for contracting on external projects.

27 *Implementation Strategies*

When the requirements and needs of your company and main stakeholders have been identified, you need to define a strategy to implement the Global Project Management Framework© at your company. This chapter explains in detail the different alternatives for the framework implementation strategy, following methods and guidelines from other management models and academic theories.

The emotional intelligence guidelines

The *Consortium for Research on Emotional Intelligence in Organisations* prepared a set of guidelines for the development of social and emotional learning, including management and executive development efforts as well as training in supervisory skills, diversity, teamwork, leadership, conflict management, stress management and stakeholder management. These guidelines can allow the implementation of the Global Project Management Framework© together with the principles of emotional intelligence (EI), as discussed in Chapter 14, and are divided into four phases (see the complete set of guidelines in Goleman et al., 2005).

PAVING THE WAY

- **Assess the organisation's needs** – using the evaluation boxes at the beginning and end of each chapter, determine the global competences requiring improvement at your company. You can assess the existing level of competences by listening to various global project managers in your organisation, and comparing the working practices and methods of successful and confident project managers with the behaviour and opinions from others who may be seeking answers to their problems.
- **Assess the individuals** – using the global competences identified in the previous step, and with the help of the global skills (discussed in Chapter 12), you can organise a team to assess individual competencies on global project management. You can prepare your assessment method using the recommendations for performance appraisals (see Chapter 14).
- **Provide feedback** (in a safe and supportive environment) to individuals on their strengths and weaknesses.
- **Maximise learner choice** – to start the implementation, organise a pilot team, selecting a group of individuals that are motivated to change their methods and learn new practices of global project management.
- **Encourage people to participate** – organise information sessions on the framework by using your key learning from the different chapters. Obtain support from senior managers and supervisors by showing them the potential benefits of the framework (refer to Chapters 6 and 8 to identify your stakeholders and prepare your communication strategy).

- **Link learning goals to personal values** – using the global skills and the results of individual assessments, help participants to understand whether the framework fits with what matters most to them.
- **Adjust expectations** – build positive expectations by showing participants that their global communication and people skills can be improved with the help of global collaboration tools and techniques and that such improvement will lead to valued outcomes. Be honest with the possible limitations of the improvements and adoption rates, and with the time it may take to implement the framework across different locations.
- **Gauge readiness** – assess whether the global project managers are ready to develop the practices in the framework and undergo training. If the readiness level is not appropriate for the implementation, revisit the previous steps or limit the group of participants in the pilot team.

DOING THE WORK OF CHANGE

- **Foster a positive relationship among the pilot team members** – appoint warm, genuine and empathic project coordinators to help you in the change process.
- **Make change self-directed** – learning is more effective when people direct their own development program, tailoring it to their unique needs, cultures and project types. Let the participants use their creativity to tailor the training approach to their individual learning styles and document their methods, so they can be used by future participants.
- **Set clear goals** – define a clear set of competencies that can be implemented within the pilot timeframe, and define clear steps to measure the learning progress.
- **Break goals into manageable steps** – identify the chapters in the framework that can be implemented quickly, to learn how to work together and how to define the good practices. Avoid being overly ambitious and divide the implementation into gradual steps.
- **Provide opportunities to practice** – encourage participants to try the new practices and techniques repeatedly and consistently in their global projects.
- **Give performance feedback** – ongoing feedback encourages people to keep their focus on the change process. Request that participants share their project documentation with you, and invite you to their meetings over distance. Provide focused and sustained feedback on their progress.
- **Rely on experiential methods** – encourage the use of development activities that engage all the senses and use new technologies or techniques.
- **Build in support** – organise regular meetings among the participants, allowing them to share their experiences and provide support to each other. External coaches and mentors specialised in global project management and cross-cultural development can be valuable in helping to support the desired change.
- **Use models** – publish the framework on the corporate website and mark with colours the different chapters being implemented or already deployed by previous steps (obtain permission from the author before printing and publishing the framework models in any communication media). Encourage the participants to study, analyse and propose changes to the framework, by using the framework web site (www.GlobalProjectManagement. org).
- **Enhance insight** – 'self-awareness is the cornerstone of emotional and social competence.' Help participants to acquire a good understanding of how their use of the practices in the framework and their behaviour affect themselves and others in the global project team.

- **Prevent relapse** – monitor progress and organise meetings so you can discuss failures and mistakes in order to improve the framework and practices. This will change the drawbacks into opportunities, and not undermine the participants' motivation.

ENCOURAGING TRANSFER AND MAINTENANCE OF CHANGE

- **Encourage use of skills on the job** – supervisors, other global project managers and global team members must adopt the practices in the framework, participate in the implementation team and be informed of the progress of the framework development and implementation. The senior management must provide a role model during the implementation of the framework (see Chapter 14).
- **Develop an organisational culture that supports learning** – obtain support from different stakeholders to value the practices of a learning organisation, building a safe atmosphere for experimentation.

EVALUATING CHANGE

- **Evaluate** – you need to evaluate the benefits of the framework, by evaluating the use of competence or skills against the situation before the framework implementation. You must also assess the success of the framework on satisfying the project needs, by using the same measures that motivated the project initiation.

The maturity model approach

If your company has already implemented, or is considering the implementation of, a maturity model such as the SEI-CMMI®, you can use the same evolutionary strategy to deploy the Global Project Management Framework©. By following the levels shown in Figure 27.1, you will improve the maturity of your organisation on global project management and achieve a higher level of effectiveness.

At level 1 (*initial*), the global projects and programs are not managed in a consistent manner. Some tools are available, but not everyone has been informed of their deployment and use as documentation and guidelines are not easily accessible. Different procedures and templates are developed according to each project manager's needs. The team members participating in different projects need to adapt to the various practices, resulting in the creation of distinct ones for their own projects and meetings over distance. Remote people management is sometimes chaotic and strongly reliant on the initiatives of highly independent team members to perform the project tasks. The time spent on unproductive meetings is widely considered as excessive.

You can increase the level of maturity by developing cross-cultural awareness, implementing collaborative technologies and global communication methods and fostering their adoption by global project managers and team members across the globe. A possible way to achieve this is to implement the practices and recommendations in Chapters 1, 6, 7, 8, 11, 16, 17, 21, 22 and 23 (as represented in Figure 27.2).

Your company has now achieved the maturity level 2 (*repeatable*). Most project managers and team members have a good awareness of how to deal with cultural diversity, and a good knowledge on the set-up, coordination of and participation in online meetings via web, audio and video conferencing. The basic rules for the use of e-mails and telephones are well established and accepted by most project stakeholders. The project managers understand the need for

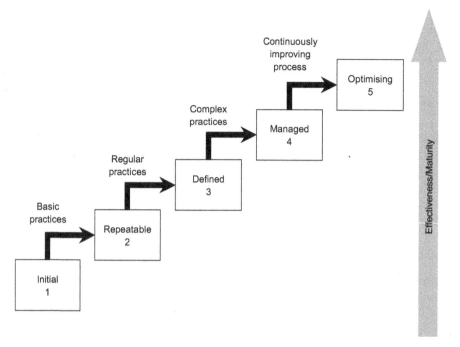

Figure 27.1   The global project management maturity levels

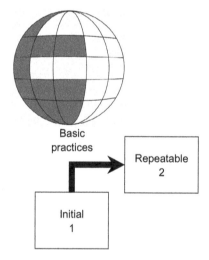

Figure 27.2   Evolving to maturity level 2

stakeholder management and know how to prepare the global communication strategies. All meetings use the same set of rules and templates to reduce the preparation effort and time required to update the project documentation and meeting minutes. Team-building exercises are common practice in project initiation phases, and most of the team know how to take cultural aspects into account when communicating with their colleagues. Less unproductive time is spent on meetings, leaving more time for efficient communication and for the project execution tasks, improving the project effectiveness and overall motivation.

Depending on the size of your company and the scope of the framework implementation, the progress from level 1 to 2 can take several months. After the objectives of this level have been achieved, your organisation can progress to level 3. As shown in Figure 27.3, you can start increasing your project and program managers' awareness of global team leadership, trust building (Chapters 2 and 3) and global communication techniques (Chapter 9), implementing the practices for global organisations (described in Chapters 12, 13 and 14) and knowledge-sharing tools and techniques (Chapters 19 and 24).

At level 3 (*defined*), everyone is comfortable with setting up knowledge-sharing spaces, and this technology is used naturally to store all project documentation, to post colour-coded reports showing the project status and during knowledge exchange activities. Trust building practices are used by most of the project stakeholders, all considering them a very positive approach. More advanced communication techniques have started to be used by global project managers, with adoption from some team members. The organisation has procedures in place to support global project teams and perform the acquisition and selection of human resources across the globe. A functional PMO has been established to coordinate the implementation of a standard methodology on project management across different locations.

The senior management can see the clear benefits of progressing to the next level, and you start to implement collaborative project management system tools and techniques (Chapters 20 and 25). Global project managers and coordinators receive training on conflict resolution techniques across borders, coaching and global creativity methods (Chapters 4, 5 and 10). Your organisation puts in place a set of guidelines for partners and suppliers that are involved in the execution of strategic projects (Chapter 15). This evolution is represented in Figure 27.4.

At level 4 (*managed*), the use of collaborative project management systems is accepted by most global project managers and team members. The online tools are used for steering committee meetings, demonstrations, brainstorming and coaching over distance, reducing travel time and costs and increasing the efficiency level. Conflict management practices are

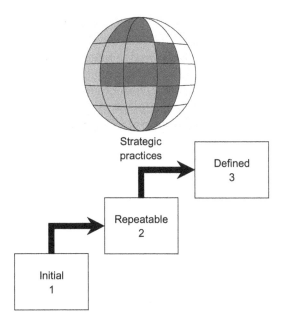

Figure 27.3   Evolving to maturity level 3

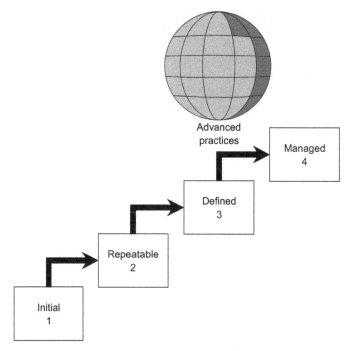

Figure 27.4   Evolving to maturity level 4

employed by all project managers, reducing the amount of ineffective communication to an acceptable level and boosting productivity and motivation. Most projects involving team members from different companies start with a kick-off session that defines the communication rules, templates and strategies. Some directors decide to establish regional PMOs to own their portfolio of programs and projects.

The framework is now fully implemented (see Figure 27.5), the last project deliverable is to establish a corporate PMO team (who will own the framework and conduct regular evaluation sessions) to identify new collaborative tools and techniques available which can continue to increase the organisation's effectiveness on global project management.

At level 5 (*Optimising*), new and improved practices are developed and the model is reviewed at regular intervals. Everyone in the company feels motivated to participate in the model construction, and a channel is open for communication between the different PMOs, project managers, team members and senior managers. The time spent on ineffective communication is reduced to a minimum, leaving more time for the project execution and social interaction among team members in different locations. As travel time is reduced, a balance between professional and social life is attained.

The first improvement expected as an organisation matures is the reduction of time spent on ineffective communication. The second improvement is an increase of the time available for project execution, as the control mechanisms and motivation levels are also improved. With more effective checkpoint meetings and with updated project documentation, the project managers can ensure the progress of the project cost, time, scope, quality and customer satisfaction. These improvements can be seen in Figure 27.6.

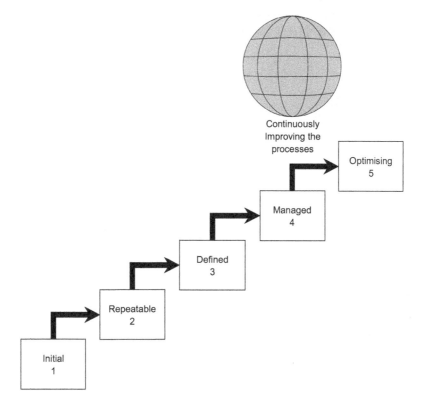

Figure 27.5   Evolving to maturity level 5

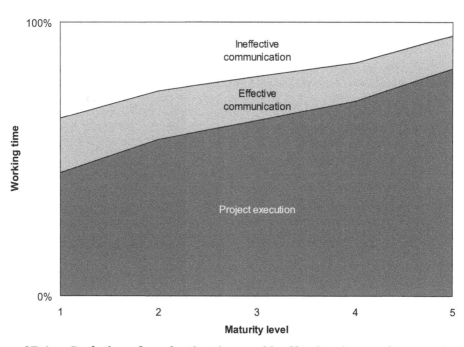

Figure 27.6   Evolution of productive time and ineffective time as the maturity level increases

REAL-LIFE IMPLEMENTATION

A typical project phases, for a successful implementation of the global project management framework at your company, would be as follows:

1. Project initiation:

    *   you identify the need for improvement in global project management practices;

    *   the project sponsor obtains the buy-in of the senior management, the project managers and other important stakeholders;

    *   a project manager is appointed.

2. Project planning – 'as-is' situation:

    *   using the assessment questionnaires in the applicable chapters, the project manager creates a map containing the areas already in a satisfactory level.

3. Project planning – 'to-be' situation:

    *   the project manager identifies the 'quick-win' areas, where the assessment questionnaires demonstrated that maturity can be achieved with minimal effort;

    *   the project manager revises these quick-win areas in a brainstorming session with other project managers, and gathers opinions on other areas to be tackled immediately;

    *   the project manager reviews the above recommendation with the sponsor and the steering committee, who take a final decision on the areas to be completed in the first cycle. The time and budget are the obvious elements for this decision, together with the expected benefits.

4. Project execution:

    *   the project manager builds a project team, ideally composed of volunteers, who believe that the processes definition can improve their efficiency in managing and participating in global projects;

    *   the areas are assigned to the project team members, who will work on their processes and good practices definition and implementation.

5. Project monitoring and control:

    *   the project manager conducts regular sessions, preferably using the good practices defined so far, to evaluate the advancement of the project and to correct deviations;

    *   these meetings also serve as brainstorming sessions where the ideas are revised, the difficulties shared, followed by peer recommendations;

    *   when the 'to-be' framework is completed, it is presented to all project managers, together with instructions for its implementation on all projects;

    *   regular reviews are held to revise the framework, the good practices and their impact on the project managers' productivity, and on the projects' effectiveness;

    *   when no additional changes are required, the framework is considered as completed, and the status presented to the sponsor and the steering committee for evaluation and decision on project closing;

    *   the same meeting can define if and when a new cycle will be started to implement another set of good practices in other areas.

6. Project Closing:
    *   a final review with the participants will document the methods developed to build the good practices, assign the ownership of the good practices after the project is dissolved, and create a 'lessons-learned' document to be used in the future implementations.

The action research cycles

The framework can be implemented as an internal project, with participation from a small group of six to 12 project managers (as project team members), following the model of emancipatory action research for organisational change. The sponsorship of senior management is mandatory (they can also participate in certain phases), and the participation of other team members in a controlled way can add more ideas to the reflection. Each research cycle would contain the following eight phases (adapted from Zuber-Skerritt, 1996):

1. **Definition of a business plan** – to explore the issues in detail, and as the study population is geographically dispersed, in-depth interviews can be conducted by video conference. The project managers' standpoints need to be identified, in order to build a list of requirements, to understand which of them are already satisfied by the existing methodologies and procedures and to determine what improvements still need to be achieved. In the same interviews, volunteers will be identified, based on individual motivation and commitment levels.
2. **Develop a shared vision** – to stimulate creative thinking and to generate data by interaction among the participants, the volunteers are gathered in a nominal group session where the requirements and suggestions (identified in the previous phase) are assembled and compared with the structure of individual practices. The tasks are prioritised and distributed for completion, each project manager becoming responsible for the elaboration of at least one individual practice.
3. **Provide strong leadership** – support from the senior managers is obtained to implement the framework and one project manager is selected to supervise the development tasks by the participants (researcher project manager). One sponsor is selected in each geographic location, to obtain the project funding and to ensure the awareness within the company.
4. **Spread shared vision to all departments** – the first version of the framework is distributed to all participants that are currently managing global projects, together with the implementation instructions.
5. **Institutionalise revitalisation** – participants are invited to apply the new practices to their particular global project to observe their strengths and weaknesses.
6. **Get feedback** – the researcher project manager collects individual impressions of the implementation phase and suggestions for further improvements. In-depth interviews can be used, according to their applicability, to understand the impact and outcomes of complex processes and issues.
7. **Monitor the whole revitalisation process** – as the reflection is shaped (refined and reflected) by group interaction, the volunteers will be gathered in a nominal group session, with the aim of achieving a common view of the efficiency level achieved (in comparison to the initial level) and the improvements to be made in the framework, to further increase the efficiency.

8. **Draw conclusions** – the findings from the previous phase must be summarised and presented to the sponsors, who will decide on the implementation of the next improvement cycle, and agree on which practices still need to be refined.

The above cycle of eight phases will be repeated – each step learning from the previous one and shaping the next – until the framework is validated by all participants, senior managers and project sponsors, allowing, 'firstly, the professional ideal of continuing openness to the development of practice, and secondly the "scientific" ideal of the continuing growth of understanding through critique and revision.' (Winter, 1989).

Part VI: Key concepts

*   The implementation of the Global Project Management Framework© can follow the principles of organisational change, maturity models or action research. Alternatively, you can define your own method and conduct a project to better coordinate the activities and obtain a formal sponsorship.

Part VI: Further reading

Cherniss, C., Goleman, D. and Emmerling, R. (2005) *Bringing Emotional Intelligence to the Workplace: A Technical Report*;

Goleman, D., Cherniss, C., Cowan, K., Emmerling, R., and Adler, M. (2005) *Guidelines for Best Practice*

These papers provide guidelines for the implementation of emotional intelligence at your company, using a process that can be also used to deploy the Global Project Management Framework©.

CMU/SEI (Carnegie Mellon University – Software Engineering Institute, 1995) *The Capability Maturity Model: Guidelines for Improving the Software Process*

The structure of the good practices in the CMMI® can be the basis for the framework contents, and for the instructions about how to use the framework and the different levels of maturity.

McNiff, J., Lomax, P., Whitehead, J. (2003) *You and Your Action Research Project*

This book can be a complete guide for the implementation of the Global Project Management Framework© at your company through the principles of Action Research.

Part VI: Interactive section

Share your experiences on the implementation of the Global Project Management Framework© in your company with the global project management community (www. GlobalProjectManagement.org):

*   Which method did you use?

- What were the advantages and inconveniences of this method? What would you change?
- If you implemented the method as part of an academic study, would you like to share the conclusions and recommendations?
- What are the main benefits achieved by the implementation of the framework? What are the limitations?

Coda

"World culture is a myriad of different ways of creating the integrity without which life and business cannot be conducted. There are no universal answers but there are universal questions and dilemmas, and that is where we all need to start"

(Trompenaars and Hampden-Turner)

After reading the manuscript for the last time before sending it to press, and seeing the stacks of books and academic papers that I consulted to write the 27 chapters, what attracts my attention are the piles of information that I did not use, and the amount of chapters I did not write. This to say there is still much to be investigated, developed and written to bring peace and satisfaction to global project managers and team members around the world.

More than a last chapter of a book, this page aims to conclude the first milestone of a long-term project: the development of a complete reference of tools, methods and practices around global project management. The Global Project Management Framework© presented by this book must be expanded to include opinions and experiences from global program and project managers around the globe, about practices and recommendations that worked well in their cultures and environment.

The website, www.GlobalProjectManagement.org, was developed using open source collaboration technologies, not only to serve as a forum to exchange the ideas around the tools and practices described in this book, but to allow the expansion of the framework.

Besides the knowledge exchange on the website, all the practices described by this book must be validated by academic studies, in order to build a solid model using a scientific approach. I will be pleased to help any effort in this sense, by supplying sources of information and reviewing your ideas.

Jean Binder
Grandvaux, Switzerland

List of Accronyms and Abbreviations

BBS	Bulletin Board System
CMM	Capability Maturity Model
CMMI ^{SM}	Capability Maturity Model – Integrated
CMU-SEI	Carnegie-Mellon University, Software Engineering Institute
ICB	IPMA Competence Baseline
IJPM	International Journal of Project Management
IPMA	International Project Management Association
OPM3®	Organizational Project Management Maturity Model
OGC	Office of Government and Commerce
PDA	Personal Digital Assistants
PMBOK® Guide	A Guide to the Project Management Body of Knowledge
PMI ®	Project Management Institute
PMO	Project Management Office
PRINCE2®	Projects in Controlled Environments – version 2
PSO	Project Support Office
SEI	Software Engineering Institute (*see CMU-SEI*)
SMS	Short Message Service
VoIP	Voice over Internet Protocol, also called IP Telephony

Bibliography

Andersen, E. (2000) 'Managing organization – structure and responsibilities' in *Gower Handbook of Project Management* (Gower Publishing Ltd, UK).

APM (2006) *APM Body of Knowledge – fifth edition* (APM Publishing, UK).

Balogun, J. and Hailey, V.H. (2004) *Exploring Strategic Change* (Pearson Education Ltd, UK).

Blake, R.R. and Mouton, J.S. (1964) *The Managerial Grid* (Gulf, USA).

Bower, D. and Skountzos, F. (2000) 'Partnering, benchmarking and alliances' in *Gower Handbook of Project Management* (Gower Publishing Ltd, UK).

Buchanan, D. and Huczynski, A. (1997) *Organizational Behaviour: An Introductory Text – third edition* (Prentice Hall Europe, UK).

Buzan, T. (2006) *The Ultimate Book of Mind Maps* (Harper Thorsons, UK).

Castells, M. (2000) *The Rise of the Network Society* (Blackwell, UK).

Cherniss, C., Goleman, D. and Emmerling, R. (2005) 'Bringing Emotional Intelligence to the Workplace: A Technical Report'. Available from: www.eiconsortium.org/research/technical_report.pdf

Clark, P.A. (1972) *Action Research & Organizational Change* (Harper & Row, UK).

Connaughton, S. L. and Daly, J. A. (2004) 'Long distance leadership: Communicative strategies for leading virtual teams' in *Virtual Teams: Projects, Protocols and Processes,* Pauleen D. J. (Ed.) (Idea Group Publishing, UK).

Cooper, D.J. (2003) *Leadership for Follower Commitment* (Butterworth-Heinemann, UK).

Dahl, S. (2004) 'Intercultural research: the current state of knowledge' in *Middlesex University Discussion Paper No. 26*. Available from: http://papers.ssrn.com/sol3/papers.cfm?abstract_id=658202

DeSouza, K., Jayaraman, A. and Evaristo, J.R. (2002) 'Knowledge management in non-collocated environments: a look at centralized vs. distributed design approaches' in *Proceedings of the 36th Hawaii International Conference on System Sciences* (HICSS'03).

Edwards, A. and Wilson, J.R. (2004) *Implementing Virtual Teams: A Guide to Organizational and Human Factors* (Gower Publishing Ltd, UK).

Fisher K. and Fisher M. (2001) *The Distance Manager* (McGraw-Hill, USA).

Gardiner, P. D. (2005) *Project Management: A Strategic Planning Approach* (Palgrave MacMillan, UK).

Gareis, R. (2000) 'Managing the project start' in *Gower Handbook of Project Management* (Gower Publishing Ltd, UK).

Goleman, D. (1996) *Emotional Intelligence* (Bloomsbury Publishing, UK).

Goleman, D., Cherniss, C., Cowan, K., Emmerling, R. and Adler, M. (2005) *Guidelines for Best Practice*. Available from: www.eiconsortium.org/research/guidelines_for_best_practice.pdf

Goncalves, M. (2005) *Managing Virtual Projects* (McGraw-Hill, USA).

Hall, D., Jones, R. and Raffo, C. (1995) *Business Studies* (Causeway Press, UK).

Hambridge, S. (1995) *Netiquette Guidelines* (IETF). Available from: www.ietf.org/rfc/rfc1855.txt

Hannagan, T. (1995) *Management Concepts and Practices* (Pitman Publishing, UK).

Haywood, M. (1998) *Managing Virtual Teams – Practical Techniques for High-Technology Project Managers* (Artech House, USA).

Hofstede, G. (2001) *Culture's Consequences: Comparing Values, Behaviours, Institutions, and Organizations Across Nations – second edition* (Sage Publications, UK).

IPMA – International Project Management Association (2006) *ICB – IPMA Competence Baseline, Version 3.0* (IPMA, The Netherlands).

Jacob, N. (2005) 'Cross-cultural investigations: emerging concepts' in *Journal of Organizational Change Management*, Oct 2005, 18:5, pp. 514–528. Available from: www.emeraldinsight.com/Insight/viewContentItem.do?contentType=Article&hdAction=lnkpdf&contentId=1515000&dType=SUB

Jolliet, Y. (2006) 'Des difficultés a gérer la connaissance à l'échelle d'une multinationale: Leçons apprises d'un projet global de knowledge management' in *The Swiss Project Management Journal (PM@CH)*, Number 1, Dec 2006.

Katzy, B., Evaristo, R. and Zigur, I. (2000) 'Knowledge management in virtual projects: a research agenda' in *Proceedings of the 33rd Hawaii International Conference on System Sciences*.

Keegan, A. and Turner, R. (2000) 'Managing human resources in the project-based organization' in *Gower Handbook of Project Management* (Gower Publishing Ltd, UK).

Kendall, G.I. and Rollins, S.C. (2003) *Advanced Project Portfolio Management and the PMO* (J.Ross Publishing, USA).

Kerzner, H. (2005) *Using the Project Management Maturity Model* (John Wiley & Sons, USA).

Khazanchi, D. and Zigurs, I. (2006) *Patterns of Effective Management of Virtual Projects: An Exploratory Study* (PMI, USA).

Kostner, J. (1996) *Virtual Leadership: Secrets from the Round Table for the Multi-Site Manager* (Warner Books, USA).

Leavitt, H.J. (1964) 'Applied organization change in industry: structural, technical, and human approaches', in *New Perspectives in Organization Research*, Cooper, W.W., Leavitt, H.J. and Shelly II, M.W. (Ed.) (John Wiley & Sons, USA).

Lipnack, J. and Stamps, J. (1997) *Virtual Teams: Reaching Across Space, Time, and Organizations with Technology* (John Wiley & Sons, USA).

Magala, S. (2005) *Cross-Cultural Sompetence* (Routledge, USA).

Mayer, M. (1998) *The Virtual Edge: Embracing Technology for Distributed Project Team Success* (Project Management Institute, Pennsylvania, USA).

Mayer, J. D., Caruso, D. and Salovey, P. (1999) 'Emotional intelligence meets traditional standards for an intelligence' in *Intelligence*, 27, pp. 267–298.

McElroy, B. and Mills, C. (2000) 'Managing stakeholders' in *Gower Handbook of Project Management* (Gower Publishing Ltd, UK).

McMahon, P. (2001) *Virtual Project Management Software Solutions for Today and the Future* (CRC Press LLC, USA).

McNiff, J., Lomax, P. and Whitehead, J. (2003) *You and Your Action Research Project* (RoutledgeFalmer, UK).

Mead, R. (2000) *Cases and Projects in International Management: Cross-Cultural Dimensions* (Blackwell Publishing, UK).

Mead, R. (2004) *International Management: Cross-Cultural Dimensions* (Blackwell Publishing, UK).

Melkman, A. and Trotman, J. (2005) *Training International Managers: Designing, Deploying and Delivering Effective Training for Multi-Cultural Groups* (Gower Publishing Ltd, UK).

Merlier, P. and Jolliet, Y. (2006) '*Mettre en place un Project Management Office: du rêve à la réalité*' (Seminar organized by the 'Societe Suisse de Management de Project' and the PMI Swiss Chapter, November 2006). Available from: www.project-management.ch/pages/DocumentationSoireesDebat.htm

Morrison, T. and Conaway, W.A. (2006) *Kiss, Bow, or Shake Hands: The Bestselling Guide to Doing Business in More Than 60 Countries* (Adams Publishing, USA).

Mullins, L.J. (1996) *Management and Organizational Behaviour* (Pitman Publishing, UK).

OGC – Office of Government Commerce (2002) *People issues and PRINCE2* (TSO, UK).

Pauleen, D. J. (Ed) (2004) *Virtual Teams: Projects, Protocols and Processes* (Idea Group Publishing, UK).

PMI (2004) *A Guide to the Project Management Body of Knowledge (PMBOK® Guide) – third edition* (PMI, USA).

Rad, P. and Levin, G. (2003) *Achieving Project Management Success Using Virtual Teams* (J. Ross Publishing, USA).

Reeve, J. (2001) *Understanding Motivation and Emotion – third edition* (John Wiley & Sons, USA).

Rees, D. 'Managing culture' in *Gower Handbook of Project Management* (Gower Publishing Ltd, UK).

Rowley, J.E. and Farrow, J. (2000) *Organizing Knowledge* (Gower Publishing Ltd, UK).

Sennara, M. and Hartman, F. (2002) 'Managing cultural risks on international projects' in *Proceedings of the Project Management Institute Annual Seminars & Symposium, October 3–10, 2002* (San Antonio, Texas, USA).

Somers, M. (2007) *Coaching at Work: Powering Your Team with Awareness, Responsibility and Trust* (John Wiley & Sons, UK).

Spencer-Oatey, H. (2000) *Culturally Speaking: Managing Rapport Through Talk Across Cultures* (Continuum, UK).

Staples, D. S., Wong, I. K.and Cameron, A. F. (2004) 'Best practices for virtual team effectiveness' in *Virtual Teams: Projects, Protocols and Processes,* Pauleen D. J. (Ed.) (Idea Group Publishing, UK).

Starr, J. (2003) *The Coaching Manual: The Definitive Guide to the Process, Principles and Skills of Personal Coaching* (Pearson Education Ltd, UK).

Trompenaars, F. and Hampden-Turner, C. (2005) *Riding the Waves of Culture: Understanding Cultural Diversity in Business* (Nicholas Brealey, UK).

Trompenaars, F. and Woolliams, P. (2003) *Business Across Cultures* (Capstone, UK).

Turner, J.R. and Simister, S.J. (2000) *Gower Handbook of Project Management* (Gower Publishing Ltd, UK).

Van Fenema, P.C. (2002) 'Coordination and control of globally distributed software projects' in *ERIM Ph.D. Series Research in Management 19.*

Wild, J.J., Wild, K.L. and Han, J.C.Y. (2000) *International Business: An Integrated Approach* (Prentice Hall, USA).

Winter, R. (1989) *Learning from Experience: Principles and Practice in Action-Research* (The Falmer Press, UK).

Zeitoun, A. (1998) 'Managing Projects across Multi-National Cultures, A Unique Experience', in *On-Target Newsletter,* 7:2. Available from: www.westmichpmi.org/NL1198.pdf (©1998 PMI Western Michigan Chapter).

Zuber-Skerritt, O. (1996) 'Emancipatory action research for organisational change and management development' in *New Directions in Action Research,* Zuber Skerritt, O. (Ed.) (RoutledgeFalmer, UK).

Further Reading

Ahern, D. M., Clouse, A. and Turner, R. (2004) *CMMI Distilled: A Practical Introduction to Integrated Process Improvement* (Addison-Wesley, USA).

Bajwa, D.S., Lewis, L.F. and Pervan, G. (2002) 'Adoption of collaboration information technologies in Australian and US organizations: a comparative study' in *Proceedings of the 36th Hawaii International Conference on System Sciences (HICSS'03)*.

Beise, C., Evaristo, R. and Niederman, F. (2002) 'Virtual meetings and tasks: from GSS to DGSS to project management' in *Proceedings of the 36th Hawaii international Conference on System Sciences (HICSS'03)*. Available from: http://csdl.computer.org/comp/proceedings/hicss/2003/1874/01/187410015c.pdf (©2002 IEEE, All rights reserved).

Benett, G. (2002) 'Working together, apart – the web as project infrastructure' in *Intranet Journal*. Available from: www.intranetjournal.com/text/features/idm0398-pm1.shtml (©2002 Jupitermedia, All rights reserved).

Binder, J. (2003) 'Open technologies for an open world' (European Masters in Interactive Multimedia Projects, Brussels). Available from: www.k-binder.be/Papers/open.htm

Brannen, J. (1992) 'Combining qualitative and quantitative approaches: an overview', in *Mixing Methods: Qualitative and Quantitative Research*, Brannen J. (Ed.) (Avebury, UK).

Brislin, R. W., Lonner, W. J. and Thorndike, R. M. (1973) *Cross-Cultural Research Methods: Comparative Studies in Behavioral Science* (John Wiley & Sons, USA).

Bryman, A. (1992) 'Quantitative and qualitative research further reflections on their integration', in *Mixing Methods: Qualitative and Quantitative Research*, Brannen J. (Ed.) (Avebury, UK).

Carroll, J.M. and Swatman, P.A. (1998) 'Building understanding of information systems practice: research in the field'. Available from: www.deakin.edu.au/buslaw/infosys/docs/workingpapers/archive/Working_Papers_98/98_12_Carroll.pdf

Chen, F., Romano, N., Nunamaker, J. and Briggs, R.O. (2002) 'A collaborative project management architecture' in *Proceedings of the 36th Hawaii International Conference on System Sciences (HICSS'03)*.

Cherniss, C. (2004) 'The business case for emotional intelligence'. Available from: www.eiconsortium.org/research/business_case_for_ei.pdf

CMU/SEI (Carnegie Mellon University – Software Engineering Institute, 1995) *The Capability Maturity Model – Guidelines for Improving the Software Process* (Addison-Wesley, USA).

Cooke-Davies, T. (2002) 'It's people who gets things done' in *Project Manager Today* (January 2002).

Cumming, E.A. (2005) 'An investigation into the relationship between emotional intelligence and workplace performance: an exploratory study'. Available from: www.opra.co.nz/hot_news/EI_Research_Cummings_Emily_2005.04.pdf

Damien, D.E. and Zowghi, D. (2002) 'An insight into the interplay between culture, conflict and distance in globally distributed requirements negotiations' in *Proceedings of the 36th Hawaii International Conference on System Sciences (HICSS'03)*.

DeLone, W., Espinosa, J.A., Gwanhoo, L. and Carmel, E. (2005) 'Bridging global boundaries for is project success' in *Proceedings of the 38th Hawaii International Conference on System Sciences – 2005 (IEEE)*.

Dubé, L. and Paré, G. (2004) 'The multifaceted nature of virtual teams' in *Virtual Teams: Projects, Protocols and Processes*, Pauleen D. J. (Ed.) (Idea Group Publishing, UK).

Dustdar, S. (2004) 'Toward integration of artefacts, resources and processes for virtual teams' in *Virtual Teams: Projects, Protocols and Processes*, Pauleen D. J. (Ed.) (Idea Group Publishing, UK).

Evaristo, J. and Munkvold, B. (2002) 'Collaborative infrastructure formation in virtual projects' in *Journal of Global Information Technology Management*, March 15, 2002.

Fernández, W. D. (2004) 'Trust and the trust placement process in metateam projects' in *Virtual Teams: Projects, Protocols and Processes*, Pauleen D. J. (Ed.) (Idea Group Publishing, UK).

Griffith, T. L. and Meader, D. K. (2004) 'Prelude to virtual groups: leadership and technology in semivirtual groups' in *Virtual Teams: Projects, Protocols and Processes*, Pauleen D. J. (Ed.) (Idea Group Publishing, UK).

Henry, J. E. and Hartzler, M. (1998) *Tools for Virtual Teams: A Team Fitness Companion* (McGraw-Hill, USA).

Hertel, T. D. (2004) 'Effective virtual teams' in *Virtual Teams: Projects, Protocols and Processes*, Pauleen D. J. (Ed.) (Idea Group Publishing, UK).

Hofstede, G.J., Pedersen, P.B. and Hofstede, G. (2002) *Exploring culture: Exercises, Stories and Synthetic Cultures* (Intercultural Press, USA).

Hornett, A. (2004a) 'The impact of external factors on virtual teams: comparative cases' in *Virtual Teams: Projects, Protocols and Processes*, Pauleen D. J. (Ed.) (Idea Group Publishing, UK).

Hornett, A. (2004b) 'Varieties of virtual organizations and their knowledge sharing systems' in *Virtual Teams: Projects, Protocols and Processes*, Pauleen D. J. (Ed.) (Idea Group Publishing, UK).

Kerzner, H. (2004) *Advanced project management: Best practices on implementation* (John Wiley & Sons, USA).

Lau, R. (2004) 'Delivering projects with virtual teams' in *International Engineering Management Conference 2004 (IEEE)*.

Maier, R. (2002) 'State-of-practice of knowledge management systems: results of an empirical study' in *Knowledge Management and Information Technology*, UPGRADE Vol. III, No. 1, February 2002.

Mayer, J. D., Salovey, P. and Caruso, D. R. (2000) 'Models of emotional intelligence' in *Handbook of Intelligence*, Sternberg, R. J. (Ed.) (Cambridge University Press, UK).

McDonough III,E.F., Kahn, K.B. and Barczak, G. (2001) 'An investigation of the use of global, virtual, and colocated new product development teams' in *The Journal of Product Innovation Management*, 18 pp. 110–120.

McNiff, J. (1994) *Action Research: Principles and Practice* (Routledge, UK).

McNiff, J. (2000) *Action Research in Organisations* (Routledge, UK).

Murphy, P. (2004) 'Trust, rationality and the virtual team' *Virtual Teams: Projects, Protocols and Processes*, Pauleen D. J. (Ed.) (Idea Group Publishing, UK).

Neece, O. E. (2004) 'Factors contributing to knowledge sharing and communication in a large virtual work group' *Virtual Teams: Projects, Protocols and Processes*, Pauleen D. J. (Ed.) (Idea Group Publishing, UK).

OGC – Office of Government Commerce (2006) *Managing Successful Projects with PRINCE2 Manual 2005* (TSO, UK).

Oja, S.N. and Smulyan, L. (1989) *Collaborative Action Research: a Developmental Approach* (The Falmer Press, UK).

Oppenheim, A. (1992) *Questionnaire Design, Interviewing and Attitude Measurement* (Continuum, UK).

PMI (2006a) *The Standard for Program Management* (PMI, USA).

PMI (2006b) *The Standard for Portfolio Management* (PMI, USA).

Ritchie, J. and Lewis, J. (2003) *Qualitative Research Practice* (SAGE Publications, UK).

Robson, C. (2002) *Real World Research: A Resource for Social Scientists and Practitioner – Researchers* (Blackwell Publishers Ltd, UK).

Rolfes, M. (year not known) *Virtual Project Management* (Term paper).

Solomon, C.M. (1995) 'Global teams: the ultimate collaboration' in *Personnel Journal*, September 1995, 74:9, pp. 49-58. Available from: www.workforce.com/archive/feature/22/19/38/index_printer.php

Thornhill, A., Lewis, P., Millmore, M. and Saunders, M. (2000) *Managing Change – A Human Resource Strategy Approach* (Pearson Education Ltd, UK).

Winter, R. (2003) 'Some principles and procedures for the conduct of Action Research' in *New Directions in Action Research*, Zuber-Skerritt, O. (Ed.) (RoutledgeFalmer, UK).

Index

Work packages, 10, 27, 31, 45–7, 55, 69, 102,
        126, 131–6, 137, 141–2, 175, 243, 252
Work-life balance, 62, 163–6, 178
Workshop, 54–9, 85, 124, 242–3
www.GlobalProjectManagement.org, 17, 20,
        49, 59, 67, 75, 77, 89, 100, 107, 115,
        126, 128, 138, 151, 161, 172, 177,
        180, 181, 186, 188, 191, 193, 195,
        198, 202, 203, 206, 209, 212, 215,
        216, 223, 230, 235, 240, 246, 247,
        256, 265, 267

XING *see* networking platforms

360-degree performance appraisal, 169
360G performance appraisal, 170, 178